THE PILOT'S HEALTH

BY ERIC G. ANDERSON

TAB BOOKS Inc.
BLUE RIDGE SUMMIT, PA. 17214

FIRST EDITION

FIRST PRINTING

Library of Congress Cataloging in Publication Data

Anderson, Eric G.
    The pilot's health.

    Includes bibliographical references and index.
    1. Air pilots—Diseases and hygiene.   2. Health.
I. Title.
RC1063.A4   1984   616.9'80213   83-20262
ISBN 0-8306-2346-9 (pbk.)

Contents

Acknowledgments

A tip of the wing to Dorothy M. Greenberg of TAB BOOKS Inc. for encouraging me to write this book on aviation, to all my physician colleagues and pilot friends who have contributed over the years to my medical and flying experiences, to Lloyd Cookson of Treisman's camera department for processing the photographs, and to Marsha Curley for again sitting down at a typewriter and producing a manuscript out of chaos.

A special appreciation to the unselfish person who does all the work of living while I get all the fun of writing: Margaret, my ever-patient wife.

Introduction

This book explains the broad principles of general health to pilots—points that are basic to consumers' understanding of their bodies. It does not deal with Federal Aviation Regulations, which are mandated more by politicians than revered by physicians.

The Pilot's Health is more interested in suggesting the fundamentals whereby a pilot can improve health than in, for example, demonstrating the mysteries of microscopic anatomy in the inner ear. The discussions in this book do not replace proper consultation between you and your private physician. If indeed your personal doctor disagrees with what is written here as it applies to you, then listen to that person—who knows *you* better.

There are a lot of women pilots and a lot of women doctors. Yet most of the time *The Pilot's Health* refers to pilot or doctor as "him." It's devishly difficult for an author to keep writing "him or her." I suspect it is, in addition, highly tedious to the reader. I hope my women friends in the fields of aviation and medicine will accept the frequent use of the third person masculine.

You may be startled to see mention in the book of so many doctors and to be given so many references. There is, of course, a reason. Medical information has more credibility if the qualifications of the authority behind it are made visible.

Besides, the physicians and research scientists who add to health knowledge *should* be given credit for their work. You, too, may wish to follow an idea or thought further with the expert concerned. If so, a telephone call—not to me, but direct to the university or hospital concerned—should give you access to the department carrying out the work that interests you.

The Harvard Medical School Health Letter has addressed itself to the subject of how the public should evaluate medical information. Recognizing that the torrent of information pouring from the media could swamp any consumer who is trying to find reasons for or discover a personal and pertinent answer to his problems, Harvard makes these points:

First, proper studies and experiments tend to be published in reputable journals where they can be scrutinized by other scientists.

Second, for studies to be significant, they must be free of bias. This requires certain controls; patients have to be treated in large enough numbers for it to be statistically valid, and results must show effect beyond simple anecdotal stories of how some individuals improved.

Third, the safety of a treatment is a major issue. There can never be absolute safety because everything in life, including medical treatment, involves risk. The consumer should evaluate claims of "safety" with a question: "safe compared to what?"

Fourth, the burden of *proof* rests with those who claim to have the answer for diseases beyond the skill of the present medical establishment, and proof is not, as said above, the recounting of a few stories and unsubstantiated claims. Says Harvard: "One should be especially wary of enthusiastic claims for unusual remedies for chronic or incurable diseases—such as crippling arthritis or terminal cancer. There are, unfortunately, some people who deliberately profit from the understandable desperation of others."

Chapter 1

Why Health?

Winston Churchill once said, "The air is an extremely dangerous, jealous and exacting mistress. Once under the spell most lovers remain faithful to the end, which is not always old age."

Yet there is magic in the air. There is tranquility and contentment and delights beyond the ken of moles and men. In the sky, pilots float in the company of the gods, over new lands—new worlds to see, to experience, to master. Let Earth and its cares drop away below them. Let men be gypsies of the skies.

And so we pilots fly serenely above our planet. We are one with our plane. We pull back and she rears up like a thoroughbred startled at the gate; we bank and she wheels like a kestrel, soaring in the sun; we reduce power, we drop the nose, and she is now a surfboard and we are surfers sliding slowly on the seas, on the waves of the wind.

> I found a place
> For boundless dreams
> Above a patchwork land

cried Nancy Stock. We all have found such a place, but there is a price.

The sky can be a harsh habitat. Flying can create problems—from the ground up. A demanding hobby and an exacting career, flying takes its toll. It hits the inattentive. It smites the lazy. It fells the incompetent. But it doesn't discriminate. It will strike down the virtuous too: those who were good pilots but tired; who were fine airmen but ill; who were skilled professionals but, at the time of their greatest need, they lacked a pilot's health.

Because you need to be fit to sit for hours in a noisy, shuddering box; to work hours that would make a hospital nurse protest or a village baker cringe; to eat and run and tell your biological clock it's Monday morning when your body knows it's Sunday night; to take your lungs from sea level to something like a third the height of Mt. Everest in several minutes; to battle your brain (and more important, your hands and feet) to make them accept the instruments and believe that you're flying straight and level when every primitive instinct you've got screams that you're not.

No wonder the original astronaut selection process was so complicated. Let's look at it:

The first phase of medical selection of military test pilots for the astronaut program was easy: height not above 71 inches, age not in excess of 39 years, a minimum of 1500 flying hours with qualifications in high-performance jet aircraft. This reduced the large number of volunteers to 69.

The second phase saw intensive interviewing on motivation, detailed questioning on technical skills, and additional examination on psychiatric strengths. This brought the number down to 31.

Today's pilots too young to remember all this excitement—and those *were* exciting times—might be interested to know what factors were considered important in the astronaut's health. The aviation doctors wanted to know if the pilots had ever traveled in areas where parasitic diseases were common and if they'd ever experienced problems with their ears, sinuses, or lungs. The pilots were tested on bicycles, electrocardiograms spewing reams of paper as they pedalled to nowhere. They were X-rayed—my God, were they ever—teeth, sinuses, throat, chest, spine, stomach, bowel. They were questioned on everything from how they felt about their childhood to how their parents felt about hazardous flying.

Then they were examined again. They were tested on tilt tables and on treadmills. They were checked on how they handled noise and isolation. They were challenged with vibrations and hypoxia. And always the psychiatrists were balancing intelligence against personality and motivation against skill. Thus the seven astronauts were chosen for the Mercury project. Only then did the world realize the awesome confrontation for America's scientists

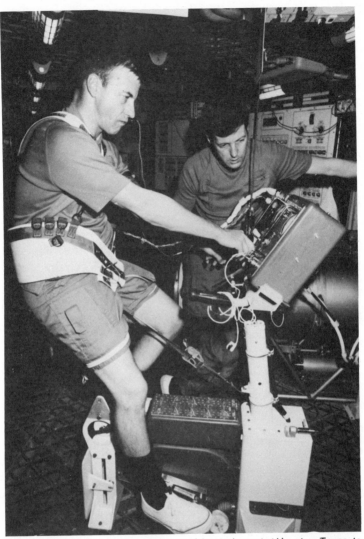

The bicycle ergometer was a simple part of the equipment at Houston, Texas, to measure astronaut fitness. (courtesy NASA)

and the frightful challenge for the new breed of pilot.

That both scientist and pilot performed beyond the dreams of the nation is now history. Indeed, so perfectly chosen and prepared were the astronauts that there were no major medical problems in the entire NASA program.

If man (and now woman) can get the human body into such

shape that the infinite—space—can be defied, surely we simpler mortals can at least improve our own health enough to tackle the finite, the mere roof of sky above our heads.

Let's see what we can do to improve the pilot's health.

Chapter 2

Tools of the Trade

Twenty-nine thousand hours, most of it spent in the left seat, and quite a bit in 747s—he'd flown Pitcairns and Pups, Stinsons, Wacos, DC-3s, and 707s. He'd owned a TriPacer and a Beech Staggerwing. My patient knew everything about airplanes, and not a thing about his own body.

Sitting on my examining table, coughing with bronchitis, he looked up, puzzled, as I thumped his chest with my fingers.

"What d'ya do that for?" he said. "I've always wanted to ask a doctor and never remembered."

It was a little surprising to be given so simple a question from so complicated a person. Here's a man who could handle sophisticated computerized technology yet didn't know that doctors bang on chests because lungs should sound and feel hollow if they're full of air.

I've even seen campers tapping on their butane and propane tanks at trailer parks to check how full the tanks are. If the percussion is dull—almost hurting the fingers—that solid feel means liquid; if the tank sounds hollow, that part is empty. Thus the level of liquid petroleum is found.

And, interestingly enough, that's how it all started in Vienna with a monograph published in 1761.

Leopold Auenbrugger, a medical student, was the son of an innkeeper of Graz and had often tapped with his fingers on his father's casks to find the level of wine. When he became a physician, he found lungs full of fluid due to pneumonia and tuberculosis. He then applied the same principle of percussion to the human chest.

Like many medical discoveries, the concept was ignored—until about 50 years later. In 1808, Napoleon's personal physician translated the report into French just before Auenbrugger died.

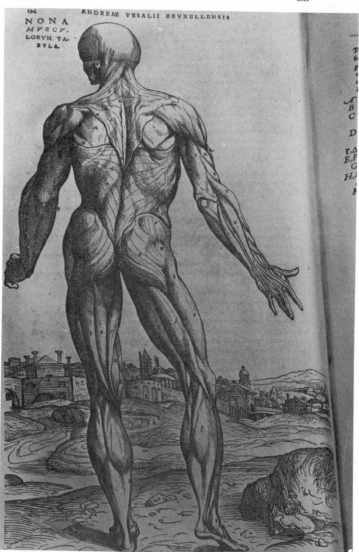

Ever wonder why your back aches after a long flight? Vesalius showed you why in 1543 in the first atlas of anatomy ever published.

Although changing patterns of disease and increasing use of X-rays make some old techniques less useful, percussing that pilot's chest still gave me important information. It also showed me that our worldly wise consumer didn't know much about medicine—a particularly unfortunate affair for a person who more than any other, has a professional life that requires good health.

And if an airline pilot who is constantly exposed to both company doctors and private physicians doesn't know too much about health, how much less must a student pilot know as he wanders over to his Cessna 152, worrying because his Class III medical is due?

It thus seemed appropriate to help pilots understand their bodies as much as their airplanes, and to talk a bit about the tools of the doctor's trade.

Maybe some of the hospital tools doctors use are a bit more complicated than what you can pick up at Sears, but there's nothing all that fancy about what we have laying around the office.

STETHOSCOPE

Take the *stethoscope*, for example, a device discovered and developed by the French physician Ren'e Théophile Hyacinthe Laennec who was born in Brittany in 1781. One day in 1816 he was trying to hear the heart sounds of a stout patient whose obesity made listening difficult. Apparently he had noticed two children at play earlier that day in a game where one scratched the end of a log of wood and the other listened. Curious, Laennec rolled a quire of paper into a cylinder and, applying one end to the patient's chest, placed his ear against the other. To his surprise, he heard the sounds of the patient's heart very clearly. Soon he had perfected a stethoscope made of a cylinder of wood a foot long and 1½ inches wide, with which many of the sounds of heart and lung disease could be elicited.

His work created great interest among colleagues—partly because at last the doctor could hear better than the old way of the ear directly placed on the patient's chest, and partly because the personal hygiene of patients at that time was pretty well nonexistent.

Indeed that is still sometimes a good reason for having the stethoscope. "How long should the rubber tubing be on my new stethoscope?" the embryo medical student will ask.

"An inch longer than a flea can jump," is the usual answer from the urbane senior resident.

OTOSCOPE

There's nothing special about the *otoscope* either. It's a light with a speculum at the end. When we stick it in your ear, the cylindrical insert parts the hairs in the ear canal and gives us a good view of the drum. There's some magnification at the eyepiece. Sometimes we blow air in or get you to do a Valsalva procedure—popping your ears. This opens up the Eustachian tube and puts air into the middle ear. Watching, we can see the eardrum move, which proves the Eustachian tube is patent.

OPHTHALMOSCOPE

The *ophthalmoscope* is another light, this time with different lenses in the physician's eyepiece. We can start by looking at the front part of the eye, then we rotate the lenses until we've focused on the very back of the retina. It's common for you, the patient, to get the sensation of small dots floating in front of your eye. You are actually seeing the reflection of the back of your own eye.

(You will sometimes get this same impression of blood cells swimming in your blood vessels if you are at a beach on a bright day. If there's a lot of ultraviolet light and you look up into a clear blue sky, you may again see this retina reflection.)

SPHYGMOMANOMETER

Another very simple gadget is the *sphygmomanometer*, the blood pressure machine. We pump up the bag while we listen. When we increase cuff tension above the pressure in the artery, we cut off the blood flow by collapsing the artery. In other words, if the pressure inside the artery is less than the outside pressure in the cuff, the artery collapses under that compression. As we release pressure slowly, we suddenly hear the flow. At that point, the *systolic* blood pressure, the strong outflow thrust of the heart, has outpointed the pressure recorded (in millimeters of mercury) in the cuff, e.g., 130 mm of mercury. As we drop pressure further, the sounds get muffled, then disappear. This is the *diastolic* pressure, e.g., 75 mm Mg. We thus record the pressure as 130/75. We worry more about elevations in the diastolic (the bottom figure) than we do about the top, systolic. Conventionally, 140/90 is considered the upper limits of normal blood pressure. (We'll talk more about blood pressure later.)

COUGH, PLEASE

As long as we are poking about your body, let me mention one other area—the groin. Asking patients to cough while we press on their groins always seemed to confuse them. When I was an 18-year old recruit in the army, word went round the shivering bare groups of soldiers that this "cough please" was a test for VD. I've actually had sophisticated college kids still ask me if this is so. The test is, of course, for hernia or rupture. Let's see how a rupture can happen.

In the last month or so of intrauterine life in male babies, the testicles drop down from where they developed beside the kidneys into the scrotum. In this location, half a degree cooler than the rest of the body, sperm is produced. To get to the scrotum before birth, the testes have to pass through an external ring in the groin. If for some reason your Maker gave you a generous ring, you will be a candidate for a hernia later and there's nothing you can do about it. Exercise doesn't help; weightlifting may well make it worse. When the doctor asks you to cough, all he is doing is testing your cough reflex to see if the ring is bigger than it should be.

REFLEXES

As long as we are sticking fingers in your groin, we might as well hit you with our hammers. Tendon hammers come in all shapes—from small "tomahawk" ones to long pliable plastic handles with something like a tire on top.

We hit your knee and it jumps—or *should* jump. Most of the time, we're banging away at your knees with our minds miles away. We're maybe thinking that it would be a nice day for flying, or that there's a good movie on TV tonight, or that we've got to remember to pick up a carton of milk on the way home.

Usually the reflexes aren't very important. The test merely demonstrates the normal continuity of an arc that goes from the tendons of a muscle in the sensory nerve fibers to the spinal cord and returns in the motor or action fibers to cause the muscle to twitch. This circle is completed faster than the brain can react from above. The test shows that one part of your nervous system is working. It *can* be a very important part of the physical examination, but if the doctor does it to you when you go to see him with nothing more complicated than a sore throat, he is either doing it from force of habit to be complete or because he's got time on his hands and wants you to see his nice new hammer.

So there's nothing special about our tools. Now let's look at something that *is* special—our patients.

Chapter 3

The Pilot as Patient

Carl Squier learned to fly in 1916. Involved in the romance of flying almost from the beginning, he had a favorite story about a fellow barnstormer. It seems this fellow had given a demonstration of flying to a midwest community several years previously and had now returned to the same farmer's pasture.

He sought out the farmer's daughter to chat over old times. To his surprise and concern he found her accompanied by a boy about two years old who bore a striking resemblance to himself.

"I would have married you," he said, "Why didn't you tell me?"

The girl replied: "Pa said he didn't want me to. He said he'd rather have a bastard in the family than a pilot."

If indeed the pilot was ever held in such low esteem, he certainly isn't now. There can be few professional pilots who don't command the respect, admiration, and envy of their fellow man. The world thinks that pilots have got it made. In a second incarnation, the only person who would not want to come back as a commercial or airline pilot and would be content to return as himself would be Hugh Hefner.

Look there! See the pilot sit in the airport restaurant. He's surrounded by the rest of the world: pale-faced wintry-eyed folks who chew hamburger and surreptitiously watch the bronzed Adonis eat his Chateaubriand, occasionally checking the time on his Rolex Oyster wrist watch.

There the pilot sits—and *that's the problem.* Sitting your way through life is not as healthy a career as you might expect.

It would be easy to start at the feet and work your way up the body, listing problems of health caused by the pilot's working life—varicose veins, for example. They're common in people who have to stand a lot without moving: barbers, beauticians, lecturers, ministers, auctioneers—and pilots. Sitting around a lot isn't much better. It tends to cause postural edema, even phlebitis in the legs.

What you sit on can become a problem, too. It's surprising they don't use pilots for the TV commercials advertising Preparation H. Piles are pilots; pilots are piles—and rectal itch and yeast eczema from sitting on vinyl all the time, and constipation. If you've got piles and are constipated, that's not much fun—but you *did* want to be a pilot, didn't you?

Simple measures to help here would include: Wear cotton underwear rather than nylon. Try to sit on fabric seats, not plastic. Drink plenty of fluids. Eat bran and drink prune juice for breakfast. And follow the very advice airline pilots give to their passengers: Walk around; exercise.

The bulging belly that the airline captain has to fight a battle with is not due to drinking beer but to the simple lack of exercise pilots get. Commuting to work, waiting at the airport, and sitting behind the yoke all allow the stomach muscles to weaken. Your doctor can give you some exercises to firm up those muscles. They are similar to those performed by new mothers after the birth of a baby.

Airline pilots, especially the younger ones, are usually able to control their weight, but it can be a constant fight. Airline management wants and expects flight crews to look efficient and sharp, and there are many pressures on pilots to look good in uniform.

Yet if it's been a long, tiring flight, it's very tempting at the end of the day to fall for the American disease coyly labelled "nocturnal hyperphagia" by Dr. E.R. Monsen, associate professor of nutrition at the University of Washington. "This is characterized," he says, "by an individual coming home at 5 o'clock, opening the refrigerator door, and staying there for the next three or four hours."

OBESITY

A study by American psychologists reveals that second to remarks about the weather, the commonest greeting when two people meet is "Hey! You've lost weight." This salutation apparently acts as a compliment to our friends (whether true or not) and demonstrates our personal interest in their welfare. It also shows our preoccupation with an important aspect of our health—our weight. Unfortunately, when Americans focus on their own weight, they do so with many misconceptions. Assailed by many "big fat lies," it's time we confronted some hearty truths.

Certain truths are obvious: There are about 40 million obese people in the United States with some age groups showing particular problems. The Metropolitan Life Insurance Company reported that 61 percent of men aged 40-49 are more than 10 percent overweight. Women have special problems. Even professional women, well removed from the temptations of the kitchen, have more difficulty maintaining their ideal weight than men.

Obesity is an ongoing problem. "Slow motion suicide," it has been called. Research has indicated 27 metabolic abnormalities in obesity, all of which return to normal when normal weight is achieved. As we dig our graves with our forks, we belch benignly and agree complacently with Charles Townsend Copeland who said: "To eat is human, to digest divine."

Not so divine is the end result and the attitudes of society toward those who are overweight. George F. Cahil, MD, of Harvard Medical School, an authority of metabolism and obesity, set out to explore any subconscious community biases against the obese. His statistics revealed 14 percent obesity in bank presidents, but 40 percent in bank clerks. Some figures even suggested that in former days it was five times harder for an obese person to get into Harvard Medical School than an applicant of normal weight.

The greatest misconception most Americans have about obesity is that it is somebody else's fault. Each individual has a favorite excuse or half truth. Let's examine the most common fat fallacies:

"It's my glands, doctor." It usually isn't. In Edinburgh, my old professor Sir Derrick Dunlop used to say, "Fat comes off your plate." Even obese hypothyroid patients lose only ten to fifteen pounds when their disease is treated.

"I was a heavy baby; I can't lose weight." Granted, there are two types of obesity and the early-onset form creates 78 billion fat cells in the child's body as opposed to the 27 billion that normal-weight children have. In contrast, the more common adult-onset obesity (after the age of twenty) is associated with an increase in adipose cell *size*, but not *number*. However, to have been an overfed heavy baby does not create irreversible damage. English researchers reported in the *British Medical Journal* of 203 infants of whom 40

percent were overweight in their first year but only 13.5 percent at the five year followup.

"I'm just bloated with fluid." A West Coast nutritional expert says his answer to that one is to say to the patient: "No, no. You're not wet. You're *fat.*" Sometimes patients (especially women) do retain fluid in the absence of other disease. Most endocrinologists believe one problem—idiopathic cyclic edema—is due to newly discovered hormones that vary with posture, the patient excreting fluid well when recumbent but not when upright. However, this is not common.

"I hardly eat enough to feed a bird" is a common statement, sometimes accompanied by a meticulous list to prove the point. Most of the time, the figures are not complete. Walter Winchell was right on target when he said, "Americans eat as if their stomachs belonged to someone else." Occasionally, a patient is being exact about decreased caloric intake but remains overweight, demonstrating both an exciting and depressing aspect of medical research—thermogenesis, the heat created by eating that burns up calories. Unfortunately, obese persons are not so efficient at thermogenesis as normal-weight people. A large meal eaten by an average person increases body heat production by 25 to 50 percent. This does not happen in the obese.

"I can't find time to exercise." Is that really true? Couldn't we park farther from the entrance, use stairs instead of elevators, and develop some pastimes, even walking? You burn off nine more calories an hour if you stand rather than sit, and 66 more calories an hour if you are the type who can "never stand still." In 70 hours of simple activity, busy people burn off one pound of body weight more than their relaxed brothers. In fact, the typist who changes from a manual to an electric typewriter will gain three pounds a year since she is working 90 calories less each day. In obesity, sloth is a more important key than gluttony.

"We're all fat in our family, doc." Yes, research shows 80 percent of children are obese if both parents are fat, and only 9 percent if both parents are normal weight, but this weight is often more an environmental factor that generic. George V. Mann, MD, professor of biochemistry and medicine at Vanderbilt University, whimsically points out that veterinarians have witnessed that pets tend to resemble their masters and that "fat masters have fat dogs. This coincidence could hardly be genetic, but it could be nurture, and it could be that they both watch the same television shows."

Television advertising significantly teases the obese. Jean

Mayer, PhD, president of Tufts University, has pointed out that the ten largest food advertisers spend 90 percent of their advertising budgets on television, and that the average child sees 8,5000 to 13,000 television food commercials a year. The National Institutes of Health revealed that Americans spend $8 billion a year on reducing aids and special diets. The companies that make those items are the same companies which produce the junk foods that make us fat.

If obesity is a disease from the neck up, can't we continue on up to find its cure? A research study showed that in France, people take longer to prepare meals, longer to eat them, and have less obesity than people in the United States. Fast and easily prepared foods have become synonymous with the American way of life. Clearly, our life styles need redefining for health styles to take priority over the American way of fat.

Of course the obese have other problems. They are more prone to gall bladder disease, high blood pressure, heart disease, emphysema, diabetes, hernias, and falls due to their lack of nimbleness.

LIFESTYLES

Does this mean that a pilot should proceed privately to a doctor for a checkup or a complete physical to see where he or she stands on the weight and balance tables for mankind?

Probably not. Certainly not if he's a typical patient who replays this scenario annually with his private physician:

"Hi doc! How's it going?" The patient greets the doctor with a cheerful grin. Looking at the slip which reads "Annual Physical," the physician groans. The patient's chart is studied: age 36, height 5'8", weight 238 pounds, smokes 40 cigarettes a day, drinks three or four highballs daily, blood sugar elevated at 152, cholesterol high at 430.

The scene seems so familiar to the physician—and it is. Last year it was the same story. The advice then, delivered not unkindly from the book: lose weight, stop smoking, drink less. The response was predictable: negative. Now, a year later, the patient is back as cheerful as before, using, for his annual physical, money which might be better spent on recreation, relaxation, or the family.

Some people would argue that it's the patient's privilege to use his cash for the reassurance of a visit to his doctor, and it's the patient's right to take any medical advice with reservations. But is the patient getting the correct mileage out of his doctor? Is the doctor charting the proper track?

When asked his views of the annual physical, a doctor's response will depend on how harassed he is in his daily schedule. (We will discuss this again in Chapter 15). Many doctors are discouraged or cynical about the results of annual assessments of healthy people, feeling that they do not identify disorders significant enough to justify the expense and time spent.

That the standard physical may not be worth the cost is the opinion of some life insurance companies that have rejected the traditional physician examination in favor of using computerized laboratory data to assess the health of insurance applicants.

Is that a better program—routine laboratory profiles rather than annual physicals? Unfortunately, laboratory normals are not absolutes and frequently are not disease-associated. A figure considered abnormal a decade ago may be within the normal limits for good health today, now that more sophisticated methods demonstrate how common that figure is in people with average life spans.

For example, the upper level of uric acid "normal" has risen from 4 to 8.5 in ten years. And even then, not all patients with elevated uric acids have gout or other related diseases. Evaluation of fasting glucose levels is quite arbitrary and even today is not definitive of disease. What is the normal cholesterol and other lipids? Are they as important as we thought ten years ago?

When I questioned the Cleveland Clinic about the value of the periodic health examination, the clinic could say only that "the answers are coming in the future." The Mayo Clinic tells me it has now scheduled less-frequent examinations for its own staff, provided the staff member feels well, has no symptoms, and no past history requiring frequency of evaluation.

Individual physicans at medical meetings cite the poor yield from subjecting healthy people to detailed workups, and some hospital pathologists have suggested to their colleagues that indiscriminate lab profiles on admission may not catch enough disease to justify the cost.

There may be justification in the eyes of the patient whose disease *is* caught by the test. If you were the one patient in 19,000 found to have tuberculosis by routine chest X-ray in one Georgia hospital one year, then the test was 100 percent effective for you. But what is the radiation safety factor?

Is widespread routine testing of healthy people a fair allocation of medical resources?

Attempts to approach health problems from the preventive

angle are already on trial. The Kellogg Foundation has funded a computerized health hazard appraisal system (HHA) at the University of Arizona to advise people of their disease probabilities and life expectancies.

At one HHA in action in Duluth, Minnesota, 336 people were assessed and the process repeated 18 months later. 80 percent of the patients had reduced their alcohol consumption; 70 percent had altered at least one bad health habit; 50 percent had cut down on or stopped smoking and 50 percent had reduced their weight by at least five pounds.

Is this the answer? Will it work? Perhaps not after the novelty wears off. We're dealing with human nature and the elusive quirks that make people different from the beasts—foibles which allow people to smoke knowing it's harmful while encouraging lip service to the bogus benefits of annual physicals.

Indeed, the same quirks of human nature make doctors avoid such exams for themselves. A recent survey showed that only about 11 percent of the responding doctors submitted themselves to annual physical examinations. The excuses of the 89 percent varied from "I don't like doctors," to "I don't know any good doctors."

Despite all this skepticism, there are two important things pilots can do: lose weight if obese, and stop smoking. Dieting may be the easier of the two restrictions.

There are two simple diets many doctors use for brief programs. They will work if followed but, like all diets, tend to become boring. Patients should not diet without checking first with their own doctors, and those persons dieting over a long period of time require particular care.

One easy diet, however, works well for many patients. It provides about 1050 calories a day and is usually well followed because it is a menu as well as a diet. In contrast to many heavily touted or bogus diets, it lacks a name and is just called:

Low-Calorie Diet

Breakfast

½ cup tomato juice

1 piece toast with ¼-½ teaspoon butter of ½ cup flake or puffed or dry cereal or ½ cup cooked cereal

1 cup skim milk

Coffee or tea—unlimited—no cream or sugar

Lunch and Dinner

1 moderate serving of lean meat or poultry or fish or ¾ cup cottage cheese or three ounces of cheese

½ cup of either potato, rice, macaroni, plain spaghetti, or plain noodles with one teaspoon butter or ½ cup of one of the following:

Beets	Green Peas	Squash (Winter)
Carrots	Pumpkin	Turnips
Onions	Rutabagas	Frozen Mixed Vegetables

Raw vegetable salad with low calorie dressing (1-2 teaspoons)

1 small apple or peach or banana or orange or tangerine—all fresh or ½ cup canned water-packed fruit

Coffee or tea—unlimited—no cream or sugar

1 cup skim milk

There is another simple diet used by many people for brief periods. The diet contains no sugar, is low in starch, moderate in fat, and high in protein. Because it allows such a wide choice of foods, it is sometimes referred to as a "free" diet.

Of course, nothing is free in life; all kinds of high-protein diets to lose weight are suspect beyond a few weeks. Consult your doctor or local hospital dietician.

Free Diet

1. Eat and drink as much of the following as you need to satisfy your hunger: Lean meat (including poultry, liver, kidneys, lean ham, bacon, and grilled sausages), fish, eggs, cheese (especially cottage cheese), salads, vegetables, fresh fruit (except bananas), fruit bottled or canned without sugar (sweetened with saccharin if necessary), nuts as part of a main dish, condiments (sour pickles, Worcestershire sauce), tea, coffee, consommes, low-calories juices.

2. You may have: (a) One half-point (284 ml.) of fresh milk daily.

(This includes all milk taken in tea, coffee, etc.) (b) One ounce (28 g.) of butter, margarine, or cream. (c) Up to 3 slices (3 oz. or 85 g) of low calories bread or 6 pieces of rye crisp daily. Instead of 1 slice (1 oz. or 28 g.) of bread, you may have either: (i) One small helping daily of plain cereal product such as cornmeal, macaroni, spaghetti, oatmeal, rice, or a non-sweetened breakfast cereal. Wholewheat bread, brown bread, or brown cereals are better for health than white bread or cereals. (ii) A glass of beer or one short drink. (iii) For those who cannot resist sweets, 1 oz. (28 g.) of a favorite item. (d) One or two potatoes per day.

3. You may have *nothing else whatever*. Note especially that this means *no* bread, except as previously mentioned; *no* cookies (dry or sweet), cake, or pastry; *no* cereals, except as previously mentioned; *no* thick sauces, thick soups, puddings, ice cream; *no* sugar, syrup, chocolate, sweets, cocoa, honey, jam; *no* alcoholic drinks, sweetened fruit drinks, or sugar-sweetened carbonated beverages [but see (ii) above]. These items all contain refined sugar or flour.

4. Weigh yourself before you begin, and once a week or once every two weeks afterwards, on the same scales, in the same clothes, and at the same time of day. You should eat three or four meals a day. Do not eat between meals. You should lose between 5 and 15 pounds (2.27 and 6.8 kg.) per month. If you cannot keep strictly to your low-carbohydrate intake, you will need to limit your cheese to an average of 2 oz. (57 g.) per day. If you wish to make the diet a little more strict, peas, beans (except green beans), parsnips, sweet corns, and grapes should be omitted. If you suffer from constipation, take up to 1 oz. (28 g.) of bran daily.

What about rest and exercise in the role of health? Is there any doctor around with some sensible fresh advice? Let's look at this prescription from a perceptive physician:

> You should get up before sunrise, wash your face and hair, clean your teeth. Then you should take a short walk before beginning the daily work. Breakfast should be a light meal, consisting of bread with a thin soup, some vegetables, cucumber, or whatnot, varying with the season, and simply prepared.

> The first meal is to be followed, during the hot hours, by a siesta in a cool, shady and retired spot. This

rest should be succeeded by a further spell at the day's occupations, after which exercise should again be enjoyed.

The chief meal of the day should be in the evening, which in summer will be just before sunset. It is to consist of fruit, vegetables, bread, and fish or meat. Then a short walk should be taken, followed by an early turn-in to bed.

If you like this simplicity, and want to try it, don't bother to write to the physician. Diocles of Carystus died in the fourth century B.C.

SMOKING

More *recent* advice from a 1981 study at Seattle University showed that an employee who smokes costs his employer about $4,789 a year more than a non-smoker, if one calculates the cost of higher medical bills, increased sickness, value of time lost, and even the increased cost of office cleaning.

Yet it is easier to diet than stop smoking. There's only one way to quit cigarettes and it's the hard way. It's called *stopping*.

Why spend money on cigarettes to fill your lungs with pollution when American industry will do it for you free? (courtesy National Oceanic and Atmospheric Administration)

However, the National Institutes of Health feel that people should first know why they have been smoking. A psychologist, Dr. Daniel H. Horn, believes that persons smoke for six reasons: because they are stimulated by cigarettes, because they need to handle something when they're busy, because of the genuine pleasure they get from cigarettes, because they get relief of stress by cigarette smoking, because they are addicted and crave the next one as soon as they put one out, and finally because they are slaves of habit.

You may want to know what the NIH tell those who quit cigarettes what to expect. Here's their story:

Immediate Rewards

"No one knows better than you that quitting smoking isn't easy and it isn't fun. Cigarettes were your constant companion for a long time. You probably had yourself convinced that cigarettes helped you through the bad times and made the good times better. By now, however, you know that cigarettes didn't really help you at all. They didn't pick you up—they let you down. Smoking cigarettes made you feed tired, gave you headaches, a cough, a foul-tasting mouth, and a case of the jitters. They robbed you of your wind, your energy and your health.

"Within 12 hours after you have your last cigarette, your body begins to heal itself. The level of carbon monoxide in your system declines rapidly and your heart and lungs begin to repair the damage caused by cigarette smoke.

"Within a few weeks, you will begin to notice some remarkable changes in your body. You'll discover that your sense of taste is returning, and if you had a smoker's hack, it's gone. Your digestive system is returning to normal. Your head is clear—no more headaches or dizzy spells from cigarettes.

"Most important of all, you feel really alive—full of energy and strength. You're breathing easier. You can climb a hill or a flight of stairs without becoming winded or dizzy.

"The psychological benefits of kicking the smoking habit are far too numerous to list here. They involve freedom from the mess, smell, inconvenience, expense, and dependence we all associate with cigarette smoking. And you know them better than anyone.

Long-Range Health Benefits

"One of every five sick days smokers miss from work is due to smoking. And one of every 10 days smokers spend sick in bed is due to their cigarette habit. Now that you've quit, you've added a number of healthy, productive days to each year of your life. Most important, you've greatly improved your chances for a longer life.

Recovery Symptoms

"As your body begins to repair itself, instead of feeling better, you may feel worse. These 'withdrawal pangs' are really symptoms of recovery. Immediately after quitting, many ex-smokers experience 'symptoms of recovery' such as temporary weight gain caused by fluid retention, irregularity, and sore gums or tongue. You may also feel edgy and more short-tempered than usual.

"It is important to understand that the unpleasant aftereffects of quitting are only temporary and signal the beginning of a healthier life."

Developing New Habits to Counter Fatigue and Weight Gain

The *Calling It Quits* leaflet available from NIH contains lots of tips on avoiding temptation, finding new health habits and coping with the "crazies" once you've quite smoking.

If you are concerned about feelings of fatigue or the possibility of gaining weight, you may want to review the suggestions provided in *Calling It Quits* that can help you avoid these side effects and develop new habits such as:

- ☐ Getting enough rest so that you are at your best, physically and mentally.
- ☐ Eating five or six small meals a day instead of two or three big ones.
- ☐ Eating foods high in protein to give you more energy.
- ☐ Drinking a lot of the right fluids: water to increase your circulation and stimulate digestion; milk to soothe your nerves and avoid fatigue; citrus or tomato juice to give you a quick energy boost.
- ☐ Beginning a habit of regular exercise.

Smoking and Your Heart

The American Heart Association has several useful pamphlets on the nicotine theme including an especially sensible one, *How to Stop Smoking!* Write for it or see your doctor.

Learn about the American Heart Association. It says it is fighting for your life. It has all the answers to the most commonly asked questions about smoking, such as:

Are there more heart attacks among smokers than non-smokers? In a study of the smoking habits of middle-aged men, observed over a number of years, it was found that the heart attack rate in heavy cigarette smokers was twice as high as in non-smokers.

Are there more deaths from heart attacks among cigarette smokers? In studies of various population groups, it was found that death rates from heart attacks in men range from 50 to 200 percent higher among cigarette smokers than among nonsmokers, depending on age and the amount smoked. The average increase is 70 percent.

Smoking is an added risk for people who are more susceptible to coronary artery disease, such as those with high blood pressure, high blood cholesterol, signs of hardening of the arteries, a family history of heart attacks and strokes in middle age, or a combination of any of these conditions.

Are cigarettes a health hazard for teen-agers? Yes, there is enough evidence of harmful effects on the body to discourage smoking even in young, healthy people. Obviously, the earlier you begin to smoke, the greater the risk to your health in future years. You may even risk a shortened life-span.

Smoking is a hard habit to break. Teen-agers who never smoke will never have the problem of trying to do without tobacco.

Does cigarette smoking cause heart disease? It has not been proved that cigarette smoking is a direct cause of heart disease. However, studies strongly suggest that it contributes to or speeds up the development of coronary artery disease which leads to heart attacks.

What are the effects on the body of substances in tobacco smoke? Tobacco contains nicotine which acts on the heart, blood vessels, digestive tract, kidneys, and nervous system. It also contains minute amounts of tars and other substances that may produce cancer and irritants which chiefly affect the bronchial tubes. Small amounts of carbon monoxide and arsenic are also present in tobacco smoke.

Ninety percent of the nicotine (and probably other substances in tobacco) is absorbed into the body when smoke is inhaled; 10 percent is absorbed when smoke is puffed without inhaling.

How does smoking affect the circulatory system? Cigarette smokers have higher levels of carbon monoxide in their blood. In most people who have been tested, smoking makes the heart beat faster, raises the blood pressure, and narrows blood vessels of the skin, especially in the fingers and toes. In normally healthy people, these changes are temporary and differ in degree according to the individual's response to tobacco. Persons who are hypersenitive to tobacco have the most pronounced reactions.

Why is smoking especially dangerous for patients with diseases of blood vessels in the arms and legs (peripheral vascular diseases)? Smoking aggravates their condition because it constricts blood vessels that are already narrowed and damaged. Patients with peripheral vascular disease are strongly warned against smoking, because those who continue to smoke increase their risk of gangrene, amputations, and even death. The effects of smoking are especially evident in Buerger's disease which occurs almost exclusively in men who smoke. This disease affects the small arteries of toes and fingers in early stages, but may later involve larger blood vessels. When the patient stops smoking the condition almost always is arrested, but a return to smoking causes it to recur.

Smoking is also dangerous for patients with atherosclerosis (hardening of the arteries) of the extremities, a disease that interferes with the circulation in legs and feet.

What other serious diseases appear frequently in smokers? Lung cancer appears much more frequently in cigarette smokers than in nonsmokers. A number of statistical studies indicate that cigarette smoking is the chief explanation for the increase in lung cancer since 1920. Studies have also shown that chronic bronchitis and emphysema (a destructive disease of the lungs) are often associated with smoking. Abnormal tissue changes related to these diseases have been observed in the lungs and bronchial tubes of heavy cigarette smokers.

Even young smokers sometimes develop a chronic cough. It is believed that a "cigarette cough" may predispose a person to emphysema or to the more serious forms of bronchitis.

How is emphysema related to heart disease? Emphysema, a chronic disease that makes breathing difficult, may result in heart failure. Smoking aggravates emphysema. In nonsmokers who develop emphysema, the disease is apt to be less severe.

Are there other effects on health from smoking? Tobacco may cause reactions in the stomach and intestines that affect normal digestion, or make gastrointestinal disorders become worse. Smoking appears to slow down the healing of gastric and duodenal ulcers and tends to make them chronic. In some other digestive problems, symptoms may be relieved when smoking is stopped.

Is there any risk in moderate cigarette smoking? All cigarette smokers run extra risk of coronary disease in proportion to the number of cigarettes smoked. Heavy cigarette smokers have higher death rates from heart attacks than moderate smokers. According to present evidence, smoking pipes and cigars does not increase the risk of heart disease, as does cigarette smoking.

Why is there less risk of heart disease among pipe or cigar smokers? Probably because the pipe and cigar smoker usually does not inhale.

How effective are filtered cigarettes? Most filters now in use reduce only moderately the amount of harmful substances in cigarette smoke. So far, there is no evidence that filters are the answer to "safe" smoking.

If you have been a heavy smoker, does it help to stop? Yes, because the death rate from coronary artery disease decreases among those who give up smoking, and after a period of years, approaches that of people who never have smoked. Also, in individuals who stop smoking, some abnormal changes in body tissues may revert to-ward normal.

Something of this advice, quoted here directly from the AHA, seems to be working. In 1981, Americans smoked an average of 3850 cigarettes or 192.5 packs per person. However, eight years previously in 1973, Americans averaged 4148 cigarettes or 207 packs that year. This per capita consumption drop of 14 percent shows that health messages are getting through—people *are* trying to quit cigarettes.

AGING

You can alter your smoking habits to improve your health but you can't make yourself any younger. The aging pilot belongs in a special category as does the aging surgeon: When should he quit?

There's no simple answer because individuals age at different speeds. I often think that in aging I'm in the left-hand lane but I have many elderly patients almost double my age who are sharp mentally and cheerful as well. After all, wasn't it Maurice Chevalier who was once asked how he liked being 80 and replied "It certainly beats the alternative!"

It's not necessarily correct that all performance suffers as a person ages. A study done at the University of Western Ontario Faculty of Medicine in Canada suggested that because children are smarter than they used to be, they show up their elders. Said Morris M. Schnore, PhD, who carried out the research, "Most of the difference in performance on intelligence tests is not due to a decline in the abilities of the old but is due to higher levels of

Nothing unusual about a Lake aircraft landing in New Hampshire, unless it's being piloted by a man celebrating his 95th birthday.

performance in successive generations." It was found, for example, that the test scores of soldiers in World War II were one standard deviation higher than those of soldiers in World War I.

There are certainly many old people whose names immediately come to mind as dynamic, busy, active persons in their late years. Winston Churchill was articulate and capable well into his 80s. In their older years, Lowell Thomas was lecturing, Richard Rogers was composing, Arthur Fiedler was conducting, Count Basie was playing, Mabel Mercer was singing, Lillian Gish was acting, and Martha Graham was dancing. Similarly peppy were Admiral Hyman Rickover, anthropologist Margaret Mead, and architect Buckminster Fuller. They all had one thing in common: It wasn't sound nutrition, adequate rest and marvelous health. No, it was *attitude*, a feeling of still being needed and still having something to offer.

Take Crocker Snow for example. He first soloed in 1926 and held the post of director of the Massachusetts Aeronautics Commission from 1939 until he retired in 1976. At that time, he was still flying the same Navion he bought new in 1946 because, as he said, "Nobody's improved on it yet." But more important was his response when asked if he was giving up an interest in flying. "No way," he said, "I'd like to see something come of all the things I've been working on."

Crocker Snow instinctively seemed to know that the key to staying young while growing old was to have an interest, a reason for being. The American Medical Association (my God, I'm quoting the AMA—there goes my credibility with some of you!) has said that mandatory retirement is detrimental to the health and even life expectancy of those who want to keep working. Some of the proof is based on the work of a former University of North Carolina researcher, Dr. Susan Haynes.

She studied in an Akron, Ohio, tire factory, retired workers who were forced to quit. She found that three years later their mortaility rates jumped upwards to a rate 30 percent higher than it should have been. Haynes believes that retired workers go through a honeymoon phase in which they delight in idleness, then a few years later they become bored and dissatisfied.

As the old Spanish saying goes: "It is pleasant to do nothing, as long as you have something to do."

It may irritate some pilots to read on but in my opinion the responsibility of being in charge of an airplane can be awesome and more than many older persons need. It's all very well to be, for example, the retired accountant who joined Bankers Life and Casualty at the age of 65 and who ultimately received a gold watch from them after 25 years of exemplary service—but *he* didn't have to make split-second decisions sometimes involving the lives of hundreds. Maybe the older commercial pilot who steps down because he wants to, or because he has to, is appropriately yielding a responsibility that differs materially from that which most elderly patients face.

Voltaire once said that what most people consider a virtue after the age of 40 is simply a loss of energy. However, there are more than two million "old old" persons in America now— people over the age of 80, and some are still private pilots. Should they still be flying? After all, Emerson declared there was a time "to be old/To take in sail."

I've looked after a lot of old patients although none of those mentioned here were ever pilots. Sara Keane, 101 years old; Grannie White, 102; Bertha Horn, 102; Lue Reynolds, 101; Alice Lovell, 102; Gertrude Bowlby, 96; Etta Plummer, 98; Sara Foley, 96; Lotta Esterbrook, 97; and Mabel Gillie, 98 years old. They were all very much with it to the end.

However, there are tests that judge whether an old person—a really old person—is disorientated. One would hope that any pilot with any of those features has already hung up his helmet and his goggles, but readers might be interested in one method of scoring mental status developed by Eric Pfeiffer, MD.

Mental Status Questionnaire

INSTRUCTIONS: Ask subject to answer all questions without reference to calendar, newspaper or other memory aids. Record and evaluate subject's response according to Scoring Criteria below.

1. What is the date today? (Month, day, and year)
   (For correct score, exact month, day and year must be given.)
2. What day of the week is it?
3. What is the name of this place?
   (Any correct description acceptable: "my home" or names of city, town, hospital or institution.)
4. What is your telephone number?
   (Scored correct if telephone number can be verified or repeated at another point in questioning.)
A4. What is your street address?
   (Ask only if patient does not have a telephone.)
5. How old are you?
   (Scored correct when stated age corresponds to birthdate.)
6. When were you born?
7. Who is the President of the U.S. now?
   (Only last name of President required.)
8. Who was President just before him?
   (Only last name of previous President required.)
9. What was your mother's maiden name?
   (No verification needed. Scored correct if female first name and last name other than subject's are given.)
10. Subtract 3 from 20 and keep subtracting 3 from each new number, all the way down.
   (Scored correct if entire series is performed correctly.)

Total number of errors

Scoring Criteria: Service intellectual impairment is indicated by eight or more errors, mild-to-moderate impairment by three to seven errors, and intact intellectual functioning by up to two errors.

These are gross criteria applying to white subjects who have had a partial or complete high school education. One more error should be allowed for subjects who have gone only through grade school or whose learning has been retarded by socioeconomic, environmental or discriminatory factors. One less error should be allowed for subjects who have gone beyond high school.

Testing thus and excluding artifacts may reveal that the old person has memory loss, disorientation, and impairment in judgement and intellect. And if that person is still flying, you may have to take away the keys.

Flying makes for exacting demands. The military experience is that pilots over the age of 45 cannot usually handle the fatigue of combat flying.

Older pilots need more exercise and fresh air. They should break their journeys for a change in routines. (courtesy Beech Aircraft Corp.)

Reflex action and quickness of response slow as we get older. Sometimes the experience and judgement of an older pilot will compensate, but the time comes when age starts to show. Older pilots can be pretty busy, for example, during landing procedures, beset as they are by slower reactions, less manual dexterity, decreased hearing, and impaired vision—especially for night flying. Indeed, the FAA declares that a pilot aged 60 may need ten times the amount of illumination as a 25-year-old.

Another thing to remember is that older pilots are more susceptible to hypoxia and exaggerated response to medication. Maybe the older years are not "prime time" after all, at least for pilots.

What can be done to delay the development of aging in ourselves, the state of old age described by Dr. Alex Comfort as "that involuntary change of dress"?

Well, sometimes you reap in old age what you sowed in earlier years. Moderation in drinking and cessation of smoking can be important as you get older. A proper diet, modified as you age, may help. You need fewer calories and more calcium and bran in your older years. Appropriate treatment of chronic illnesses may be significant.

Interestingly enough, studies in Evans County in Georgia, Abkhazia in Russia, Amsterdam in Holland, and in other foreign countries such as Pakistan and Ecuador have shown that a lifetime of toil and poverty have in some cases produced longevity. The subjects, the reporters said, had been spared the blight of affluence.

Choosing your ancestors wisely can be important. Oak trees seem to produce oak trees.

And finally, remember again that word—*attitude*. When people met in ancient China, a common greeting was "How many glorious years do you have?"

Chapter 4

The Importance of Health

MacKenzie Hume's neck was hurting that morning. With his Spitfire squadron, he had landed without difficulty on an airfield full of shellholes and bomb craters. The airstrip's desolation was par for the course for any field heavily bombed in the Battle of Britain in 1940. However, it was now 1944 and quite unexpected was the sudden jolt in the jeep that catapulted him out of the vehicle as it bumped over the uneven ground.

Pilot Officer Hume stood there rubbing his neck. Exhausted from many combat missions, he wondered whether to go to bed or report sick. He was meant to be back on duty in another four hours, and a fighter pilot who couldn't twist his neck to look to the rear for one second every three would soon be dead. This was why fighter pilots wore white silk scarves. Without them, their coarse collars would have gradually worn through their skin.

Suddenly the siren sounded the alarm: German aircraft approaching!

The squadron scrambled, Hume taking off with the others. His neck was on fire. There was no way he could stand the pain of moving it. If it came to a dogfight he was dead. Perhaps he would be lucky. Perhaps it was a false alarm. Perhaps . . .

The Focke-Wulf 190s were among them in a moment, snarling, scratching, biting. The sky was aflame. Planes, fluttering like bats, fell tumbling out of the skies. In seven minutes it was all over and the air was suddenly as calm as the center of a hurricane.

The Spitfires limped home—those that could—to fight another day. As Hume turned final, he suddenly realized his neck was no longer stiff. In wonder, he wiggled his neck, shrugged his shoulders, and tilted his head—no pain. He was cured. He'd stumbled on an unusual treatment for wry neck: seven minutes of intense physical therapy. He smiles now, 40-odd years later, as he stands beside his glider. "I know I couldn't move that neck," he says, "but I guess the fear factor cancelled out the pain factor."

A DEMANDING CAREER

Seldom is a pilot's health that important at any normal given moment, but those who fly do live in a very precise environment. This is not the place for the lame and the halt. In the skies, there is no generosity. There are many jobs and hobbies that allow casual attitudes, even daydreaming. Flying is not one of them. Flying is a demanding career. It's an activity intolerant of incompetence. It does not accept a performance less than your best. Unfortunately, the act of flying takes a continuous toll. You may be at your best when you start a flight but fatigued when you end it, and the ending—the landing—may be on occasion the most stringent challenge of your day. Peter McGowan points out that "the air will forgive almost any error, while the ground will not."

You need to be healthy to be a good pilot. As a recreation, flying is a rather humorless hobby. It hardly fits the description of a fun sport given by Dr. Scout Lee Gunn, head of the graduate curriculum in leisure counseling at Oklahoma State University. Recreation, she says, should have spontaneity, flexibility and creativity; it should be playful, joyous, and ideally provide "lots of giggles." I don't know any pilots who giggle. In contrast, I believe some private pilots would think Mary Duncan, head of the department of recreation at San Diego State University is right on target when *she* says, "I've known lots of people who have embarked on their leisure time activities for reasons of status. They're skiing or surfing or ballooning just because it's the 'in' thing to do. Many of them are spending far more than they can afford. Going bankrupt can sure take the fun out of recreation."

It sure can. So can a crash. Yet your personal health is as important as your aircraft's soundness. If you learn to control your body as well as you do your plane, not only are you less likely to crash but, in the event you do, you are more likely to survive the catastrophe.

MacKenzie Hume, now a Massachusetts pediatrician, knows

Flying has always attracted dynamic; aggressive people. Just remember, the war's over. Relax to fly, fly to relax. (author photo at San Diego Aerospace Museum)

this from his flying career. He has another military memory that sits on his spare frame like an albatross.

It was his thirteenth mission to Europe. When the flak exploded, his Spitfire staggered and started to lose altitude. The engine quit at 5,000 feet over the English Channel and Hume baled out. He tightened his Rolex watch strap on the way down, and carefully stowed his expensive sheepskin gloves, a parting gift from his mother-in-law.

The water was icy.

His Squadron Commander wheeled overhead to send a bearing on that small spot in the ocean, then left for home, his fuel exhausted. Darkness fell, then a Sea Otter amphibian arrived overhead. Hume knew if the plane landed in those heavy seas it would never be able to take off again. The pilot knew this, too.

Hume had stopped shivering and was reconciled to his fate. The aircraft *couldn't* land. Yet with a roar and a mighty splash the Otter hit the water and taxied over to him! Hume struggled into the cabin and lay panting and shivering on the floor. A flight sergeant pulled him over, and cradling the frozen airman in his arms like a baby, brought his warm stubbly cheek to Hume's icy face.

The seas thrashed the puny Sea Otter and it started to founder. Just before the plane went down, an Air Sea Rescue launch arrived to save them all. The Sea Otter pilot, a New Zealander, received the Distinguished Flying Cross. (And Hume got a new Rolex when that company found out he had ruined his watch.)

He was up in the air within a week, his zest for flying unquenched despite his near-drowning.

As Hume's Air Sea Rescue launch approached the chalky escarpment of England, he saw from sea level what every Allied airman back from the Hell over Europe headed for: the White Cliffs of Dover.

EAGLES WITH CLIPPED WINGS

Those same cliffs had welcomed Julius Caesar in 55 BC and greeted St. Augustine in AD 595 when he arrived with his fellow traveler, Christianity. Here arrived William the Conqueror after the Battle of Hastings in 1066 and in 1909 came the Frenchman, Jean Louis Blériot.

Blériot, that cold morning of 25 July 1909, was far from well. He stood painfully on crutches, shivering despite a tweed suit, a woolen khaki jacket, and blue engineering overalls.

The dawn broke. Blériot looked out to sea and shuddered again in the cold wind. What nonsense for a man on crutches, a handicapped man, to attempt the greatest flight in history! *Mon Dieu*, the foot hurt.

It was no surprise for the few townspeople up that early morning to see their countryman on crutches. Bleriot had shown interest in flying from the very beginning, but between 1900 and 1908 had crashed 50 times, always miraculously avoiding serious injury. However, just twelve days before, his engine had caught fire between Étampes and Orléans, the flames blowing back to his cockpit, badly burning his left leg.

How could a handicapped man hope to be the first to fly from Calais to Dover? Did not a pilot need perfect health—and even then, what hope would an airman have tackling so futile a flight?

The burly figure in the helmet seemed to shrug his shoulders. Blériot rubbed his drooping red walrus mustache, looked at the sky and asked the small crowd, "Where is Dover?"

They pointed. He swung his left leg painfully backwards and forwards, then suddenly announced. "If I cannot walk, I will show the world I can fly." He hobbled to the plane—a tiny dragonfly-like aircraft weighing less than 500 pounds—threw away his crutches, and climbed in.

Thirty-seven minutes and 25 miles later he was over England

"by following his nose." He cut the engine and dumped the plane, his three-cylinder Blériot *No. 11* on to a grassy meadow in Dover.

There are still people alive today in Dover who recall that marvelous moment. One, William Sutton, for example, remembers how he ran up to Dover Castle that summer day. "We were very excited to see him up there," he says, "but disappointed that it wasn't an Englishman."

Blériot went on to become (in 1912) the first man to loop the loop. By the time he died in 1936, he had designed 300 types of aircraft and built 10,000 flying machines. Yet he never did anything more significant than when he ignored a disability and threw away his crutches. Thus he became the most famous man in the world, so important were those 20 or so miles of sea.

Two oceans away, in Hawaii, other handicapped persons have also flown high with the seagulls. One program was started at Honolulu International Airport by a flight instructor Jack Gentry. He became interested in the plight of the wheelchair-bound when he met a 50-year-old-woman, the bookkeeper of the Hawaiian Civil Air Patrol, who'd had polio as a child. Challenged by the situation, he took her up in an Ecroupe and taught her to fly.

Gentry had a theory that persons weren't handicapped until they *proved* that they couldn't do something. He was soon contacted by a Dutchman, Robert Van Wittenberger, a man paralyzed from the waist down. Wittenberger showed great determination and became the first handicapped person in Hawaii to obtain a license, an event soon followed by the successful flight test of the CAP bookkeeper.

Wittenberger was in fact a psychiatrist. He got his license in the Ercoupe, then progressed to a Cherokee fitted with hand controls. You would expect a physician to have special awareness of the problems of the handicapped, and a psychiatrist especially so. Dr. Kyle Hamm, a New Orleans psychiatrist, is no exception. Contracting polio as a senior in high school, Hamm nevertheless went on to medical school on crutches which he still uses. Like many disabled persons he has learned what is important is the attitude rather than the handicap itself.

"There's very little I can't do if I want to put the time and energy into it," he says. "I've spent lots of time proving that I could do things. I once climbed halfway up a pyramid in Mexico."

Dr. Frank Jirka agrees that attitude is important. He has worn two artificial legs since a shell hit his gunboat off Iwo Jima in World War II. He feels it is very important for handicapped persons "to set their sights and go." If they do, handicapped people can overcome their difficulties. Jirka, a Chicago kidney specialist, entered medical school six months after his injury and has taken only two days of sick leave since he started practice. "You'll find that true of many handicapped workers," he says. "They often have better work records than other employees."

Jirka lives what he says. He enjoys boating, swimming, fishing and hunting. Many of his friends and patients are unaware of his difficulties until something unusual happens, such as the time he was dancing and suddenly one of his feet turned backwards!

Steve Carrell, a medical reporter, tells of another physician, now a resident in physical and rehabilitative medicine at the St. Paul-Ramsey Medical Center in Minnesota: Dr. Frank Zondlo. Zondlo lost a leg and nearly died in a car crash during his senior year in medical school. He developed a massive infection requiring a toxic antibiotic which carried a risk that it might cause deafness. Zondlo survived as a deaf amputee, his biggest problem— communication.

He had difficulty learning to lip-read and thinks that the natural talent to do this is rare. His friends suggested he become a pathologist—"I guess because somebody thought dead people would be easy to lip-read"—but now he is busy, often with an interpreter, in treating other disabled persons. He feels there are probably about 18,000 disabled physicians in America and that 25 percent of them could work again if they had proper rehabilitative services.

Disabled persons should be aware of what is happening in the field of rehabilitation. For many, flying could well be the pasttime to get them up and going—literally. Many professionals are devoting their lives to helping the handicapped. One, for example, is Dr. Theobald Reich, codirector of NYU's Rehabilitation Engineering Center. Reich is working with mechanized wheelchairs and electronics environments where controls are activated by blowing into a tube, speaking into a voice box, or flicking a switch. The controls can work door locks, light switches, television knobs, even telephone dials. "At least one of these controls can be operated by virtually any disabled person," Reich says.

In contrast to this *Star Wars* technology are the Tarzan tricks which can be taught to monkeys—capuchin monkeys, the kind formerly used by organ grinders. "Tricks" is an unfair description for the sophisticated experimental program being developed by Dr. Mary Joan Willard in Boston at Tufts University. There, just as guide dogs are used by the blind, so small monkeys are being trained to vacuum, dust, change tape cassettes, and otherwise do a myriad number of tasks for their quadriplegic paralyzed owners. (Can you imagine this? "No wonder my last landing was a dog; it was done by a monkey," would be a marvelous excuse and hanger-tale.)

The reason we're talking about handicapped problems in this book is because conscience dictates it. Those patients don't really get fair treatment from us. They're not asking for pity, just fairness. Some of them could learn to fly and a whole new world could open up for them. Look at what has happened in other activities. Take New Englander Larry Buchine for example: at age 35 he skis and plays volleyball, tennis, and golf. When he was a boy he "didn't do anything except watch TV." Then he lost his leg at the age of 15. Now he *teaches* sports. "Society says handicapped people can't do things," he declares, "so some handicapped people believe it and don't try."

The University of Minnesota is attempting to make handicapped persons try. A program developed with the help of Minnesota Outward Bound encourages disabled persons to rise above their negative expectations of themselves. Robert Blum, MD, who started with this program, accepts that there will be some moments of failure. "If you don't slip, you don't know how far you can go," he tells his people. He believes that you can have devastating illness and still be, in a way, healthy. "We all have limitations," he says. "To be able to live near that edge of what you're capable of doing—to me, that's health."

If you know a handicapped person, consider if flying might not be a possible pastime for him or her. If you know a pilot who quit after an accident, find out—tactfully—whether he could use help to get back in. The factors that make a difference appear to be age, education, cultural background, degree of family support, and amount of two-way communication that develops.

FLYING WITH A HANDICAP

If you want to follow this more fully here are some addresses:

National Handicapped Sports and Recreation Association.
Skiing, waterskiing, golf, horseback riding, whitewater kayaking and rafting, scuba diving

Box 18664
Capitol Hill Station
Denver, CO 80218
Tel: (303) 978-0564

National Wheelchair Athletic Association
All competition is in wheelchairs.
Archery, swimming, table tennis, track and field and weight lifting
40-24 Sixty-Second Street
Woodside, NY 11377
(212) 898-0976

National Association of Sports for Cerebral Palsy
Ambulatory and wheelchair soccer, archery, billiards, bowling, cycle
racing, horseback riding, rifle practice, swimming, table tennis, track
and field, weight lifting
Box 3874
Amity Station
New Haven, CT 06526
(203) 397-2280

Peter Burwash Tennis International
Suite 1507
1909 Ala Wai Boulevard
Honolulu, Hawaii 96815
(808) 946-1236

Winter Park Handicap Ski Program
Box 313
Winter Park, CO 80482
(303) 726-5514

North American Horseback Riding for the Handicapped Association
Box 100
Ashburn, VA 22011
(703) 471-1621

If you wish to fly with a disability, listen to Robert Bornarth, former director of AOPA Pilot Service Department:

The FAA has issued medical certificates to several paraplegics and people with missing limbs.

Choose a local FAA-designated medical examiner and make application for a Third-Class medical certificate. The local doctor will conduct the standard examination and indicate on your application the exact nature of the physical deficiency. The doctor sends the application to the FAA Aeromedical Certification Branch in Oklahoma City for a decision on whether a medical certificate can be issued. In cases of certain static functional losses, such as loss of an extremity, the FAA can issue a medical certificate with the limitation "valid for student pilot privileges only."

When the "student only" certificate is issued, the FAA informs the pilot that authorization to take a medical flight test will be granted as soon as the pilot is ready to take the regular private pilot flight tests.

The pilot then sends the request for authorization back to the Aeromedical Certification Branch. Sometimes the authorization will be handled by the regional flight surgeon.

The authorization for medical flight test, a new medical certificate without the student-only restriction, a Statement of Demonstrated Ability ("waiver"), and instructions on how to conduct the medical portion of the flight test and what to look for during the test are sent by FAA in Oklahoma City directly to the FAA General Aviation District Office where the pilot has indicated he is going to take his flight test. At the conclusion of the flight test, assuming it is passed satisfactorily, the FAA flight inspector issues a temporary private pilot certificate and the new medical certificate and waiver. Appropriate limitations may be placed on the pilot and/or medical certificate. For instance, in the case of a paraplegic pilot, the certificate may carry a limitation that is valid only with respect to airplanes having two controls and a handbrake. In the case of a pilot with an artificial leg, the medical certificate may state it is valid only while the prothesis is worn.

The waiver must be carried along with the medical certificate when flying. When renewing the medical certificate, the waiver should be shown to the doctor. As long as the condition for which the waiver was issued has not worsened, the doctor can issue a new medical certificate without the necessity of any additional tests or red tape.

To fly with a defect may be possible. It is not always safe. The studies on disability defects and flying accidents are difficult to assess. Much of the original work was reported by C.R. Harper, MD, in 1964 in *Aerospace Medicine*.

John D. Dougherty, MD, helped to clarify the data four years later. He found that if normal pilots without defects were ascribed the value 1.00, then pilots with bone and joint defects had a relative risk of accident of 3.80. In other words, they were almost four times as likely to have an accident.

Strangely, this is not the experience in automobile accidents, where the opposite results are obtained. Dougherty, a flight surgeon with the Massachusetts Air National Guard and a fellow at Massachusetts General Hospital, felt the reason for the discrepancy between airplane and automobile was that on the highway, the handicapped drivers learned to drive defensively; by anticipating problems and reacting to them early, they obtained a superior record in road accidents. In the air, all trained pilots fly defensively and therefore to exhibit this trait does not make the handicapped pilot cope better than others.

The risk of accident for pilots with cardiovascular defects was 2.60 in the Dougherty/Harper study; 3.09 for nervous complaints; and 4.65 for muscular defects. Age too played a part. When the figure for below 35 years was given the value of 1.00, the rate for those over 55 years was found to be 1.22. However, as Dougherty said in an article in *Aerospace Medicine* in May 1968: "The combination of information from automobile and aircraft accidents suggests that the increased risk of age is actually associated with physical defects accumulating with age rather than age itself."

Each year over 7,500 Aviation Medical Examiners process the applications of about half a million airmen. Slightly more than one percent of those persons are turned down medically. This group is often unsure of its rights. The FAA describes the system thus:

Just as AMEs are delegated the authority to issue medical certificates, they also have the authority to deny certification when medical standards are not met. To assure the rights of applicants, several avenues of appeal are available. An applicant denied a medical certificate may request reconsideration by the Federal Air Surgeon. If the denial is sustained, the applicant may petition the FAA for a grant of exemption from the applicable standards and/or petition the National Transportation Safety Board (NTSB), which will hold a formal hearing to review the applicant's case. Should the NTSB affirm the FAA's denial, the applicant has the right to take the matter of eligibility to the Federal Courts.

Airman medical standards were originally established during World War I, when more pilots were fatally injured while learning to fly than while flying operationally. These standards merely defined the level of risk and predicted success in training and mission completion. As flight training and pilot replacement became costly, the standards were broadened to incorporate preventive medicine. Today, medical standards are established to maintain fitness of pilots, and other personnel connected with civil aviation, and to ensure that safe environmental conditions and appropriate human-machine relationships exist.

Studies are being conducted to investigate the need for change in the frequency of certification examinations, and to determine if standards are adequate in light of recent medical and technological advances. For instance, studies indicate that an annual evaluation of medical standards—particularly in the area of neurology, endocrinology, and vision—may be beneficial. This activity in the future will draw from abnormal and pathological certification findings to correlate them with accident statistics. This may provide clues as to the detection of disease, gather additional data on crew skills, and more definitively evaluate physiological requirements in present and future aircraft.

Consumers with chronic disease should know about the various organizations formed to help them. They can be found in the *Yellow Pages,* and include:

The Allergy Foundation of America
The American Cancer Society
The American Diabetes Association
The American Foundation for the Blind
The American Heart Association
The Arthritis Foundation
The Epilepsy Foundation of America
Fight for Sight
The Leukemia Society of America, Inc.
The National Association for Visually Handicapped
The National Council on Alcoholism
The National Easter Seals Society
The National Foundation for March of Dimes
The National Hemophilia Foundation
The National Kidney Foundation
The National Multiple Sclerosis Society
The National Paraplegia Foundation
The National Society for Prevention of Blindness
Muscular Dystrophy Association of America

Chapter 5

The Pilot's Challenges

He was old. He was bent up and dried up and old, but he could fly.
He'd known Chamberlin, Mollison, and Wilkins. He'd met Mermoz,
Earhart, and Doolittle. He was on speaking terms with Juan Trippe,
Bill Boeing, and Don Douglas. Eaglerock Biplanes? He'd flown 'em.
Lockheed Vegas? Yup! Stinson Trimotors? You bet! He'd cut his
teeth on 0-M3s. And F.5-Ls and B-6As. You name it. He'd flown it.
He could handle anything.

Except carbon monoxide. It killed him.

He was an old guy. He'd sit hunched up in the right seat of the
ancient Apache, scowling out the window. He'd never look at the
dials. He'd fidget in his seat, peering out at his memories. His frown
would deepen—grumpy old coot. He was supposed to be teaching
me multiengine flying, but there he was, fussing beside me, staring
out at the sky, miles away, probably asleep.

"Fly straight and level, Doc," he suddenly growled, "Don't you
ever watch your instruments?" He continued to glower out the
window, his back turned to me. The dials were a whisker out. Very
gently, imperceptibly, I corrected them.

"That's better," a voice like gravel said, "Now hold it like
that."

He was flying aerobatics before there were talking pictures.
He was as comfortable upside down as any other way. There was no
hair to fall mussed into his face; his leather tanned head was as bald
as the proverbial billiard ball. His face was lined with furrows like a

ploughed field—no, it looked more like a baseball catcher's mitt. It was a lived-in face, as brown and wrinkled as a walnut. His eyes were blue, deep blue, but maybe that's because they were always turned up to the sky—that is, if they weren't turned on you with an unblinking stare as he asked you, his student, a question.

His hands were gnarled—bits missing here and there, left behind in a Wright Whirlwind engine at Hadley Field and in a Hispano-Suiza at Old Orchard Beach. Not to mention other cuts from Argus and Jupiter and Hall-Scott engines, and marks from the struts of a Bellanca, the undercarriage of a Consolidated Fleetster, and the wings of a "Flying Washboard."

Yet those hands on a stick could do anything—provided of course his blood pulsated rich and red, not pink, as it was the day it killed him.

He was flying inverted, getting ready for the Labor Day Parade he'd held every autumn at his small airport. That special New England nip was in the fall air. The trees were early that year and already starting to turn gold and red. He flew down the runway upside down—"brains in his feet" he used to say. He came over the numbers and ever so gently flew into the ground.

His son and I stood immobile, frozen.

The Decathlon slid across the blacktop in a shower of sparks, then exploded. What was left of the body showed carbon monoxide poisoning. What was left of the plane showed where the leak had come from.

He was a great old guy, an original, a pioneer. We loved that old cuss—worshipped him. He could do anything in the air. He could handle anything.

Except carbon monoxide.

CARBON MONOXIDE

It's a colorless, tasteless, odorless enemy. It creeps up like a thief, and what it steals ruins everything.

Carbon monoxide is not usually present in the body in significant amounts except in smokers. Some student pilots get confused between carbon *dioxide*, which is present normally in air expired from the lungs, and carbon *monoxide*, a gas found when combustion occurs in conditions where fresh air or oxygen is not plentiful.

For the body to function, oxygen must be transported through the *entire* system, but the brain is particularly vulnerable to oxygen lack. Oxygen in the lungs passes through the air sacs into the tiny blood capillaries where it combines with a chemical called *hemoglobin* in the red blood cell.

In normal situations there is no problem. For example: Breathe in—a deep breath. Good. That big breath flooded your lungs with air and sent a great gust of oxygen slapping into your blood where it immediately stuck to the red cells like flies to flypaper. The combination called *oxyhemoglobin* gives oxygenated blood a bright red appearance.

The gas carbon monoxide (which, incidentally, is classified as a chemical asphyxiant), reacts competitively with oxygen for the hemoglobin. But carbon monoxide has a great, tragic advantage: It finds hemoglobin with an affinity for it at body temperature that is 218 times heloglobin's affinity for oxygen.

If there's any carbon monoxide around, the oxygen has to fight for its place on the red blood cell—and it loses. It's like being number 219 on standby for a 747 when the desk calls out that there's one seat available. Blood full of carbon monoxide has a horrible pink look to it, an appearance which persists and gives a clue to the pathologist doing the post mortem examination.

Yes, post mortem, because they *die*, those victims. They do die. This is for keeps.

You can pick up a newspaper in the Northeast any winter and read about some night watchman asphyxiated behind a closed-up stove in his small hut. There's also usually a story about a young couple found dead at a drive-in movie—ignition on, engine running, heater turned up, windows closed—the car park empty, everyone gone home except two who never will.

The risks are always there for the general aviation pilot because most single-engine aircraft are warmed by air that has passed over the exhaust manifolds, and if the manifolds have a crack, carbon monoxide mingles imperceptibly with the air breathed. The pilot may be lucky: He may smell exhaust fumes rather than the odorless carbon monoxide. He may notice that he's not as sharp as usual, that he feels tired and sleepy. He may become dizzy, uneasy, and develop headache. If he's fortunate, he'll catch on, open the windows, and turn off the heater.

If he has oxygen in the cabin, he should put on the mask and flush out his body for at least ten minutes. But he should land promptly and have his plane checked out.

Such a pilot would be unusually lucky. Normally, a pilot who smokes already has up to 10 percent carbon monoxide concentration in his body at peak periods of smoking. Alcohol potentiates the problem too, as does altitude. More likely is that the pilot would not smell exhaust fumes and would just drop off to sleep at the wheel with tragic consequences.

It doesn't take much carbon monoxide to create a problem. A typical airplane engine, running rich, will have about 7 percent carbon monoxide in its exhaust; a leak into a 50-cubic-foot cabin will soon give a concentration of one part carbon monoxide to 20,000 parts air, a dangerous amount.

Although an FAA Central Region study once suggested that more than 20 percent of aircraft flying have detectable amounts of carbon monoxide present, and one in a hundred has *dangerous* levels, you can actually get into difficulties with an airplane that's normal.

Just as policemen on point duty sometimes become ill from the exhaust fumes of traffic around them, so you can become poisoned just by following in the traffic pattern close to other airplanes—especially jet aircraft. Try not to sit for ages waiting to take off while a jet blows its exhaust around you. You could become an unsuspecting victim of this silent enemy.

Most pilots who end up ill with carbon monoxide poisoning are, however, casualties of poor maintenance on their own aircraft. It is not enough to arrange an inspection at the start of cold weather.

Whether it's an old Pinto or a 24-year-old Cessna, it's more likely to have carbon monoxide in its cockpit than the latest from Detroit or Wichita.

Some winter experts say your heating and exhaust systems should be checked after every 25 hours of flight use.

Inexpensive carbon monoxide detectors can be bought at any pilot shop. Use them and keep them fresh, especially if you're flying an old aircraft.

We are seeing a lot of drivers with carbon monoxide illness in winter emergency rooms these days as more and more people continue to drive old cars because of the high price of new ones. But even new cars that are stationary with engines running can allow carbon monoxide to enter the vehicle when there is no slipstream to wash the exhaust away from under the floor.

I remember one cold night going off with my wife to attend a hospital Christmas party but stopping for a house call on the way. I left Margaret in the car with the engine running and went into the house. An old lady had fallen, bruised her shoulder, and become a bit excited. It took me about 45 minutes with the help of the patient's brother to get this old woman squared away. (She didn't want to go to bed and all 100 pounds of her fought us all the way.)

When I finally returned to the automobile—a new Mercury—my wife was confused, drowsy and had a splitting headache, clearly from the fumes that had entered the car. I had to cancel the party, so that was *two* fights I had that night with little old ladies.

COLD WEATHER

Heaters—with their risks of carbon monoxide—are not so necessary if those folks out in cold weather would just dress appropriately. If you pile on the clothes in layers, you may not need a heater. A warm hat, warm boots and gloves with perhaps a snug scarf can make all the difference. See what the pilot shops have in the way of government surplus items.

Failure to dress appropriately for cold weather is a common mistake for the pilot whose travels may take him in a single day from one extreme of climate to another. If a pilot goes from a warmer atmosphere to a colder one and from a lower level to a higher one, he is really challenging his body's ability to maintain the status quo.

William J. Mills, Jr., MD, a consultant on cold injury to the U.S. Army Surgeon General and physician with the U.S. Public Health Service in Alaska, was once critical of climbing catastrophes on Mount McKinley and Mount Foraker in 1976, where ten climbers died and many became ill with high-altitude mountain sickness.

In high terrain, the pilot may be hypoxic even on the ground. Watch density altitude. (courtesy FAA)

Most of those afflicted were experienced climbers and some were Swiss guides.

Their mistake was in getting too high too soon—the method: landing by aircraft from altitudes from 8,000 to 13,000 feet then rapidly climbing higher. This is the disadvantage of the airplane: It can dump a person suddenly at altitude to face all the problems of cold and hypoxia without aclimatization.

Mills feels that the serious problems of frostbite and frostnip are nothing compared to the slow, insidious danger of *hypothermia*. This sometimes-fatal drop in body temperature occurs especially in tired persons in poor physical condition who have been overexerting in hypoxic situations. Inadequate clothing and deficient fluid intake are other factors.

It's hard to get pilots to drink enough fluid when they're dehydrated. Research on endurance athletes such as competition cyclists and marathon runners show that by the time an athlete is thirsty, he's about four pints down. But not only is the person in cold weather or high altitude not drinking enough—he's also *losing* too much. The dry air creates a situation where every breath out takes body moisture with it. At times, a pilot may find his throat so dry that radio communication becomes difficult. If he's on oxygen, the dry throat is even worse.

The "dry nose" that pilots get is not due to the coldness of the air but to the dryness of it. In cold climes, every breath has to pass through the nasal and throat passages where it is warmed and humidified. This invaluable process dries out the lining of the nose but it certainly protects the deeper structures of the lung. In 1945, two internists, Moritz and Weisiger, reported on the case of a wounded airman who was exposed in a damaged gun turret for three hours to an outside temperature of $-58°F$ and an airspeed of 160 mph. Despite a frozen face and swollen upper air passages, there was no evidence of injury to the lungs themselves, and the aviator survived.

The opposite of dry nose is "nose drip," which occurs when the moist air is exhaled. This simple condensation at the end of the nose can be a constant irritation for any pilot struggling through his preflight in cold weather, and surely there is no colder place in winter than a windswept open airfield.

There is evidence that some pilots hurry through preflight examinations in winter, certainly the very time that extra care is needed to confirm that the airplane is ready for whatever the weather ahead may offer. The most important part of the preflight should be done first, before any cold-confusion makes you speed up dangerously on what you are checking. Pilots should load luggage and get the cockpit squared away at an earlier stage, not as part of the preflight. This enables the pilot to do his examination of the aircraft in segments, returning to warm up before carrying out the next part. Only this discipline prevents rushed preflights in cold weather.

Dr. Ove Silson, director of the Institute of Aviation Medicine, Linkoping, Sweden, reminds pilots not to wash their hands before preflighting an aircraft. If your hands are moist and you remove your gloves to touch metal, your skin will immediately freeze to the metal. Even cold liquids will give your frostbite if you spill them on your hands in Arctic weather. And remember too that spilled fuel in low humidity/high static electricity environments can cause explosions.

Frostnip and its more serious form, frostbite, are now better understood. In frostbite, tiny crystals of ice form in the tissues, usually in exposed extremeties like ears, nose, hands, and feet. Fast rewarming by any method is the best treatment. Rubbing the affected part with snow is *not* appropriate, even though old medical texts suggested it was. All this does is injure the part already in trouble and cool it further as the snow melts.

If you believe you've been nipped by the cold, get back into shelter, get a warm drink into your body, and hold a warm hand against the cold ear or tuck a cold hand into a warm armpit. Plunging the part into hot water makes sense unless you're going out into the cold again.

The basis of cold weather protection is to dress in, layers starting with wool, flannel, thermal, or polypropylene underclothing. Every aviation authority seems to quote the U.S. Air Force advice for winter clothing suggestions. Let us do the same; military personnel have been fighting cold weather for generations.

The U.S. Air Force recommends that:

> Airmen wear at least three layers of clothing in wintry areas. The first layer, next to the skin, should be loose-fitting wool (the best woven material for heat retention), loose twill, cotton, or quilted thermal underwear. Looseness is stressed because tight-fitting garments restrict the all-important circulation of blood.
>
> The inner garment should be cuffed at the neck, wrists, and ankles to retain warmth. The second layer should be a medium-weave, medium-weight one or two-piece garment—again, not tight-fitting. The outer layer should be wind-resistant, like nylon, and must include a hood. Clothing that will protect windchill should not be waterproofed or rubberized. Material which does not "breathe" may soak the wearer in perspiration during active periods, and the imprisoned dampness will add to his discomfort.
>
> For working around an aircraft in cold weather, a light nylon glove worn under a heavy glove or mitten is recommended. This permits the nylon gloved hand to be used for careful work with frozen metals without risking skin damage.
>
> Paradoxical as it may sound, it is possible to become both frostbitten and badly sunburned at the same time. Skin creams can do double duty in protecting sensitive areas like the lips, nose, ears, and cheeks from intense sun, while also reducing exposure to cold.
>
> Winter sun can also be a hazard to the eyes, especially if there is snow on the ground. A good pair of

sunglasses should be placed in the upper pocket of the parka and kept there in a case; forced landing could easily damage or destroy the glasses worn while flying, and snowblindness could hamper a drowned pilot's efforts to remain alive and comfortable until rescued.

In theory, a man trained to survive under rigorous conditions could provide himself with virtually all of the shelter he needed from the materials found at hand in the area where he lands. But the fact is that the great majority of pilots are not so trained, and although one tends to learn fast under conditions of stress, there is no reason to make survival contingent on luck, labor, or ingenuity. The thoughtful pilot who *wears* his basic sheltering equipment can fly with much greater ease of mind than the shirt-sleeved, carefree airman who closes his eyes and relies on good luck rather than on good sense.

But respect cold weather. It can defeat even the trained athlete who is appropriately dressed: There were 76 cases of frostbite during the 1979 pre-Olympic trials at Lake Placid.

So much for winter.

You can put more on in cold weather but for the opposite type of threat—heatstroke—there's a limit to what you can take off.

HEATSTROKE

Much of the terrain overflown by the American pilot is desert. If he's on a vacation trip, he's often flying the desert in summer, the hottest season. Even if there are no problems and the flight progresses on schedule, the pilot and his passengers are being subjected to a considerable challenge of excessive heat.

The human adult body loses about five pints of water a day in the form of excreta, moist exhaled air, and sweating. If you lose 2½ percent of your water weight you may become unwell and irrational, and losing 10 percent of your water weight may cause such irreversible changes that it could be fatal.

Yet a peculiarity of those subjected to heat stress is that they will not drink enough and thus suffer from "voluntary dehydration." Persons in trouble surrounded by water have had to be reminded to drink.

Some of the best information we have on heatstroke has come from the USAF School of Aerospace Medicine at Brooks AFB in

Dehydration can occur rapidly in the American Southwest. Keep up your fluid intake—don't forget to drink.

Texas and the Heller Institute of Clinical Research, Tel-Hashomer, Israel, because military organizations certainly have to confront the problem of heat.

The description of the high motivation of military recruits could well be the explanation of why pilots, under pressure to perform, are also at risk of heatstroke in desert flying. In portraying those altruistic, dedicated, professional soldiers as candidates for heatstroke, Shibolet in Israel says, "Under other circumstances, these same individuals would have rested when tired, taken liquid when thirsty, or remained at home when ill."

He points out that heatstroke is more easily prevented than treated. The advice seems logical: Take adequate rest and fluids before physical exertion in heat, and rest during work to cool off and to drink adequately. Don't wear impermeable polyester clothing in hot countries. Get aclimatized slowly. Reduce alcohol but not fluid intake. Rest more.

Despite widespread use of salt tablets by athletes in the American South in summer, there is still argument as to whether this is needed. A normal diet contains 10 to 15 grams of salt daily, more than you could ever lose in sweat. Sometimes gastrointestinal flu with fluid loss will hit people and predispose them to heatstroke later.

It's not always the outside heat that is important, but rather the inner source of heat the person produces. An Australian physician, Sutton, has described cases of heat injury where the outside temperature was 16°C. However, in the United States, the hot summer of 1980 caused more than 1,000 deaths, many of them elderly persons who could not handle the heat or could not be induced to drink enough fluids.

Road runners should understand their fluid needs in hot weather. An athlete should drink half a pint of water 15 minutes before starting a marathon race and should continue to drink the same amount every two miles. He should not judge his needs by whether or not he is thirsty.

Pilots, however, have more problems than thirst. If you fly a lot in the American Southwest, you will already be using space blankets in an attempt to keep cabin temperatures down in parked airplanes (Your avionics will thank you.) You'll tie down in the shade, and over grass rather than above white concrete. And you'll open up an airplane to ventilate it before you even start your preflight. Nevertheless, the oven-like heat inside a parked vehicle is unbelievable. During World War II, a temperature of 190°F was recorded in the seat of a jeep at Imperial Valley Navy Station in California.

If you suspect that any member of your party is suffering from heatstroke, get that person rapidly into the shade, start fanning, and keep the skin wet. Try to get fluid into the patient quickly. If the

In desert flying, always note where you last saw water. In a crash/survival situation, it can be lifesaving.

patient is ill, attempt rapid cooling by any method: alcohol sponges, air conditioning, ice packs, ice water baths. Call a doctor.

Even if you're able to avoid heatstroke, you can still fall to severe sunburn. Norman Levine, MD, a dermatologist at the University of Arizona Health Sciences Center, Tucson, states that in hot climes persons should avoid the hours of greatest sunlight concentration—10 a.m. to 2 p.m. He feels that mineral oil, baby oil, and all the other lotions "neither protect from sunburn nor allow a better tan to develop."

His program to avoid sunburn is the time-honored one: Start your exposure with a small "dose" of sun—about 15 minutes' worth—and gradually increase the amount. Don't be deceived by cloudy hazy days because ultraviolet light can penetrate clouds. Watch out for reflected light from sand, water, or pavement. Wear appropriate protective clothing when not swimming or sunbathing. Use sunscreen creams and, since they are water-soluble, reapply them after swimming or perspiring heavily. Don't forget to protect your lips.

But sunburn pales beside the significance of heatstroke. This threat is important. It kills: urban dwellers, high school athletes, sauna enthusiasts, Mecca pilgrims, and military recruits. It starts wars: Of 146 Englishmen imprisoned in the "Black Hole of Calcutta" in 1756, 123 died in one night. It loses battles: King Edward's men in armor in the Crusades forfeited the Holylands to Arab horsemen and heat prostration. It's part of our heritage: The Old Testament is thought to discuss heatstroke in II Kings 4:18-20.

MOTION SICKNESS

I've vomited in the *Queen Elizabeth* in mid-Atlantic, in a French ferry boat in the English Channel, and, God forgive me, in a harbor-cruise boat on the glassy millpond calm waters of Scarborough Bay.

I've thrown up in a DC-3 over Ireland, a Britannia turboprop above Gander, and I also think I once showed my true colors in a Constellation over Kansas.

However, I don't believe I've used a barf bag for about 20 years, so maybe I *can* talk about motion sickness.

It can happen to just about anyone, and probably Kent K. Gillingham, MD, PhD, at Brooks Air Force Base, Texas, knows as much about this subject as anyone. Yet even his answers are frustrating: "How can the volumes of scientific data and numerous anecdotes dealing with motion sickness be incorporated into a coherent theory?" he says. "At present they cannot, at least not to the complete satisfaction of all who study in this field."

Nevertheless, it seems that motion sickness can result if there is abnormal stimulation of any of the sensations that the body analyzes to stay oriented in its sphere. Thus, misinterpretations from vision, from hearing, from the vestibular balance center in the

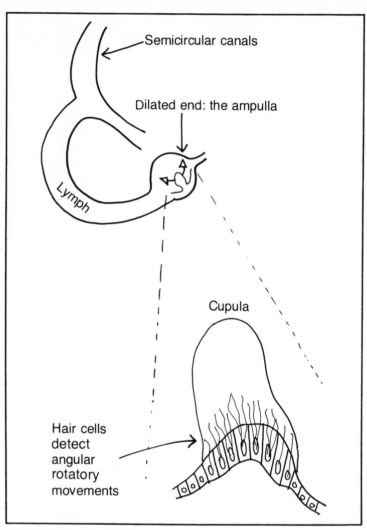

Semicircular canals

Dilated end: the ampulla

Lymph

Cupula

Hair cells
detect
angular
rotatory
movements

Semicircular canals of the inner ear.

inner ear, from the sensation of touch, or from the impression of movement may all contribute. Fear, apprehension, and insecurity may predispose a person to airsickness, as well as memories of previous episodes. Malodorous aircraft compartments don't help. There is some evidence suggesting that inflexible, rigid personalities are most susceptible to motion sickness.

With those concepts and the drawing of the inner ear before us, we can see how some problems develop. Heaving ship decks or rapidly accelerating elevators stimulate the nerve organs, the *otoliths*, in the part of the inner ear called the *vestibule*. This gives information to the brain about linear motion and about the position of the head. The otolith has tiny bone-like crystals of calcium carbonate that are three times as heavy as the endolymph fluid in which they float. Changes in position of the body displace briefly those tiny so-called octoconia crystals to send nerve sensations to the brain.

I recall reading, when I was a medical student, of experiments on fish where the octoconia crystals in the otoliths were replaced

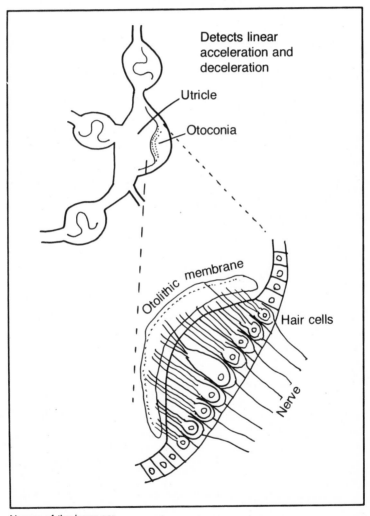

Nerves of the inner ear.

somehow by metallic particles. The fish continued to swim normally, but when they were exposed to a magnet they developed such apparent disorientation that they became seasick.

Incongruous visual references can induce motion sickness. Here the eyes tell you one thing and your sense of balance another. Thus "antigravity" houses constructed on a slant in amusement parks, and roller coaster rides or car chases in motion pictures can all create enough conflict between eyes, seat of the pants, sole of the feet, and the vestibular balance center to occasion nausea. Aerobatics and complex maneuvering make fluid swirl turbulently through the semicircular canals. It is thus no surprise to find airsickness can be a problem for pilots.

Looking at the record of military flight schools in World War II is instructive. About 10 percent of student pilots became airsick during the first ten flights. In other cases, some aircrew members had airsickness rates as high as 50 percent. In very unfavorable weather, airborne troops were so disabled on landing that they sometimes produced figures as high as 70 percent.

I remember well the National Guard parachute jump when I slipped my first lumbar disc. The flight, a mere 20 minutes long, was so turbulent that we were all puking and jumping at the same time but glad to be out of the airplane. We were only 40 seconds in our parachutes, but talk about air pollution! The landings, too, were less than elegant.

I recall that trip for other reasons, too. If you'll permit me to stray off the subject, let me tell of a military adventure that started as badly as it ended. The first part will be an old story to military pilots.

It was the 1950s. Although I had been a captain in the British National Guard Parachute Regiment for some years, I was looking at my first C-119, the Flying Boxcar. My unit usually jumped from British Hastings aircraft and the American plane was new to me.

Headquarters had chosen this day of all days to change the rules. Henceforth, the pre-jump inspection of aircraft would be the responsibility of the Army paratroops, not the Air Force.

As the stick commander I therefore climbed clumsily into the airplane, blinked at its vast size, and tried to follow my checklist. Assigned to me was a member of the aircrew, a tall, languid Texan who appeared from his casual dress to have been called away from a baseball game.

I started my inspection muttering to myself: "All exterior

projections hinged; check. Door edges padded, no rough edges; check. Static wires anchored; check."

I moved down the aircraft. "Red light, okay; green light, okay." It seemed things were moving along. This was no sweat, I thought. The guy with the drawl and the funny hat doesn't know this is all new to me.

I moved to the rear and pulled with its attached tube a plastic cylinder resembling a Thermos cup away from the central pedestal. I blew into it and said, "Testing, testing, one, two, three," but there was no response.

I gazed up at the baseball player, raised my eyebrows and said, "Doesn't your intercom work?" He stared at me for a moment, looked up the plane, then down, took off his hat and said quietly, "The intercom works fine. You're holding the urinal."

It was no better when we finally got to Germany for NATO maneuvers.

In the exercise, my task as leading point platoon commander was to capture and hold a river crossing. Charging over the bridge, we ran into an umpire who immediately sent us back with a shout that the bridge had in theory, been destroyed. In true paratrooper tradition, the brigade commander was up front, near enough to see our return. "Damn you, Anderson," he shouted, "get over that blasted bridge!"

Attempts to communicate were ignored by the commander, and since I could see his imperious pointing finger and the umpire was no longer visible, I gathered my force again and dashed over the bridge—to run into another umpire.

"There's technically no bridge here and you should all be listed as drowned," he shouted, "but I'll let you go back since we haven't marked the bridge destroyed."

Back we galloped, to hear the frenzied bellow of my general: "Anderson, blast you! Get back over that bridge or I'll —"

It didn't take me long to decide between a brigadier general whom I would see many times a year and a captain umpire I hoped never to see again.

"The bridge, men!" was my half-hearted cry. We crashed across at last to reach the far side and, of course, our second umpire surrounded by a group of curious German civilians who had seen the whole charade.

"You're all dead—that's it!" cried the umpire, scribbling on his note pad.

"On, Anderson, on!" came the faint cry from behind us.

I caught a strange, embarrased expression in my sergeant's eyes and asked him what was wrong. "Well, sir," he replied, "I understand German, and I just heard one of those civilians say to his friend, 'Herr Finkel, one wonders how we lost the war!' "

So airborne troops have difficulties beyond those due to airsickness.

Nevertheless, the dilemma of motion sickness is big when you realize that in World War II 65 percent of navigators became airsick and 5 percent were eliminated from training because of that problem. Recent USAF figures suggest that in flight training, 18 percent of student pilots develop motion sickness symptoms severe enough to interfere with control of the aircraft. Yet people adapt. Intractable airsickness eliminates only 1.4 percent of USAF student pilots.

Prevention is easier than treatment in light aircraft. Since it is impossible to stop the airplane, the best alternative is to get the victim to lie down and keep the head still. Sometimes allowing an outside visual reference may help, and having the person come forward and "fly" the airplane under supervision may keep the patient busy and distracted from the nausea.

Cooling the cabin by blasting an air vent at the ill person may be effective. Try oxygen. Loosen clothing.

It is helpful for attendants to take action promptly and for sufferers to notice and report symptoms early. Usually the patient becomes apathetic and loses appetite with sudden stomach-awareness. Salvation starts and the patient becomes pale and begins to perspire. Headache and nausea develop, then vomiting and prostration.

If a family member has frequent attacks, try to break this recurrent cycle to prevent conditioning where, for example, your child may vomit at the mere sight of your tied-down aircraft. There are many nonprescription drugs available such as Dramamine or Bonine. Some doctors favor Phenergan, but the Air Force still seems impressed with combinations using the old drug scopolamine in a dose of 0.3 to 0.6 mg by mouth one hour before flying.

This is the drug your grandmother probably got for "twilight sleep" in obstetrics. It is now enjoying quite a comeback, available for adult sufferers as a transdermal adhesive patch that you actually stick behind your ear. This slow-acting continous release form of 0.5 mg scopolamine lasts for three days. The medicine is absorbed

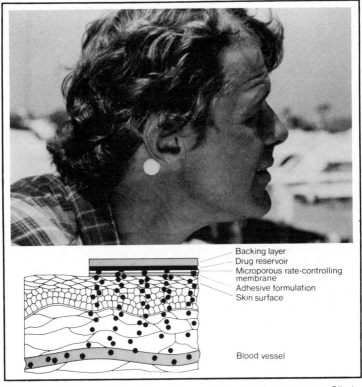

Backing layer
Drug reservoir
Microporous rate-controlling membrane
Adhesive formulation
Skin surface

Blood vessel

One method of preventing motion sickness is to *wear* the treatment. Ciba's Transderm-Scop delivers the medication through the intact skin behind the ear and can be worn for 72 hours.

through the skin. Ciba calls it Transderm-Scop; your doctor will discuss it with you.

Motion sickness has afflicted many famous figures in history: Lord Nelson suffered from seasickness and Lawrence of Arabia is said to have developed nausea from riding on a camel. Interestingly enough, 30 percent of the American astronauts and the same percentage of Russian cosmonauts in space have experienced motion sickness.

When Richard Truly soared above the earth in the space shuttle Columbia he wore the Ciba Transderm-V ear patch. With its help, Truly completed his assignment with no symptoms of motion sickness. Now NASA physicians have decided that every astronaut making a first flight into orbit must use nausea medication prophylactically.

All this seems a better treatment for motion sickness than the traditional Cunard cure at sea which said "in case of seasickness, have patient sit under a tree."

VERTIGO

Pilots probably understand this phenomenon better than medical students. They've certainly heard more about it. (Vertigo as a sense of rotation will be touched on again later.) Vertigo is sometimes a concomitant of motion sickness. In the airman's vocabulary, it means the pilot can't tell up from down and is in a state of disorientation.

For many pilots who fly under Visual Flight Rules, the cause of vertigo is that they lose good visual reference in bad weather. They develop conflicts between what they see—or think they see—and what they feel from their other sensory systems. This disagreement between what they feel in the muscles and skin in their buttocks, what they hear in the engine note, what they believe they are being told by their vestibular balance center, and what they see or can't see out the window or on the instrument panel is all so confusing that the brain briefly gives up like a computer overwhelmed by too much input.

Vertigo may resolve once the VFR pilot gets good visual reference or learns to read his instruments, but even IFR-trained pilots can be at risk. For example, one military pilot took off in a jet fighter, and copying his clearance, dropped his pencil. He bent to pick it up as he rotated. The resulting vertigo was so severe that he had to eject from the aircraft.

Perhaps man was meant to function on the ground. As was once said: "Perhaps if the good Lord had meant man to fly, he would have supplied him with a built-in gyro." Vertigo can threaten even in level turns where the rate of change is not enough to activate the semicircular canals and in protracted turns where the canal fluid movement stabilizes, giving the pilot an illusion of straight and level flight. Vertigo can ensue even in straight and level movement in flights parallel to another airplane but at a different speed.

You can get into trouble flying between cloud layers where you wrongly believe the layers to be truly horizontal, or in gradual ascent or descent where the otoliths are not subjected to enough force to be stimulated, or on approaching fixed lights because of misinterpretation of the relative motion.

The FAA has some very useful succinct advice on this subject:

The only way a pilot can safely operate an airplane in a low-visibility environment is by using and trusting instruments.

Man's orientation senses—visual (eye), vestibular (inner ear), and proprioceptive (associated with muscles, tendons and other tissues)—are not designed to cope with the artificial environment of flight when external visual references are obscured by clouds, fog, haze, dust, darkness, or other phenomena, unless visual reference is transferred to aircraft instruments. When the visual sense is provided with reference points such as the earth's horizon or aircraft instruments, there is usually no problem with aircraft attitude control since the visual sense overrides the other senses.

It is in situations where visual references such as the ground and horizon are obscured that trouble develops, especially for pilots who lack experience and proficiency in instrument flight. The vestibular sense in particular tends to confuse the pilot. Because of inertia, the sensory areas of the inner ear cannot detect slight changes in the attitude of the aircraft nor can they accurately sense attitude changes which occur at a uniform rate over a period of time. On the other hand, false sensations are often generated which lead the pilot to believe the attitude of the plane has changed when in fact it has not. This not only compounds the confusion of the pilot but also makes him more susceptible to motion sickness which often accompanies disorientation.

If a disoriented pilot actually does make a recovery from a turn, bank, or spin, he has a very strong tendency to feel that he has entered a turn, bank, or spin in the opposite direction. These false sensations may lead to the well-known "graveyard spiral."

Every pilot should be aware of these illusions and their consequences. Flight instructors should provide each pilot with an opportunity to experience these sensations under controlled conditions.

Every pilot should consider his training incomplete until he has learned to fly by instruments and has gained proficiency in instrument flight techniques.

Every pilot should be somewhat conservative in

judging his capabilities and he should use every means available (weather check, postponed or delayed flight, 180° turn-around, unplanned landing at an open airport, etc.) to avoid flight environments which overtax his ability.

If inadvertently caught in a poor flight environment, the pilot should immediately make radio contact with the nearest Federal Aviation Agency facility and follow instructions. Calmness, patience, and obedience to instruction represent his best chance for survival.

HYPOXIA

Paul Bert was worried. Previous balloon ascents had returned with the aeronauts ill and incapacitated by the thin air they had penetrated. This expedition in 1875 would be *different*. Bert provided his balloonists with bags of oxygen and showed them how to use their crude equipment.

And so with France's roar of approval, the balloon *Zenith* rose into the skies to a record height of 28,820 feet.

When it returned, it contained aviation's first fatalities of altitude hypoxia: the bodies of heroes Croce and Sivel and the barely living Tissandier who nevertheless survived to tell the story. They had waited before breathing the oxygen in order to conserve the meager supply and delayed so long that they were in the grip of hypoxia before they could open the valves.

Since 1875, a century of war has sharpened the need for men to fly high and fly strong. It almost seems as if there is nothing left to learn about altitude and hypoxia, but new discoveries are, in fact, constantly being made. The present interest is in the deterioration of performance in situations of *mild* hypoxia.

It has now been demonstrated that mild hypoxia impairs the performance in learning complex tasks. In one experiment, reaction time of volunteers studying a new procedure was 58 percent slower for those being taught at the equivalent of 7,000 feet compared to controls taught at ground level. If a task had been well-learned, however, performance did not drop off until the equivalence of 10,000 to 12,000 feet. Yet the subjects in the experiments remarked they felt as tired after two and a half hours at 8,000 feet as after six hours at ground level.

Those observations of Ernsting at the Royal Air Force Institute of Aviation Medicine in Britain are interesting when compared to a theory of a Canadian physician, Don Campbell, who was formerly with the Civil Aeromedical Research Institute in Oklahoma City. Campbell felt that high density altitude errors on takeoff were being made because the Koch charts or Denalt computers were being used, studied, and calculated by an airman *hypoxic from the very density altitude he was trying to evaluate.* Campbell's suggestion was that the pilot should put himself in oxygen for ten minutes before he did his figuring and used his computers.

Since most light aircraft lack oxygen facilities, it will be hard to prove Campell's hypothesis, but it seems logical—to us at ground level.

It's appropriate to spend some time on the subject of hypoxia because it does tend to come back to haunt us. The word itself is simple: "hypo" means below or under. For example, a *hypodermic* shot is one below the skin. The opposite term is "hyper" as in *hyperactive* and *hyperglycemia* (too-high blood sugar). Thus hypo-oxia—hypoxia—simply means too little oxygen in the blood.

As you go high in the air, whether you're flying an airplane or just driving a car in the mountains, the atmospheric pressure drops. Not only is there less oxygen in the air you're breathing, but the pressure that forces oxygen from the lungs into the blood is less too, giving you quite a double whammy at altitude.

Most student pilots have had so many discussions on this that the subject of hypoxia, like the subject of vertigo, probably needn't be hammered to death in this book.

Death, however, is what can happen with hypoxia—because a pilot either drones on, at high altitude oxygen-deficient but on autopilot and not aware that his brain is turning blue and dying, or because he makes a fatal error due to the oxygen starvation and impacts the plane in a steep dive before the lower altitude he's plowing through can revive him.

This is all rather grim stuff but the pilots I know at sea level in New England are pretty casual about needing to understand much about oxygen. Some local pilots I've met in the Rockies are similarly blase. Yet I can't see much difference between a pilot deeply unconscious at 25,000 feet and a patient brought in by ambulance to our emergency room who has had a cardiac arrest without support that lasted, say, ten minutes. Both patients are likely to die.

We have touched on acute mountain sickness earlier in this chapter, but pilots need to be reminded that you can become hypoxic on a mountain *outside* your plane. Severe problems were encountered by physically fit young Indian soldiers who were brought abruptly to 12,000 feet in that country's border wars with China in the early 1960s.

This difficulty confronting pilots who fly high terrain can be severe. A cardiologist and professor of medicine at Stanford University School of Medicine who is also chairman of the medical committee of the American Alpine Club, Herbert N. Hultgren, MD, states that if a unacclimatized pilot flies to 14,000 feet and then starts hiking, he has an 80 percent chance of developing acute mountain sickness and a 20 to 30 percent chance the symptoms will be bad enough to incapacitate him.

I wish pilots would check their oxygen supplies as thoroughly as scuba divers fuss over their air tanks. Remember, oxygen starvation is a bit like carbon monoxide poisoning. It creeps up on you, disturbing judgement, dulling thought, and preventing reaction.

If you're a smoker or in poor training or if you're a drinking man, flying without oxygen will take its toll earlier. And if you're old and tired and fat and wondering if you're past it, then flying above 8,000 feet without oxygen will show you that you are.

It is agreed that individuals vary, and of course acclimatization plays a part, but the difference isn't all that much—maybe a few thousand feet. You can't try to examine yourself for characteristics of oxygen starvation. If your brain is truly deprived, you won't be able to make the correct assessment.

Respiration rate depends on carbon dioxide stimulation rather than oxygen lack. Thus, shortness of breath does not necessarily mean you are hypoxic. If you are under a lot of nervous pressure,

Your aircraft may have the performance for mountain flying. Do *you* have the same stamina? (courtesy Cessna Aircraft Co.)

The effects of mild hypoxia can be experienced under controlled circumstances by any pilot who wants to learn to recognize the symptoms. (courtesy Civil Aeromedical Institute)

your respiration rate is increased by hyperventilation to further confuse the clinical picture.

If in doubt, use oxygen. If you are a lowlander and adding temporary oxygen equipment to an airplane for a special flight, you'll probably find a local industrial oxygen supply house cheaper than going to a pilot shop. However, explain your needs carefully. Some medical forms of oxygen contain water vapor that could freeze at altitude and block the tubing.

Let us look for a moment at the FAA advice on oxygen needs. Their ideas make a lot of sense. Notice we're not talking about the Federal Aviation Regulations, but how the FAA actually advises young, healthy pilots:

> There is one general rule: Don't let hypoxia get a foot in the door. Carry oxygen and use it *before* you start to become hypoxic. Don't gauge your "oxygen hunger" by how you feel. Gauge it by the altimeter.
>
> Here are some general suggestions which apply to young, healthy fliers:
> Carry oxygen in your plane or don't fly above

12,500 feet. If bad weather lies ahead, go around it if you can't get over it.

Use oxygen on every flight above 12,500 feet. You'll probably need it, and when you do, you might not realize it.

Use oxygen on protracted flights *near* 12,500 feet. It won't hurt you and you'll be a lot sharper pilot.

Use oxygen on all night flights above 5,000 feet. If you want to give your night vision the best protection, use oxygen from the ground up.

Breathe normally when using oxygen. Rapid or extra-deep breathing can cause loss of consciousness also.

Flying above 12,500 feet without using oxygen is like playing Russian roulette—the odds are that you *may* not get hurt, but it's a deadly game! At 20,000 feet your vision deteriorates to the point that seeing is almost impossible. The engine sounds become inperceptible, breathing is labored, and the heart beats rapidly. You haven't the vaguest idea what is wrong, or whether anything *is* wrong. At 25,000 feet you will collapse, and death is imminent unless oxygen is restored.

If you're on a long cross-country, you'll want to fly high. You get into less turbulent air, you can lean your mixture and conserve gas, you may have more favorable winds, and you'll certainly be faster. If you're VFR, you'll see your checkpoints better. If it's midsummer over desert, you'll be cooler. If it's winter over mountains, you may not *want* to fly higher but you may have no choice.

Harold N. Brown, MD, former president and present director of safety and education for the Flying Physicians Association feels that supplemental oxygen may be helpful if the airman is tired or uneasy on a long flight over unfamiliar high terrain or is in bad weather, especially if the person is older than 35 years, has recently been ill, or knows that he tolerates altitude badly.

Says Brown: "The pilot must understand the relationship between man and the aviation environment or he misses the major link of safe piloting since the airplane fails far less often than does the pilot."

Chapter 6

The Pilot's Special Senses

The Air Force medical officer was becoming concerned about one of his best pilots. True, there was nothing wrong with the man's wish to visit his girlfriend every weekend that he was off duty, nor was it surprising that the youngster chose to use a fast motorbike as his method of travel.

No, what was worrying the doctor was the evidence of the pilot's increasing hostility towards a farmer whose fields he passed on his weekend trips. The stories tricked back to camp. First, the pilot grumbled about the smells that he detected as he raced past the farm. The stink was repulsive, worse than any other odor around a pig farm. Moreover, it increased each time the pilot went by. Soon the pilot started shouting obscenities as he passed the farmstead.

Finally one day, almost overcome by the stench, the pilot rushed into the farm, started an argument with the owner, and knocked him down. Then his rage lessened, and the air became once more fit to breathe. He looked down in some bewilderment and helped the farmer to his feet.

He was brought thus to his doctor. The explanation was all too simple. On approaching the farm, the pilot had to ride down an avenue of equally spaced trees behind which lay the setting sun. This flickering light gave a so-called photostimulation and produced an epileptiform seizure. The seizure precurser and warning was the misinterpretation of smell sensations and the increasing temper.

Each incident was potentiated by the previous episode. The ultimate occurrence would have been a full seizure with loss of consciousness at speed on a motorbike. The pilot was indeed fortunate to have been caught before this happened. Even the farmer, rubbing his jaw, could see grudgingly how lucky the patient was to have had this problem revealed in time.

Such flicker effects of light will give seizures to photosensitive eptileptics if they look at a TV station that has signed off for the night, or if they fly a plane into the light and watch the spinning propeller.

SMELL

Perversions of smell are sometimes found in highly-strung patients who are anxious. Misinterpretations of odor can occur in mentally disturbed persons such as paranoid psychotics, or in patients who have tumors or "space-occupying lesions" in the brain. There's no spare room inside the skull for a brain cyst or growth and even an enlargement of a cranial blood vessel can put pressure on the brain and irritate the delicate nerves of smell.

However, common causes of difficulties with the sense of smell would include a simple cold (always a reason for not flying), a sinus infection, or a bout with allergy. Loss of taste often goes hand-in-hand with loss of smell.

Heavy cigarette smoking also spoils the sense of smell. The heavy smoker at the aircraft controls thus not only ruins his vision for night flying and impairs his proficiency at altitude but also destroys his ability to detect odors in an environment where the sense of smell can mean safety. Aviation records reveal many situations where a shorted electrical wiring, a malfunctioning radio, or a burning item in freight were detected first not by instruments but by a crew member's nose.

It is easy to test your sense of smell. Remember those Boy Scout competitions or party games? Get someone to select a few common non-irritating odors like oranges, cloves, coffee, vanilla extract, peppermint, camphor, turpentine, tobacco, even perfumes. Close your eyes and have the person test you.

You never know when a sense of smell will be useful. James E. Crane, MD, an FAA medical examiner in Connecticut, tells of the time when "The airplane was leaving 29,000 feet on descent when a peculiar odor permeated the cockpit. The pilot had never smelled anything like it before. Smoke quickly followed. The flight engineer rushed back to the unattended galley and found vaporous matter billowing from the oven. Stewardesses had put in the oven hand towels that were soaked with shaving lotion; they forget all about them."

HEARING

If a keen sense of smell can save lives in the air, so can sharp hearing. Hearing, however, is hard to protect in today's noisy, mechanized world. We are subject to noise all our lives, at work and at leisure. When we leave our business environment with all its machines, we come home to children playing stereos and neighbors using chain saws, the sounds of the kitchen and the noise of the TV.

We've lost the magic of silence once described by physician Oliver Wendell Holmes as a "poultice which comes to heal the blows of sound."

Pilots don't realize how noisy their airplanes are and how fatiguing this can be for crew and passengers. A doctor friend of mine, John M. Sherwin, MD, a former president of the New Hampshire Medical Society and an orthopedist, has flown his Bonanza throughout America in all sorts of weather bad enough to ground ducks, vampires, and even avenging spirits. He once rented a Grumman American Traveler for a weekend. He and his wife brought it back an hour later, exhausted by the noise of that light aircraft. Spoiled by his smooth-running and quiet Beechcraft, he had forgotten how noisy most smaller aircraft are.

You will hear mixed medical reports about the value of ear plugs in the prevention of swimmers' ear infections but *no* negative statements about the usefulness of wearing plugs to reduce noise. Ear plugs can be found in any pilot shop. Buy the best you can get. Try them out. Use them if you fly a lot. They are especially recommended for flight examiners who have prolonged periods of cockpit noise in excess of 100 decibels. Some of those tired jokes about old copilots being deaf in the left ear and captains deaf in both are based on fact; premature deafness in rock musicians is a well-established entitiy.

Someone once said that "If there is a construction slump in your area, then build an airport; within five years it will be surrounded by homes." Taking advantage of the way houses creep up to noisy airports, Dr. Gareth Watkins of the Institute of Psychiatry reported in 1981 on a study he had done on 5885 persons living in the vicinity of London's Heathrow Airport. He found that people habitually exposed to noise tended to utilize health services more and buy more over-the-counter drugs than other persons.

Excessive noise damages the cochlea, that part of the inner ear responsible for hearing. The exact mechanism of damage is not certain. Probably high, intense stimuli cause eddies in the fluid in the cochlea that tear away the fragile hair-cells.

As far back as 1961, Doctors Glorig, Ward, and Nixon had shown that four years in a noisy work environment would cause substantial hearing loss in the high-mid range of sounds. That is, those afflicted could hear deep bass notes but they lost the ability to detect high-pitched, shrill noises. In 1964, Doctor Burns, Hinchcliffe, and Littler showed that ten years in the textile industry caused weavers to have a greater hearing loss than spinners, whose environment was quieter.

In 1969, the federal government recognized the problem of hearing loss in the workplace and established industrial noise standards. For example, a worker cannot be exposed to more than 90 decibels of noise for more than eight hours a day, 95 decibels for more than four hours, 97 decibels for more than three hours, or 110 decibels for more than a half-hour a day.

However, hearing activity (like sex) declines with advancing years, the dip starting around the age of 65. Darrell E. Rose, PhD, head of the audiology section of the Mayo Clinic, feels that workers get the best noise protection from soft-foam plugs.

His method is simple: "The foam should be rolled between the fingers and the thumb until it is small enough to insert in the ear; it conforms comfortably to the shape of the ear canal. The plugs, which also can be custom-fitted, are inexpensive and can be worn repeatedly. They can be cleaned with a mild detergent, although to avoid disintegration they should not be washed too vigorously. The plugs, which can provide up to 40 dB of attenuation at high frequencies, can be worn underneath earmuffs; however, little benefit is gained by wearing both devices after 50 dB of attenuation has been achieved."

You can still hear the aircraft radio wearing ear plugs. In fact, by suppressing background noise you've actually improved your ability to receive radio communications. If you are wearing plugs to prevent further hearing loss, and already have a problem, you should have an audiogram run on your hearing at frequent intervals, say six months.

If you are unimpressed by all this discussion, then try this experiment: Fly with only one ear plug in. Then, when you land, get a friend to whisper in both ears. The deafness, which lasts for an hour or two in the unprotected ear, can be quite striking.

The noise that pilots are exposed to in light aircraft is a combination of factors: engine din which itself is about 100 dB; vibrations from the propeller; amplifications from the metal airframe; resonance from instrument panel; and added sounds from airflow through air vents and seal gaps.

Many flying authorities have suggested methods for increasing the soundproofing of your plane. It may be important to try to deaden noise in your plane, especially if you fly it regularly and often. An FAA Cockpit Noise Study, several years ago, looked at the level of noise in twenty of the most popular single-engine and light twin aircraft. It concluded that "engine noise in the cockpit of any light aircraft may cause irreversible hearing loss when a person is exposed to it for more than three or four hours a week over a period of a few years."

Noise pollution is tiring. It took me 35 hours once to fly in an old Cessna 175 from Boston to Los Angeles. My reaction on landing surprised me. It was: "Oh God, I've got to fly all that way back." I tried to analyze this response and found it wasn't the worry of the Rocky Mountains a second time in a 13-year-old airplane with an impaired service ceiling. It was the thought of all that *noise* for another 35 hours.

Consider again 100 decibels from your Lycoming or Continental engine. How loud is that? Well, an alarm clock at two feet, a garbage disposal unit, and a printing press at full steam all create 80 dB; an electric shaver is 85 dB; a food blender hits you with 90 dB as does a Lamborghini Countach S loping along at 90 mph. A 6″ skill saw produces 100 dB; a punch press can develop 110 dB; an electric power substation reaches 120 dB (the threshold of pain); and a pneumatic street drill zonks you with 130 dBs.

We've come a long way with our present powerful light aircraft from the Early Birds. Then, listening intently was one of the skills of flying. As pilot Sammy Mason explains it: "Engine performance was mostly determined by sound. If it was noisy, it was running; if it was quiet, it had quit."

People with impaired hearing live in a cruel, empty world. To begin with, their handicap may not be noticed. They may have difficulty in understanding others, and complain that their friends don't speak clearly. At work this can create problems and reduce competence. Efficiency falls. Their own speech changes—usually they start to speak more loudly. They miss remarks on television and stop attending movies or theater shows. Conversation drops off, especially at the table where their own chewing may drown

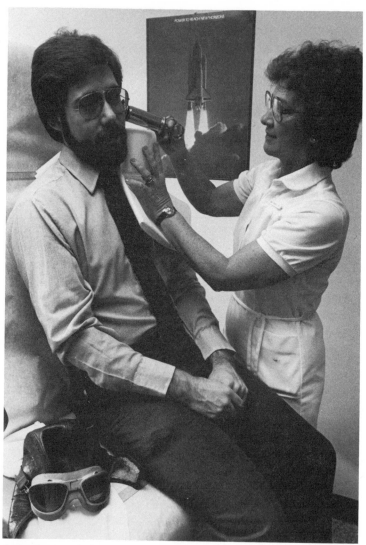

A simple ear syringing can work wonders for pilots who feel they're becoming deaf.

their awareness of remarks made by others. There is, finally, emotional withdrawal on their part and social ostracizing on the part of others who find that jokes, repartee, and rapid conversation can no longer be responded to.

Deaf persons are surely not given the sympathy accorded to the blind.

The pilot should certainly want to protect his hearing. Incidentally, a point to mention to any pilot who's losing activity of hearing: Go and see someone who can put a otoscope in your ears and look in. Lots of people form wax. A brief course of Debrox or Cerumenex followed by ear syringing can work wonders for the poor pilot who has in each ear a plug of ear wax the size of a champagne cork. Eh?

VISION

To stand in the radio communications room of the *Queen Elizabeth II,* the greatest liner in the world, is to be surrounded by the most magnificent satellite equipment ever made by man. To gaze forward from the bridge is to stare into the unknown, into the silent seas where man is a puny, insignificant speck.

And the greatest navigational aid available on the bridge of the *QE2?* Says Stuart A. Trundle, the second officer and navigator, a lithe, fair-haired, earnest man: "It's a Mark I Eyeball. The human eye is still the prime navigational instrument at sea. We still use bionculars, even though we no longer stand on the bridge with a sextant in one hand and the wheel in the other."

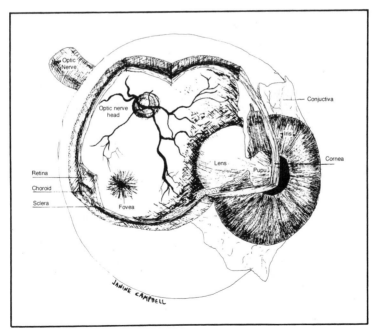

Elements of the eye.

The human eye was more than a navigational aid in two World Wars. It was a weapon. All the greats among the fighter pilots had two skills, and flying ability wasn't either of them. What the aces had were a competence in firearms—they were all excellent shots—and a talent for sharp vision. They could see a spot on the horizon and recognize an enemy plane before any other pilot had sensed he was no longer alone.

The eyes have it. Of all the senses, eyesight has to be the most important for any pilot.

If you think that statement is for the birds, you've made a point. Bird eyesight is far superior to human vision. Anatomical studies of birds' retinae have shown a great preponderance of the cells required for acuity of vision. That's why a swallow can alter its flight path to snatch an insect in midair and why a hawk can see its dinner from thousands of feet of altitude.

Indeed, the U.S. Coast Guard has been experimenting since 1979 with a five-pigeon bird rescue detachment. As reported by *Time* magazine, the birds are harnessed on the outside of a helicopter to a cage which has a transparent observation window. The pigeons have been taught to peck at an electrical button any time they see the conventional colors of emergency equipment: red, orange, or yellow. And in test flights, the birds saw the targets six times in seven before the human eye did; 90 percent of the time the birds saw the floating targets on the first pass. People could score only 38 percent.

If only they could be taught to speak.

The human eye is most at rest when it is focused in the distance. Probably in the days of pioneer America, people spent more of their working days with their eyes lifted to the horizon. Now it seems we go along bombarded by visual insults that occur at closer range. On any street we are assaulted by neon signs, bright colors, and flashing images. It's as if our eyes are constantly producing results in our brain like a telephoto lens in a camera. Our perimeters have closed in on us. We read more. We watch TV.

Is it any wonder that we have eyestrain? Is it any wonder that headaches are common? Yet headaches are not so commonly due to eyestrain as you might think. It used to be said: "You know it's time to change your glasses when you start getting headaches," but a careful analysis of this theme does not substantiate it. Dr. Thomas R. Hedges, professor of ophthalmology at the University of Pennsylvania School of Medicine, Philadelphia, the oldest medical school in America, believes that only about 10 percent of important headaches come from eye problems.

In general, headaches, made worse by reading or using the eyes, continue to get worse if the eyestrain continues. The symptoms include an aching around the eyes and a heaviness of the

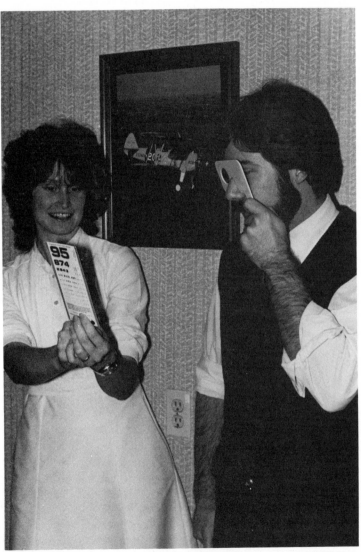

Examination of vision is an important part of any pilot's health checkup.

eyelids. This discomfort may intensify, spreading to the temple area or even to the back of the head. However, headache following intense reading such as study for your FAA examinations might be caused by tension brought on by anxiety rather than eye problems themselves. And headaches on awakening are surely not due to eyestrain. We will talk about headaches again later.

The usual eye difficulties are, first, imbalance of the muscles that move the eyeball. This can be treated by, among other things, practicing eye exercises that strengthen the ability of the muscles to converge. Second, there is the bother of *astigmatism* which can be handled by using special glasses. The third common eye trouble is *hyperopia,* the problem caused by growing older—or, as some persons say, having arms that are growing shorter.

It happens to us all, usually when we're in the mid-forty age group. You're flying along watching for traffic and you glance down for your instrument scan. It takes longer to focus on the dash than usual and the numbers may not be as sharp as before. Or you're reading a map and you have difficulty deciphering some of the place names. Or you're thumbing through the telephone book and you find the surname easily but can't quite make out the number.

Friend, you have arrived. Your future is here. I remember how Bill Kearney, MD, my opthalmologist, broke it to me. He was initially more interested in telling me about his new Piper Arrow than in listening to my symptoms. Boy, was he cheerful about my problem.

"Yup, Eric, " he said, "It's happened. You need glasses. You've avoided this for 45 years but we eye doctors get y'all sooner or later. Yup," he said, whistling away, "It's like catching fish in a barrel. You throw in your line and catch you a fish."

It's actually no big deal to wear eyeglasses. The improvement in visual acuity is so striking that the patient tends to be both relieved and satisfied.

There are, however, other eye problems that bring the pilot to the doctor. Redness of the eyes may be a sign of purulent conjunctivitis where infection has hit the eyelid or white of the eye. It can be caused by an associated cold or upper respiratory infection, or it can be a primary condition where a hand that rubbed a nose (which always contains germs) then touched an eye.

Infection is usually demonstrated by crusted debris, yellow in color, along the eyelids. When the patient awakes he often finds the eyelids stuck together. The periphery of the eye, not the pupil part, is red and itchy. Conjunctivitis may respond to simple eye washes with an old fashioned solution like boric acid but you'll probably need antibiotics. This is quite a contagious condition. Eyes have little resistance to infection. If a child gags when I'm examining a throat and I feel something hit my eye, I can hardly wait to reach the sink to wash my eye out.

An unrelated point is that if you ever get a chemical in your eye, wash it out fast with anything. Water is excellent. The days are over when you would try to neutralize a specific chemical like an acid with its proper remedy. Use copious fluids to irrigate. Just about any liquid is appropriate. Usually a kitchen refrigerator contains a big container of milk. Grab it. Bend over the sink and dump the contents, in a fast flush, into your eye, then go under the water faucet. (Another golden rule in eyes for parents is: Don't let your kids buy BB guns, but that's getting away from our subject.)

Distinguished from conjunctivitis which hits the periphery of the eyeball is iritis, a serious condition that gives a red appearance to the center of the eye, the pupil area. The circumference of the pupil has a hazy red look not unlike photographs of the flare around the sun. There may be blurring of vision, tenderness of the eyeball, and considerable pain. Iritis is not so common as conjunctivitis but is much more important. If you suspect it, get to a doctor.

Another painful and significant eye condition is glaucoma, where the pressure inside the eyeball starts to increase. Glaucoma probably accounts for about 20 percent of all eye complaints and can lead to blindness. The types that strike adults can be sudden or slow in onset. The chronic form is more common. The first indication to the patient may be blurred vision but, on testing, the doctor may find already considerable decrease in the visual field.

The acute kind usually causes severe pain—bad enough to give nausea or vomiting. Vision may become blurred. Halo effects may be seen around lights as when, for example, a street lamp is surrounded by fog.

Glaucoma clearly can be a very serious matter and older people, who are more likely to have this problem, should have glaucoma pressure testing done as part of their regular visits to an eye doctor. A city often has community clinics run by service organizations. If you don't have any of those occasional "health fairs" in your area, approach your nearby Lions Club and ask them to run one.

The Lions Club movement has a long history of dedication to helping the public keep its eyesight. Lions will be genuinely pleased to help you. I recall the first time the newly formed Londonderry,

New Hampshire, Lions Club arranged such a health fair, the first time the Alexander Eastman Hospital in Derry, New Hampshire, had been associated with a community clinic. The first volunteer to be tested for glaucoma was the president of the Lions Club himself. I couldn't believe the results—it seemed too much of a coincidence. I called over the supervising ophthalmologist who confirmed my findings. The president of the club had glaucoma and needed immediate surgery!

Cataracts are less threatening and more obvious. In this condition, the lens becomes frosted or opacified, restricting vision. This problem is also more common in the age groups above 50 years. Surgical treatment has been greatly improved in recent years.

There are many other less important conditions that bother the eyes. You can get allergic reactions in eyeballs and allergic swelling of eyelids. There are styles or infections of one of the glands in the lid margins, and chalazions or cysts of the eyelid plates. There's shingles or herpes zoster, which, like cold sores or fever blisters, can attack the orbital area with important after-results. There are foreign bodies which, even if small, always feel as big as the Rock of Gibraltar.

Let's talk about foreign bodies because many a pilot or mechanic spends quite a bit of time under his aircraft. The reason for protective goggles in industry is to protect eyes. The goggles are not meant to make the work easier. You're not meant to *like* them; you're meant to *wear* them. If a piece of debris gets into an eye and doesn't immediately wash out with water, then see a doctor—especially if the fragment is made of metal, because rust results if a metallic foreign body lingers too long on the eyeball. Often the debris is easily removed but the "rust rim" needs extra handling. Eyes are valuable. See a doctor promptly if you have a foreign body in an eye or even if you simply get a severe blow to the eyeball.

Black eyes can be bad news. Remember that ice compresses are always useful; start as early as possible. The easiest way to make a cold compress for a black eye is to wrap some ice in a towel, hit it with a hammer, then shake the crushed ice into a Saran Wrap bag. It'll leak—so you'll get wet—but that's okay.

If you wish further information about eyes, you can call the National Society to Prevent Blindness (79 Madison Avenue, New York) and ask them to send you pamphlets.

People without eye problems may still have questions about eyesight aids. The field of contact lenses is changing rapidly. Contact lenses were first developed in Europe more than a hundred years ago. The indications have always been medical, athletic, and cosmetic, but only recently have the lenses become comfortable. It is no longer true that 90 percent of all contact lenses sold reside virtually permanently in a top bureau drawer.

Contact lenses have now become big business and your eye doctor will be more than pleased to talk to you about it.

What about another aid, also becoming more and more expensive: sunglasses? Says Dr. James R. Gregg: "The glaring truth is that sunglasses may make you look good but see badly. They can cause headaches, fatigue, and fuzzy vision and can be a downright nuisance if they aren't just right for you."

He has many hints for those buying. Go to a place with a broad selection of quality brand names like Bausch & Lomb (RayBan), American Optical (True Color), and Polaroid. Get a proper fit, paying attention to temple-length and bridge-width. Don't buy too small a pair; you need to keep out light at the edges. The best colors are brown, neutral gray, and greenish gray. "When you put on a sun lens," he says, "the world should appear in its true colors, though not as bright."

Be prepared to pay for quality but test the glasses outside before buying. Spend the money on lenses rather than designer frames, and check the glass for flaws.

Most pilots have found that they need sunglasses because few persons can adjust to the range of brightness involved in flying. Not only do sunglasses protect against ultraviolet and infrared rays but they help to preserve night vision sensitivity before that dangerous time in flight when the sun suddenly goes down, leaving you over a dark world.

Even in daylight there are demands on the pilot's eyes. The pilot is flying into a formless field. There's no spot to focus on, and no orientation in depth. The pilot tends to overfocus and search the far distance with eye muscles that hold his eyes focused to a closer range. This can be very tiring, yet the stress induced continues to make the pilot overfocus.

Use every means to relax your focusing. Get laid-back to infinity. Check the ground to verify that you are focused for far off and not for the dead bugs on your windshield. Remember, too, as you search your skies, respond to peripheral vision also. It is so easy to be using central vision all the time that you can end up tuning out your periphery. You need this part of your vision to get the full 180° arc. Peripheral vision also detects movement better than central sight. The eye cells that respond to light are called *cones* and *rods*. The cones occupy the center of the retina and give sharp vision and color appreciation; the rods are more prominent in the perimeter of the retina, contributing especially to night vision.

If you're having trouble developing a good scan technique while flying, either discuss it with a flight instructor (preferably one who is an instrument instructor too), or write to the Aircraft Owners and Pilots Association requesting a copy of their excellent "Scantraining program to minimize collisions."

Remember that statistics show five percent of flying fatalities come from midair collisions. Most accidents occur at or near uncontrolled airports during daylight hours on weekends. Most of the airplanes involved are on pleasure trips, not on a flight plan, and are flying in uncongested airspace. Final approach and the landing flare are the most common midair collision situations and although pilots with fewer than 100 hours are frequently involved, the disaster can strike any pilot. Indeed, instructors, in one series, were involved 37 percent of the time. Says pilot Sammy Mason, "Flying through the airspace is like walking through a haunted house; you sense that something is there but you can't always see it." And he said that *before* the air traffic controllers' strike.

Mason feels one of the problems is that pilots have been spoiled by complicated cockpits which deny the wide field of vision enjoyed by the first pilots. Recalling those days, he says, "The intrepid birdman sat out in the open, usually well forward in his flying machine. He had better than a grandstand view of what was ahead. Because his was usually the only aircraft in the air, everything worth looking at was ahead. The machinery following him was too frightening to look at anyway."

Mason is not the only one critical of any cockpit design that obscures vision and creates blind spots. One airline captain had this to say: "In a British plane, you sit in a huge, comfortable cockpit perched on top of a flawed machine that seldom works. The American pilot, however, is astride the most marvelous and wonderful piece of engineering man has devised, but he's bent up in a tiny cabin which the builders forgot to add to the design until the last moment."

Cockpits can contain distorted glass that will polarize light; the pilot wearing polarized sunglasses may find that the combination produces blind spots. This is especially true if the plane approaching you is painted a non-contrasting color, although bright colors seem to be spotted only from four miles off. Every time I pick up a fast exotic sports car for a magazine road test, I groan if I find it

In the early days pilots used all their senses. If your ears weren't ringing, your eyes rolling, your fanny shaking, and your nose twitching, it wasn't flying. (author photo at First Flight, Kitty Hawk, North Carolina)

brightly colored as it so often is. A flaming red BMW M1 or Lamborghini Countach is surely going to be noticed by everyone including the State Police. Have you noticed how often you see bright yellow or fiery-red Corvettes slinking along slowly in the right-hand lane? They've previously been spotted and have already collected their share of speeding tickets for the year. Bright colors attract. God know that psychology guides the average airplane manufacturer when he paints his planes so bland and indifferent a white.

Remember, too, the difficulties as you approach an uncontrolled airstrip if you have the sun behind you. You are in your own shadow to planes facing you. You have to be twice as careful to look out for the other guy. While flying in the pattern, check your shadow on the ground. You'll sometimes see, with a start, that it's awfully close to the shadow of another not-yet-noticed aircraft.

Californian Mason has his own horror poem about near misses:

> "Breathes there a pilot with rapid
>   breath,
> With windshield filled with the threat of
>   death,

Who never to himself hath said,
'Where did *he* come from?'   "

You need good vision as a pilot. You also need good color vision
to identify the red, green, and white colors used so often in aviation.
Imagine the danger of a colorblind pilot who couldn't respond to
light-gun signals, or at night recognize the navigation lights of an
approaching plane. Be wary also if you hold a Third-Class medical
certificate passed with borderline 20/50 vision. The meaning of this
relative impairment is that you see at 20 feet what a normal-vision
pilot sees at 50 feet. You are thus at a considerable disadvantage.

Do everything in your power to protect and conserve your
eyesight. World War II Navy pilots used to fear failing eyesight
more than any disablement. It was often the thing that grounded the
pilot.

Save your eyes. Get them checked; wear glasses for reading if
they have been prescribed. Remember, TV has been called "chewing gum for the eyes." Give your eyes a rest now and then.

See a doctor promptly if something happens. Be wary of sports
involving BB guns, or bows and arrows. Tidy your basement. Clear
your garage. Don't have free-hanging junk dangling from ceilings in
darkened cellars.

The FAA is very clear about your duty:

> As a pilot, it is your responsibility to make sure you
> have good near, intermediate, and distant visual acuity.
> Near vision is required for checking charts, maps, fre-
> quency settings, etc. Near and intermediate vision are
> required for VFR operations including takeoff, attitude
> control, navigation and landing. Distant vision is espe-
> cially important in mid-air collision avoidance.

Chapter 7

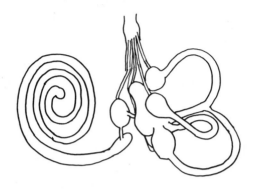

Common Problems

They do certainly give very strange and new-fangled names to diseases.
—Plato (427-347 BC)

It wasn't one of my better days. I felt a bit light-headed as I got up—probably rose too quickly, I thought. Maybe a touch of postural hypotension. Felt a bit weak in the shower. Tilting the head does it, y'know. And if you're pushing 50 (years, that is, not pushups) you *can* kink your neck blood vessels. It's no real problem. Slight dizziness pulling on a tie. No big deal—probably catching the flu.

Doctors, you see, are hopeless at self-diagnosis. Usually the spouse does all the diagnosing and treating in a physician's home.

Some shivering on opening the closet door—probably catching a chill. I bent into the cupboard to pick up some socks, and the room turned upside down and spun to the left. I fell to the right and vomited into my shoes. After a thousand years, I crawled out whining like a baby.

It was mere vertigo from a simple attack of labyrinthitis—the bug, but a severe remainder of a phenomenon that can make any pilot impotent in the sky.

VERTIGO

Vertigo knows no frontiers. It felled another physician I heard of, a prize pain, whose pride and conceit made him feel he was God's gift to the world.

"My prescription for my patients was myself," said this confident society-doctor. "I called it 'prescribe the doctor.' It never failed until I was summoned to a new high-rise to see a sick child."

He strode from the express elevator and swept into the penthouse. His tall frame showed the world that the illness was now *his* problem and the burden could be taken off the shoulders of the parents. Aware of the majesty of his bearing, he asked the parents to bring the child from the darkened bedroom to the stately living room. While he waited, he sauntered to the vast plate glass windows, glanced down, and immediately fell to the floor with an attack of vertigo.

"They brought the child into my presence to find me pouring with sweat, reeling on the floor, and vomiting into the fig trees—a picture of medical impotence."

If this is mere vertigo, imagine if you will the extra blows of deafness with a constant roaring in the ears and you have *Meniere's Disease*. This is one chronic illness to make a pilot hang up his helmet.

Meniere's Disease is about as distressing an affliction as a person can have. It is frightening as well as disabling, and many patients live in fear of the next episode. Each attack can further impair hearing and the typical patient, a person of either sex aged 30 to 50 years, ends up with deafness, a persistent rumbling sound in the ear like the roar of the ocean (tinnitus), and rotational dizziness which is usually so severe that vomiting results. Fortunately, convulsions or loss of consciousness do not occur, and modern treatment is more effective than what used to be offered.

THE COMMON COLD (CORYZA)

About this we know as little as we ever did. There are so many rhinoviruses in the nose, so many different families of germs, that we'll probably never have a vaccine. If we did, the immunity would last about a month.

Nose drops may help for a few days but don't get trapped into becoming a habitual user. Afrin or Neo-Synephrine are popular brands. Compound congestion pills like Sinutab can be bought over-the-counter and used if you are not flying. A product like Chloraseptic spray might soothe your throat. Aspirin helps.

Antibiotics are useless unless your sputum (spit) turns yellow or green. This is sometimes a warning of a secondary bacterial infection. If you are a heavy smoker or have emphysema or recurrent sinusitis, your doctor may wish then to start you on a broad spectrum antibiotic. A simple cough remedy like plain Robitussin may be useful. Sinusitis and other upper respiratory infections are treated similarly.

Don't fly with the cold. From handling dozens of flight attendants and aircrew out of Logan Airport, Boston, I would say that the airlines would expect them to work with a broken leg but *never* with a common cold.

If you get barometric damage to your eardrums, you may have residual problems for ages. Yet you might be overnighting miles from home in some obscure corner of America. Isn't there anything you can do to get back home with a cold? Nothing beats driving, but there are two minor things that help.

Menthol Inhalations

This old-fashioned remedy can be very helpful in resolving some of the symptoms of respiratory congestion. Menthol crystals are sold over-the-counter at pharmacies without a prescription and usually at a very low cost. Ask the pharmacist for the smallest bottle available. This product is very concentrated and little is needed.

Place one or two crushed methol crystals in a basin, cup, or bowl, and pour boiling hot water on top. Put a towel over your head, and through the nose and mouth freely breathe the fumes that are released from the mixture. This should be done for 10 to 15 minutes. More crystals may be added so that a constant strong menthol odor is released. Don't go out into the cold night air for one hour after carrying out this treatment. The menthol inhalations may be done as often as you wish, but twice a day and at bedtime is sufficient. You can use Vicks VapoRub or Mentholatum if the drug store does not have the crystals.

Salt-Water Sniffing

Wintertime brings dry air with the frost. Homes become excessively dry, especially where insulation is good and where log fires are burning. Doctors have long realized that simple attempts to humidify the nostrils reduce some so-called allergic symptoms in winter and can prevent nose bleeding.

Even if the home has a humidifier (and most bedrooms should), salt-water sniffing can improve symptoms of colds and sore throats. The program is as follows:

Mix a teaspoon of salt and 8 ozs. of water and put them in a jar in the bathroom. Shake this jar each time it is used. Cup the hand, pouring some salt water into it. Bend over the sink and sniff the mixture repetitively up each nostril until the fluid is gone. Repeat several times. Occasionally tilt the head back and let some run down the back of the throat. Initially, you should use the full 8 ozs. several times on the first day, but as you improve you can use less and less. Try it; it doesn't work unless you try it.

The problem in the middle ear with the common cold is the block in the escape valve, the Eustachian tube, a valve that usually balances the pressure in the middle ear with outside atmospheric pressure. Air trapped in the middle ear at the time of the block will expand if you ascend in your plane, and contract if you descend. Even if the Eustachian tube is congested, you can usually open it on climbout with maneuvers like yawning or swallowing. As you climb further, the increase in pressure itself usually forces more air out of the swollen Eustachian tube into your mouth and nose.

However, on descent, the Eustachian tube can't suck extra air into the middle ear to raise the entrapped air pressure. You can try Valsalva maneuvers and pinch your nostrils to "pop" your ears, but it may not work. At this point, your eardrum could implode to fill the middle ear with blood. On occasion, you may be able to delay your descent and climb back to an altitude where your ears feel better. If

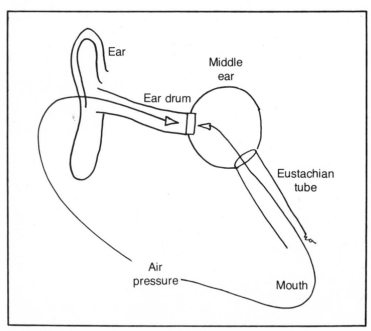

Eustachian tube.

this helps, perhaps you'll manage to land comfortably if you take it very slowly.

The condition called *aerotitis* or *barometric otitis media* was virtually unknown until pressurized jet travel became popular. Dr. C. Richard Wolf, an epidemiologist at California's Department of Public Health in Berkeley, in one survey found 2015 cases occurring between 1964 and 1969; 1786 of these problems were among airline employees. He feels that this disorder is now well-known to crew but not to passengers. He believes the airlines should put a discussion of this condition on plastic cards in the airliner seat pocket as they have done for emergency drills. It can be that important. The rules therefore seem clear: Don't ever fly with a cold. Don't scuba dive with a cold. And for Pete's sake, don't do both on the same day.

I remember once on a magazine assignment in Bermuda, floating with a slight head cold in the open sea, about a mile out, in a mere 40 feet of ocean. I was as sick as a dog but didn't want to admit it to the diver I was interviewing. I had been taking photographs with a Nikonos as he went overboard. In the ocean swell, the effect of looking through a wide-angle camera creates the same result as peering through aircraft binoculars does on a Search and Rescue mission on a bumpy day.

Twice I filled my face mask with vomitus and each time had to rinse it out in the Gulf Stream. Finally we dived—or rather, the party dived and I sort of sank with them. I didn't want to declare that I, a commercial pilot, was seasick but maybe my bubble trace showed I was hyperventilating or maybe one of the guides snorkeling above us was just very perceptive. Anyway, this curly-headed bugger suddenly dived from the surface, popped my Mae West, and sent me up to the surface like a cork from a champagne bottle.

I just had enough wits left to think "God, here comes the pulmonary embolus," and exhale fast before I hit the surface belly-up like a dead whale. My ears screamed as if they'd never forgive me.

At times like this, it's a great help to have a wife who is an ex-flight attendant, speaks English, and knows where you've hidden the travelers' checks. The trip back was not one of life's better moments. What idiot said: "Life is a journey, not a destination"?

Michael B. Strauss, MD, a lieutenant commander in the Navy who has previously served as a medical officer for underwater demolition teams, feels that of all the problems in diving, about 75 percent are associated with middle ear and sinus spaces. (We'll meet this Navy doctor later when we talk about panic and survival.)

Strauss points out that the difficulties are not confined to inexperienced divers. Even the Japanese professional women divers, the Ama, can develop ear injuries.

With 830,000 pilots in America and two million certified scuba divers, not counting 20 million who snorkel, there are plenty of opportunities for people to get aerotitis.

Another reason you shouldn't fly with a cold is because you are not at your best for flight planning on the ground and decision-making in the air. You are less alert and not so observant. Both judgement and reaction time can be impaired. Fatigue is more likely. Even if you've given yourself sufficient time for a cold remedy to be out of your body before flying, there may be some residual effect on even unknown allergic reaction setting in.

Your eyes will be watering more and your ears will be less keen. Even your sense of smell will be impaired, and this can be quite protective as we have previously seen. Radio communications will not be so easily handled either.

The best place for a bad cold is a warm bed, not an aircraft seat.

HEADACHE

Forty-two million people in the United States suffer the misery of the humdrum headache. They spend four billion dollars a year on their affliction and visit their physicians 12,000,000 times a year, hoping that the medical world has the answer. It hasn't, but it has had, over the centuries, a lot of suggestions.

Galen (130-200 AD) favored strong purgatives, but later the physicians and barber surgeons of the Dark Ages leaned to blood-letting. A graduate of my medical school—Edinburgh,—contributed to the death of George Washington by this practice. The Incas used surgical trephination, where holes were bored in the skull to release the evil devils and demons. Sometimes this "ultimately relieved the patient's headache by killing him."

More ahead of his time than he realized was Robert Burton, whose 1630 *Anatomy of Melancholy* announced that milk and all that comes in milk are not good for those that are subject to headache. Indeed, food allergy is now known to precipitate some forms of migraine, the most interesting of the headache group.

Headaches are more than interesting to the unfortunates prone to them. Patients can be quite overwhelmed and we can only speculate how many affairs of honor, matters of high intrigue, and events in history have been altered by headache.

"I'm very brave generally," said Tweedledum in *Through the Looking Glass*, "only today I happen to have a headache."

We've not really come a long way since the old days. Aspirin on occasion, or Tylenol if you can't handle aspirin, seems adequate. For a pilot with a hangover, a whiff of oxygen is said to be the traditional cure. Get your eyes tested, your sinuses looked at, and your blood pressure checked if the problem continues. Remember, facial ache like neuralgia can sometimes be due to dental problems, and air trapped in dental cavities can expand painfully at altitude.

MIGRAINE

Migraine is a special type of headache with its own folk tales and superstitions. In my family, four members out of five have it; I thus have much personal experience.

Patients sometimes believe that the word migraine just means "very bad" and often use the term casually out of its context. Migraines headaches sure are bad but they are *not* part of a sequence: bad; worse; migraine. They are forms of headache in their own right.

In migraine, the blood vessels in the head somehow go into spasm. Because the brain needs blood and oxygen more than any organ, it is very sensitive to reduction in blood flow and cannot function well without oxygen. The most susceptible part is the visual cortex, the area at the back of the head that interprets what the eyes see. If you are short of oxygen there, the visual cortex will play tricks on you.

Thus in the classic forms of migraine, patients have visual problems at the beginning of the attack. Indeed, patients who understand their condition can often anticipate the headache and take specific treatment if they are lucky (if that's the right word) and have this aura or warning that a migraine headache is starting. Common visual disturbances include fortification figures, which are zigzag lines passing across the field of vision; they get this name because to some patients they look like the top of a calvary fort in Indian Territory. Other patients describe them as resembling the top of a mountain range, or like the teeth of a saw. One patient said they were "like the prisms of light reflected from the crystal border of a mirror" and I knew exactly what she was talking about.

Sometimes the aura will produce light flashes as if a camera flashgun had gone off. Just about anything can happen. Frequently there are visual field defects—holes or shadows in what you are looking at. If you gaze at a door, for example, you may not see the door handle but you may see the hinges. Move your head slightly. Now you can see the door handle but not the hinges. If you're looking at a newspaper, you will notice areas missing that you can make appear and then disappear by moving your head. One of my patients walked past a movie theatre showing Paul Newman in *Absence of Malice*. He saw: Pau   in *Absence of Malice*, and by moving his head saw: Paul Newman in *Absen*   and therefore worked out the name of both star and movie.

On occasion, patients will have blurred vision as if they are looking along a heat shimmer on the highway, or as if they are peering through a windshield that has water running down it. Consequently they may complain that focusing is difficult during the aura. There is, infrequently, a telescoping effect to vision, simulating a view through the wrong side of a telescope. This shrinking effect gives the migraine patient difficulty in judging distance, and can even make viewed objects or people appear smaller. Lewis Caroll, who wrote *Alice in Wonderland*, suffered from migraine and it is now believed that his description of Alice's shrinking small enough to pass through a rabbit hole was the result of those visual aberrations he'd previously experienced himself.

Another way the human body is distorted in these visual oddities is where only half a person may be seen. For example, the migraine sufferer may not see the right-hand side of a person's face or body, and may even not be able to see her own. I say "her" because the patient is indeed usually female.

I recall one person who had her first and only attack of migraine as she drove a school bus down a steep hill. The dash mirror was vibrating on the bumpy road and she couldn't adjust it to her satisfaction. She was actually in the first stages of a visual migraine aura, but did not know it. She then attempted in vain to see properly out of the outside driver's mirror. She rolled down the window as the bus tore down the hill. She put out her hand to steady the mirror, but still couldn't see properly.

She glanced down at the wheel and into the same visual field defect and couldn't see her right hand. In a panic, she thought: My left hand is on the outside mirror; my right hand isn't on the wheel. God, where is my right hand?

Shaken badly, she limped into the office convinced she must have a brain tumor. A first attack of classic migraine can be as fearful as a first period to an unprepared young girl. This patient had reason to be frightened because her attack—the only one she ever had—

was of the so-called *hemiplegic* type where the patient has a temporary weakness or paralysis down one side as if a stroke had occurred. Symptoms clear, however, in a few hours and there is no permanent damage. With this type of migraine, the features can be quite bizarre. Often there are numb feelings to the face, gums, or teeth as if a dentist had given a novocaine shot. There may be clumsiness or tingling to one hand; the eye may water or feel funny.

Some migraine episodes abort at this stage without resultant headache. Patients with this subclinical or abortive migraine are lucky even though, until the diagnosis is made, they may be more scared. The real misery of migraine is the resultant headache which tends to follow the aura by 20 to 30 minutes. It is usually on one side only, often felt behind the eye as a pounding aching, synchronous in time to the heartbeat. It may last from two to three hours to several

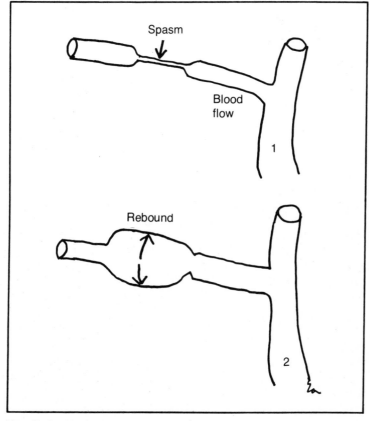

Vasodilation in migraine.

days. There is often associated photophobia (aversion to light), and there is usually noise sensitivity, Nausea and vomiting can ensue. Rarely, abdonimal pain occurs where the trouble is in the belly blood vessels as well as the brain.

The headache is easy to understand. After the initial spasm and contraction of the cranial blood vessels, there is a resultant rebound opening-up or *vasodilation*. The surging stretching of the wall of the blood vessel is very painful, and no wonder—the tiny nerves in the wall are being stretched too.

Specific treatment requires the patient to take medicine to prevent this stretching *early*, at the first sign of the visual aura. There are now, fortunately, other useful medications that can prevent frequent cluster attacks in patients. More preventive treatments need an understanding of the whole patient. Some migraine sufferers clearly have food allergies. They will develop migraine if they eat chocolate, aged beef, aged cheese, meat tenderizer, monosodium glutamate food preservative, or Chinese food. Red wine and some other forms of alcohol likewise can cause trouble.

Other migraine victims seem to be tense, rigid, inflexible, perfectionist personalities. They have the cleanest children, the tidiest homes, the neatest desks that always have the sharpest pencils and so on—marvelous persons to have working for you but not always the easiest to live with. It was once said that migraine and high intelligence went hand in hand; a recent study debunked this idea but I'm not going to dwell too much on this theory.

Another approach to migraine is biofeedback. Here some patients who have cold extremities can be taught techniques to raise their body temperature and vasodilate the blood vessels of their fingers, hands, and presumably brain. The methods are relatively simple to learn and represent a new trend, and a desirable one, where the patient is cooperating with the doctor in his or her own cure.

I have seen patients with recurrent headaches due to migraine who are now free for the first time in years because they have started biofeedback treatments. Thus, persons previously unable to seek employment have found themselves once again fit to fight that regular grind we call our working day.

Migraine strikes pilots. The disease appears to select dynamic, busy, enthusiastic people. Flying seems to attract people as much for the challenge as for the fun. It is not a restful career or pastime. For some, flying is a compulsion—an obligation to get more ratings the way a Boy Scout shoots for all the merit badges.

For some, it is a pressure to achieve more than before: longer cross-countries, faster doglegs, higher altitudes, quicker touch-and-goes. Aviation as a hobby should be your servant, not your master. If flying is causing tension, rethink your situation and ask why. Don't be like the longtime golfer once overheard by Dr. Carl Adatto, a New Orleans psychiatrist, to say: "Thank God it's raining today, so I don't have to play."

ALLERGIES

There are more allergy sufferers than those who simply endure migraine. The National Institute of Allergies and Infectious Diseases believes that 31 million Americans are afflicted by hypersensitivity.

In allergy, the individual situations are as striking as the total statistics: A Detroit autoworker gets blisters on his lips every time he kisses his wife. A Dallas executive finds a skin rash on his hands if he touches a dogwood tree. A Boston housewife suffers diarrhea each time she tastes spaghetti sauce. A Las Vegas mortician nearly dies after eating lobster.

Probably, we've all had an allergic episode without realizing it. As our world becomes more complicated, our environment more altered, and our skies more polluted, the problems are going to get worse, not better.

The medical profession has not, however, succeeded in understanding allergic disease the way, for example, infectious disease has been clarified. It will take a couple of generations of medical students before we know the role of allergy as well as we comprehend the action of penicillin.

In my medical student days I treated a wretchedly poor woman who lived in miserable conditions in a seedy tenement. I got her to see an allergist. The backroom scientist ran his tests, then told me blithely that the destitute woman was allergic to *caviar*. I wanted to strike a colleague whose tests were so divorced from reality and whose contribution to any patient's welfare was so worthless.

I have often been asked by patients about the value of an allergic workup. The answer is not always easy. I tell them that in some ways our knowledge of allergy today is about the same as our attitudes toward mental illness were in 1793. In that year Philippe Pinel, a warm and compassionate physician at the Bicetre hospital in Paris, looked at his mental patients whose treatment had consisted of being chained to their beds for years. One patient had been chained for 40 years, another for 36 years. Pinel decided that this was not appropriate and boldly ordered all the mental patients released. In anger, the city rose up against him, the mob attacked, and he was apparently saved only by the intervention of a patient he had just released.

It took a whole century before a young man, working in Charcot's clinic in Paris in 1885, clarified the illness called "the divine madness" and established a scientific basis for appropriate treatment of mental illness. His name was Sigmund Freud.

If awareness of allergy at the end of the 20th century is truly comparable to 18th century knowledge of psychiatry when mentally ill patients lay on straw mattresses in chains, then we indeed have a long way to go in understanding a disease caused because the patient is oversensitive to an agent that strikes from the shadows of his environment.

Nevertheless, progress is being made.

The word comes from the Greek for "changed work," and even then Hippocrates had observations on this phenomenon. Later, two 19th century British doctors, personal sufferers of summer symptoms, investigated why they had such problems under the hot burning sun. They felt that the heat itself was the problem. It took the intuition of a patient to divert the research in "hay fever" to the pollens themselves.

Some of the bacteriological research by Pasteur in France and Koch in Germany gave clues to the factors involved in allergy, and finally a Baltimore pediatrician, von Pirquet, showed that reactions to diphtheria antitoxins were not due to the antitoxin but to the horse serum contained in it.

The rules of allergy are, however, hard to write. The allergen, an irritant to you, that causes a reaction does so because it is your personal poison. It doesn't help to get angry about the problem. It makes as much sense for you to rage at the doctor for this as it is for him to fume at you for having this personal idiosyncrasy.

It's understandable that an allergic patient would show resentment to the doctor, the spouse, or to life itself. It's a rotten problem. Allergic patients pay $135 million a year for drugstore prescriptions and another $100 million for injections. In addition, their allergies provoke about three times as many visits to the doctor as other people have to make.

Dr. Alice S. Mills, a Chicago allergist, believes that the nation loses 36 million school days a year because children have allergies. Military doctors state that for every sixteen recruits rejected because of medical problems, one has been refused because of allergic difficulties.

Respiratory allergy is more common than any other kind. Probably about 75 percent of allergic sufferers have trouble with their nose or their lungs. Fortunately, knowledge and treatment of this form of hypersensitivity is light-years ahead of how we handle food allergies.

In my area of New England, spring allergy to trees and shrubs starts in April, summer allergy to grass sets in about June, and fall weed allergy begins around September. Mold allergy can be common in summer or winter, as can dust allergy, although symptoms may be more common in bad weather when the house is barricaded up against the cold.

Most doctors feel that patients should see an allergist if symptoms last longer than a season of a few weeks, and are not helped by oral antihistamines; if the allergy is causing failure to thrive; if it creates school difficulties in children, or work absenteeism in adults; if it makes life miserable and suffering intense for any age.

TURISTA

A lot of conflicting advice has trickled down over the years about travelers' trots. Probably the best thing to do is drink lots of fluids and let the diarrhea run its course. This gets the bug out of your system. Pepto Bismol helps in huge amounts (it'll make your stools black).

You probably will end up requesting some Imodium or Lomotil tablets to cut down the bowel irritability, and maybe some Vibramycin to kill germs, but most doctors are skeptical about the value of those drugs in this setting. A previous favorite, Entero-Vioform, is now considered quite the wrong treatment.

The germs are everywhere. Watch the ice. Watch the water. Watch out for lavish desserts or fancy buffets that have taken long hours and many hands to prepare. In tropical countries, don't open your mouth in the shower and don't brush your teeth with tap water—use distilled.

You'll still get turista. It is written.

A conference of gastroenterologists once met in Mexico City to discuss this traveler's diarrhea, sometimes called the Aztec Two-Step, Delhi Belly, Montezuma's Revenge, and so on. About 280 doctors came from all over the world. They booked into the best and cleanest hotel in Mexico City, yet the seminar was cancelled the next day when just about all the physicians developed turista and were confined to their rooms.

IRRITABLE BOWEL (Spastic Colon)

Next to the common cold, irritable colon is the commonest cause of absenteeism from work in America. The symptoms can be like those of turista but usually the recurrent pattern is established in any one patient who is aware of the simple diagnosis and the way it constantly hits.

The features vary. There may be loose stools with mucus or slime, cramping with much spasm and pain, nausea, and irritability. Blood is not present in the stools. Attacks can be caused by tension, by prior bowel infections, or by dietic indiscretions. Food allergy may occasionally provoke it.

The treatment should be easy. It is, after all, a recurrent problem and you would expect the patient to be able to handle it. In my experience, however, instead of being reassured by recurrences of symptoms (which indeed confirm the diagnosis), patients seem to treat each episode as a potentially new problem and always come needing reassurance.

A paregoric-like product with a mild tranquilizer—Donnatal or Librax—is usually sufficient. Patients may need to stay home for a day or two until their angry bowel settles.

Charles Darwin, the naturalist, was said to suffer from this problem so severely that any long journey in a train that did not have a corridor or toilet was an agony. As Jefferson said, traveling makes a man wiser, but less happy.

ACUTE GASTRITIS (Gastric Flu)

There's a whole spectrum of illnesses that cause vomiting, some important. This is why over-the-counter remedies always carry the caution "see a doctor if no improvement."

Important illnesses are sometimes associated with abdominal pain but not always so. Doctors worry if patients vomit blood, which can be either fresh or old, making it look like coffee grounds. Yellow liquid in the vomitus is often bile. This is sometimes of significance. Usually, ill people who vomit first empty their stomachs, then progress to retching up gastric or digestive juice.

Common illnesses causing vomiting include virus stomach infections and food poisoning. Some of the problems of turista give similar symptoms, and diarrhea is often a feature. To some degree you can avoid food poisoning by being cautious, especially during the summer months when germs grow quickly.

Be careful with sandwiches sitting in Saran Wrap bags baking in the sun's heat on top of your instrument panel. Watch out for mayonnaise in summer—it can go off quickly. It is probably a good idea for pilot and copilot to eat different foods in restaurants. If you are vomiting, it can be helpful to reduce your diet to drinking clear fluids only: ice chips, Popsicles, tonics, Jello, water, and maybe sherbert. Tums or Rolaids on occasion are useful as are antacids like Maalox, but Maalox can cause loose stools, and if you've got that tendency already, Titralac, which tends to constipate, may be better.

If the illness is severe or recurrent, see your doctor.

URINARY TRACT INFECTION

Infections in the lower urinary tract are more frequent than any trouble in the upper regions of the kidney. Kidney infections present themselves a bit like flu with backache, fever, and chills, and often the patient has no urinary symptoms.

Lower tract infections are common. Acute cystitis—bladder infection—is essentially a woman's problem. The symptoms easily identify the condition. There may be frequency and discomfort on voiding. Often there is delay in emptying the bladder (you have to wait a bit for things to happen) and sometimes feelings of inadequate emptying occur, necessitating the patient's returning often to the restroom. Frequently the patient has to get up at night, often more than once.

Women are more susceptible because of their anatomy. They have a shorter tube from the bladder and this tube, the urethra, ends in proximity to the vagina and rectum. Any sweat or moisture in the saddle area may carry germs from the anus to contaminate the urethra. A woman may be socially clean after a shower or bath, but not bacteriologically sterile.

Snug nylon briefs, leotards, pantyhose, and polyester clothing tend to prevent proper ventilation of the saddle area. This compounds the problem for women, as does their peculiar tendency not to drink as much as men.

Indeed, a first attack of bladder infection will almost always clear if the patient forces a lot of fluids—a *lot*; eight pints a day for a couple of days. Repeated attacks suggest you should see your doctor.

VAGINITIS

This is hardly an emergency but it is a common problem in women who often don't know all the answers to it. Because we have been referring to the pilot so often as "he" this handout for women from our office may be a courtesy for women pilot readers.

Vaginitis is an irritation or inflammation of the vagina. The chief symptom is a sudden, abnormal discharge, generally followed by itching and soreness of the vagina and external genitalia. Some discharges are the natural and normal mucus secretions of your reproductive system, but these are usually clear, odorless, and non-irritating. If you notice a change in the color, quantity, or odor of your usual discharge, and it is accompanied by itching, consult your doctor.

Vaginitis is not generally very serious. Gynecologists estimate that one out of every two women will have vaginitis at least once. Most will suffer nothing worse than a temporary annoyance.

Vaginitis is usually caused by infection by a fungus, bacteria, or other microscopic parasites. Chemicals in commercial douches and vaginal sprays can sometimes cause a "non-infectious" vaginitis, which is why many physicians discourage their patients from using such preparations.

Some women may be infected by their sexual partners. (Men rarely have symptoms, but they are often carriers of the infective organisms). In other cases, bacteria from the feces may get into the vagina because of careless wiping after a bowel movement.

However, many cases of vaginal infection are not "caught" in the regular sense of the word. There are always lots of tiny microbes or germs living in our bodies. Normally they do not cause any problem. Sometimes, though, the chemical balance of the vagina is altered, causing one of these microscopic organisms to grow out of control and cause infection. This chemical imbalance may be caused by excessive douching, antibiotics, oral contraceptives, even an emotional upset. Pregnancy also makes you a likelier candidate for vaginitis, as does diabetes. As with all infections, vaginitis is more likely to take hold when your resistance is lowered by illness.

Moniliasis

Moniliasis is caused by a fungus, and is probably the most common form of vaginitis at this time. It is also known as *candidiasis*, thrush, or yeast infection. The main symptom is a thick white discharge that looks like cottage cheese and produces marked genital itching. The victim may find sex uncomfortable, even painful. Monilia is easily treated. Your doctor is likely to choose from a variety of medications: vaginal tablets, suppositories, creams, solutions, ointments, or oral tablets.

Trichomoniasis

Trichomoniasis, caused by a microscopic parasite, usually comes on the heels of your period. It produces an odorous, yellowish-green discharge. There may be itching in and around your vagina. Urination is frequent and painful. Sex may be painful, too.

Your doctor is likely to prescribe an oral medication for you *and* your partner, so that you don't reinfect each other during intercourse.

Nonspecific Vaginitis

Nonspecific vaginitis results from an outgrowth of normally harmless bacteria in your vagina. You can also get it during intercourse or because of improper wiping. Symptoms vary; you may have a gray discharge, a whitish discharge, or a yellowish one. As with trichomoniasis, the discharge will be odorous. There may be itching and burning. In treating nonspecific vaginitis, your doctor may find it necessary to try two or three different kinds of medication, usually creams, suppositories, or antibiotics.

Viral Vaginitis/Herpes

Viral vaginitis is caused by a virus related to the organism that causes cold sores, except that instead of cold sores, you're probably going to get genital blisters that hurt when you urinate or have intercourse. You may also experience itching and watery discharge. Your doctor will prescribe an ointment or lotion to relieve any discomfort you may feel because of the blisters.

Atrophic Vaginitis

Atrophic vaginitis occurs only in women who are well into the menopause or have had their ovaries removed. As the body's supply of estrogen diminishes, the vaginal walls become thinner and more susceptible to infection. There may be itching and a watery discharge; intercourse may be painful. Your physician will relieve the distress of atrophic vaginitis by prescribing a cream, suppository, and/or oral medication.

Mixed infections are quite common and, like all forms of vaginitis, should be diagnosed by your doctor.

Your doctor will want to know if you've been ill lately and the names of any medications you may have taken. You will be asked if you think you may be pregnant. And you will be examined, with a sample of your discharge taken for diagnosis. That's why it's important not to douche before your appointment; you might wash away all the evidence.

Often the cause of your infection can be pinpointed just by inspection of your genitals or examination of a drop of the discharge under the microscope. If your doctor is still in doubt, a sample of the discharge will be cultured—a technique that encourages the organism to grow and makes it easier to identify.

If you are itchy, don't experiment. Check with your doctor, and do what he or she recommends. The prescribed medication will soon stop the itching. If you are particularly uncomfortable, your doctor may also recommend some additional measure to sooth your irritation and itching.

You may feel better within a few days, even a few hours. But though your symptoms have vanished, the organisms that infected you will probably still be active. Play it safe. Follow your doctor's instructions to the letter. Take your medication for as many days— and as many times a day—as your doctor's prescription indicates. Then come back for a follow-up visit. That's the *only* way to know if you're *completely* cured.

Check with your doctor about giving up sex while on treatment. If intercourse is likely to bother you, it may be recommended that you give it up until well. When your sex life does resume, your doctor may recommend that your partner wear a condom while the danger of reinfection exists. If you've been wearing a diaphragm, you may be instructed to get a new, sterile one.

Reinfection happens. There is no assurance that you won't get this again, but you can minimize the chances by following the rules of good hygiene: clean underwear, clean bathing suits, frequent baths or showers. Make it a point to wash the inner surface of the external genitals with a mild soap, then dry carefully. Remember that infectious organisms thrive in hot, moist environment, especially those created by nylon panties and stockings with a garter belt. Skirts and looser pants may also be advisable.

Avoid the problem of getting bowel bacteria into your vagina by always wiping front to back after a bowel movement. If you use a vaginal spray, don't direct the spray into your vagina. Finally, if you don't have a steady, dependable sexual partner, it may be wise to insist that your friends wear condoms.

HEAD INJURY

There can't be many pilots who haven't walked into a wing or some other part of an aircraft. The resulting blow sends them on their way with a bump on the temple and a ringing head.

Pilots elsewhere also forget to duck like any other person. They bang their heads skiing or skating. They fall downstairs. They've even been known to get into fights.

There's a lot of misconception about what follows if a blow on the head has been bad enough to knock a person out. Sometimes the bruising of the brain happens at the site of impact. Sometimes the bruise appears on the opposite side to the blow—*contre coup*—as the brain slides across the hollow skull, skidding like a beer down a bar counter, to stop suddenly against something solid.

An emergency-room doctor may choose to admit the patient for observation. However, if you are in a less-than-ideal situation or have chosen for some wrong reason not to be checked by an emergency room, you might want to know what advice is commonly given in follow-up.

Friends and attendants often get it all wrong. They will call the doctor and proudly say that they've walked the poor victim, and I do mean *victim*, around the bedroom all night to prevent his falling asleep. There's nothing wrong with letting the patient fall asleep. You may have no choice if he's drunk as well as injured. Just verify later that he *is* asleep and not unconscious.

This means confirming after a few hours that the patient can be roused and wakened. It is usually sufficient to shake the patient, waken him, allow him to mumble something coherent, then let him slide back to sleep. Repeat this several hours later.

Follow-up advice to head-injured patients and their friends often runs like this:

1. Waken the patient twice through the night, the first night, to verify that he is asleep and *not* unconscious.
2. Call the doctor immediately if any of these symptoms occur:

   ☐ Difference in size of pupils
   ☐ Persistent vomiting
   ☐ Increasing sleepiness or stupor from which patient cannot be aroused (see 1 above)
   ☐ Bleeding or discharge from ears or nose
   ☐ Increasing headaches or facial weakness
   ☐ Persistent dizziness or difficulty with balance

MEDICAL MAYDAYS

A patient's perception of what constitutes an emergency may not always be valid. However, the majority of doctors would regard an emergency as *anything* that threatens the life of a patient and could cause permanent significant damage to his well-being. Although patients should attempt to anticipate problems and not seek medical care in a crisis-oriented fashion, there are times when a lot has gone wrong, and the patient is getting into trouble and needs to be seen urgently.

Such illnesses include:

- ☐ Severe chest pain which is unexpected, unfamiliar, and unexplained; sudden pain felt in the back, shoulders, neck or abdomen; severe palpitations.
- ☐ Significant loss of blood in the stool, urine or vomitus; heavy vaginal bleeding.
- ☐ Convulsions, unconsciousness, severe confusion, sudden weakness.
- ☐ Sudden mental breakdown; attempted suicide.
- ☐ Significant injuries: major burns; broken bones; head or back injuries; gunshot or knife wounds; eye injuries; lacerations needing stitching; poisonings; drug abuse; animal, snake, or poisonous insect bites; near-drownings; electric shock.
- ☐ Sudden life-threatening problems: severe difficulty in breathing; loss of vision; dramatic simultaneous diarrhea and vomiting; intense allergic reactions.

If in doubt to whether you should go to your nearest emergency room, and if you can't get hold of your private physician, you may wish to call a hospital emergency room and speak to the emergency room nurse in charge. She is usually a most experienced person. Remember, a hospital emergency ward, a crowded waiting room, a busy harassed medical and nursing staff are all the best place for a genuine middle-of-the-night emergency call and the worst place in the world for ongoing delivery of care for a chronic problem.

Chapter 8

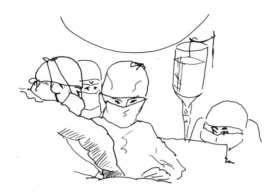

Surgical Adventures

A doctor, so the saying goes, is someone who still has his appendix, tonsils, and adenoids. There can't be many bodies in America that don't have at least one scar, although no American can compete with the patient in Sydney, Australia, who has undergone 87 major operations.

A back surgeon was once challenged by a *Newsweek* reporter: "How come you guys always want to operate?"

The reply came promptly: "When you go around carrying a hammer, you tend to believe everything you see is a nail."

So how is the consumer to decide? How is a pilot, perhaps miles away from his home base, going to decide on the appropriateness of surgical advice?

The old way—*become informed*. Understand your body.

Sometimes, there's no question. If you've been injured somehow and your ear is hanging off, you're going to want it stuck back on. But elective surgery is different. This is where you have a choice.

The most common operations done in America are hernia repair, D & C (dilatation and curettage of the uterine body), and removal of the gall bladder, the uterus, the appendix, and piles (hemorrhoids).

Let's get to the bottom of all this. Let's start with piles.

PILES

Hemorrhoids have been the affliction of man since he first stood upright, grimacing and snarling, to rise above the other animals. He's paid the price with piles.

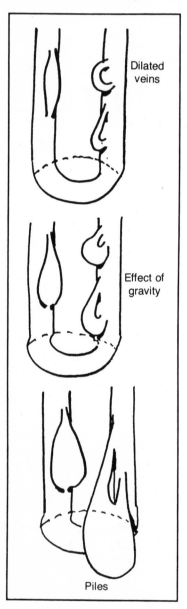

Dilated veins

Effect of gravity

Hemorrhoids.

Piles

These are simply distended varicose veins in the wall of the rectum. Piles are merely the result of the action of gravity and, to a smaller degree, the tourniquet behavior of the anal sphincter muscle. Some people appear to have weak-walled veins or absent venous valves. Other exciting causes include constipation, straining at defecation, prolonged standing, and heavy lifting. Pregnancy in women and enlargement of the prostrate gland in men can precipitate the problem of piles.

By the way, piles and hemorrhoids are one and the same condition. Patients seem to prefer "hemorrhoids"—it's more elegant, and certainly the Old Testament refers to piles as "emerods" or the plague (Deuteronomy XXVIII.27).

Whatever they're called, they can be a miserable affliction. The symptoms are rectal bleeding for first stage piles and a feeling of something coming down for Stages Two and Three. "I can't raise my gear," a pilot once told me, "I can't get my undercarriage up!"

Piles are classified as Stage Two if swollen veins protrude during bowel movements, but go back up again once the straining is over.

Stage Three piles hang down as soon as the patient stands erect and are an indication for surgery. Stage One patients probably will avoid the knife, but the blood count should be checked to confirm that anemia has not resulted due to surreptitious blood loss. Stage Two patients may need surgery.

Fortunately, not all piles progress from Stage One to Two and Three. Patients with difficulty learn to avoid the problem of constipation and to give up long meditation while on the throne.

If there is much itch, an over-the-counter cortisone cream may help and soothing suppositories like Wyanoid or Anusol can comfort internally. In young adults the disease is usually a primary problem without any deeper significance, but in older persons piles may be secondary to other disease further up the bowel.

You really should see a doctor. This is a hard place for do-it-yourself health nuts to handle.

You need surgery if the piles are always down, the bowel movements are always bloody, and you are always miserable.

DIVERTICULOSIS

Let's stay in the bowel for the moment and mention a common problem: *diverticulosis* and, if things get inflamed, *diverticulitis*. At least 5 percent of people of both sexes over the age of 40, on barium enema, show the presence of diverticula or small bulges, pockets,

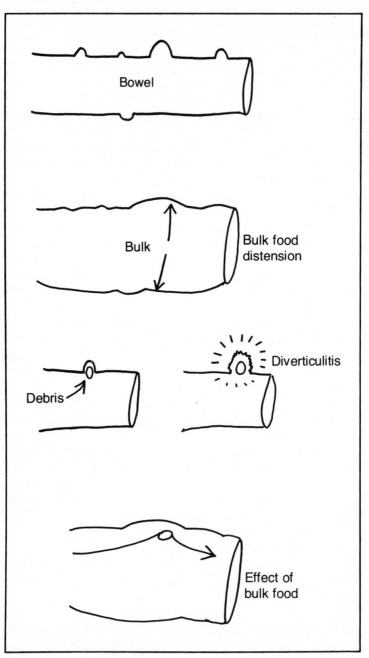

Diverticulosis.

or herniae in the wall of the large bowel. There may be just a few in the pelvic part of the bowel, or there may be many all the way up the large bowel.

It's no big deal to have diverticulosis. Doctors have swung away from the former advice about avoiding roughage. The old idea was that seeds or indigestible food matter would block those blind pockets and cause inflammation. Now physicians believe that patients with this condition should eat bulk—bran for breakfast every day—in the hope that this will stretch out the bowel and make the pockets shallow and more open. Thus, bowel contents will move along without sticking in the diverticula.

Sometimes these things bleed and if a diverticulum gets blocked and irritated, the problem has progressed to diverticulitis. This is an important cause of abdominal pain; it is usually in the lower left abdomen. If the swelling bursts, it's as bad as appendicitis. Probably 30 percent of those with diverticulosis have an attack of diverticulitis over the long haul, and about 15 percent of patients with diverticulitis get into trouble and need surgery. Older persons with many areas of diverticulosis are most likely to have problems.

It's probably a good idea for a pilot over the age of 45 who is often away from his home base, if he has vague lower abdominal pain, to know his blood type and have a barium enema to clarify if he has diverticulosis. This is especially true since the many moves around the world that some pilots make predisposes them to constipation. As someone said, "Aeronautical man is a constipated biped with backache."

Constipation should be easy to handle: a couple of glasses of warm water on awakening, bran and prune juice for breakfast, with fruit and vegetables included in the diet. If this doesn't work, get more exercise, drink more fluids, consider occasional use of milk of magnesia, mineral oil, or a bulk-additive like Metamucil. Avoid constant use of laxatives.

You need surgery if you have such severe abdominal symptoms that the doctor isn't sure of the diagnosis, or whether or not you're perforated.

APPENDICITIS

This is a disease of our century. We started to understand it about the same time as Orville and Wilbur got the hang of those winds at Kitty Hawk.

Yet bizarre reports have occurred in the medical literature. As far back as 1581 there were discussions of fatal suppurating disease of the bowel low down on the right side. It was then called "perityphlitis." Claudius Amyand actually did an appendectomy in 1736 in Britain when he found an inflamed appendix punctured by a pin in a hernial sac. It was not, however, until Reginald Fitz, a professor at Harvard, read a paper at the first meeting of the Association of American Physicians in 1886 that the disease received recognition.

The first successful operations for appendicitis were carried out about 1888 by Dr. Thomas Morton in Philadelphia and Sir Frederick Treves in London, but the most famous one was in England in the first decade of this century; the patient was King Edward VII two days before his coronation. This story brings the disease a royal full circle because an acutely inflamed, perforated appendix has been found preserved in the mummy of a young princess of Egypt.

What is the appendix? It's just a simple short dangling tube, like a worm, that hangs down from the start of the large bowel. It falls into the pelvis or is tucked up behind the bowel. It has no use and merely creates problems. The tube is hollow, normally big enough to admit a matchstick. The appendix is found only in man, in certain anthropoid apes, and—strangely—in the wombat (a nocturnal burrowing Australian marsupial).

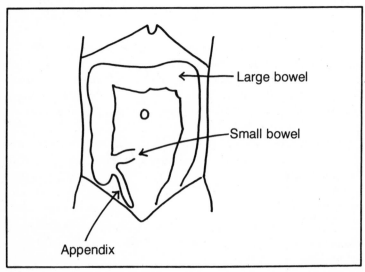

Appendix.

What causes appendicitis? Who knows—there are so many factors. It may run in families, perhaps associated with familial unusual positions that the appendix may occupy. The disease seems more common in civilized nations which may be because they have departed the simple diet rich in cellulose. This cannot be the whole explanation, for acute appendicitis has occurred in lifelong vegetarians and even in babes at the breast.

Strong laxatives may play a part. Medical students are taught in undiagnosed cases which may be appendicitis that "purgation means perforation." Many surgeons blame obstruction. They often find at operation small hard lumps of bowel movement resembling rabbit pellets stuck in the appendix. It's as if those so-called fecoliths have inflamed the appendix.

Appendicitis is a riddle. The condition has risen from relative rarity to the most common serious intraabdominal affliction of the Western civilized races. Yet it now is quite definitely less common. Why, nobody knows, so everyone has a theory. The probable reason? *Nobody knows*. It is certainly not common after the third decade, but it is a *very* important condition. It is so important that, in the past, applicants for expeditions exploring primitive countries or distant lands have had to submit to elective appendectomy before they would be considered for travel to those far-off areas.

By the way, although a passenger in an airliner expects accuracy in his pilot and to be landed at the correct airport, don't be too startled if a member of your family undergoes appendectomy and afterwards the appendix is found to be normal. A surgeon can't bat better than 800. He *has* to operate in the grey areas of doubt. It's better to take the risk of surgery sometimes than to sit on a hot appendix and see your patient perforate. Perforation adds greatly to the patient's problems. You need an operation if you've got appendicitis and clearly not settling. It would be hard to find a bigger nuisance, yet the appendix is only three to four inches long.

GALL BLADDER DISEASE

Before we leave the digestive tract, let us mention another four-inch terror: the gall bladder. This is a simple bag about the size and shape of an empty balloon tucked under the liver. It functions as a reservoir for bile.

A normal adult on a normal diet makes about one-half pint to two pints of bile per day. The gall bladder stores this and concentrates the bile tenfold for conservation of water. The idea was sound, but something went wrong. Gall bladder disease even has its

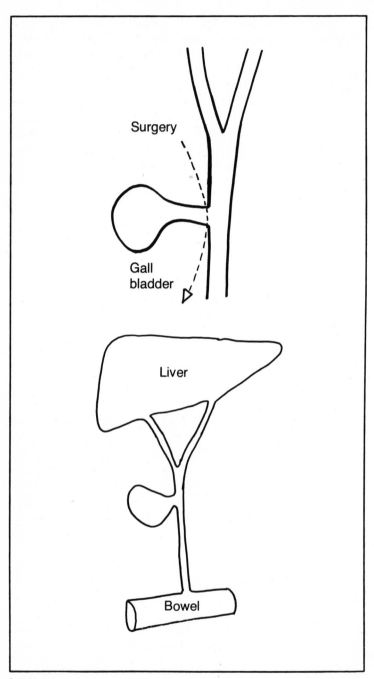

Gall bladder.

110

own Murphy's Law. John B. Murphy was professor of surgery at Northwestern University, Chicago, before he died in 1916. His name has been given to the sign when an examining hand thrust deep into the right upper quadrant causes pain at the zenith of inspiration if the inflamed gall bladder comes down on it.

Gall bladders can become inflamed for many reasons, such as stagnation of bile or irritation from juice from the pancreas (sweetbread), but in 85 to 95 percent of the occasions it is because stones have formed in the gall bladder, crystalizing out from the molasses-like bile. Often previous infection was a factor in stone formation. Lord Moynihan, the famous British surgeon, used to tell his students "Every gall stone is a monument to a germ which lies within it."

However, the reason for the meteoric rise in gallstone formation in America is not clear. Most stones in the United States are about 70 percent cholesterol. Diet clearly plays a part. Bile is needed to digest fat, an excessive component of the American diet. Stagnation plays a role in stone formation as it does in infection of the gall bladder. Hormones do too; both pregnancy and birth control pills make the bile viscous and more likely to develop stones. Racial factors are important, but it is difficult to separate dietary habits here. For example, the Masai of Africa don't get gallstones, yet look at the Pima Indians: 70 percent of their women have gallstones by the age of 30 and 70 percent of males by age 60.

The problem of gallstones is indeed more likely to hit women than men, and once the classic sufferer was described as the fat fertile flatulent female of forty, but the disease now strikes younger people, sometimes children in their teens. As I write this, one of my patients, a girl aged 13, is preparing for surgery.

At the other end of the age spectrum are elderly patients who have gallstones yet no symptoms. It was felt until recently that gallstones were always an indication for removal of the gall bladder. The concept was that it was better to get a cholecystectomy when you are younger, well, and prepared properly for an elective operation than to get it when you are older, vomiting, dehydrated, and receiving an emergency procedure in the middle of the night.

Now the surgeons are not so sure. Maybe persons *can* be left to their gallstones if patients are old and the stones silent. About 10 percent of patients over the age of 50 undergoing autopsy are found to have gallstones that have not contributed to the cause of death.

Yet many medical studies have suggested that it is rare for gallstones to be silent if the patients are followed closely. In one study of 3012 patients with gall bladder irritation and stones, only 134 had no symptoms attributable to gall bladder disease.

It would seem prudent for a pilot with gallstones to have them removed. I remember a private pilot, the president of a small manufacturing company in New England, who was my patient and unfortunately my next door neighbor—unfortunately because he kept reminding me of the episode.

We had arranged a gall bladder X-ray on a day the pilot, unknown to us, was flying his personal Beech Musketeer from Boston to Philadelphia. The X-ray showed gallstones. However, the pills taken to demonstrate these shadows on X-rays caused him violent diarrhea the whole day. On his flight to Philly he had to land five times—once, he said, in a farmer's field. The last I heard of Alec, he had given up flying and was hiding his gallstones someplace in Los Angeles. You need surgery if you have gallstones or an inflamed gall bladder that's not settling.

HIATUS HERNIA

Before we leave the abdomen let us consider two types of hernia. The first, hiatal hernia, could be more of a problem for pilots because its symptoms can mimic heart disease and cause chest pain.

Hiatal hernia does not occupy many pages in most surgical textbooks partly because the handling is often medical—the patient is treated as if he has an ulcer—rather than surgical. However, any doctor with a few years in private practice has seen a tremendous number of distressed patients with this problem. Essentially what happens is that, in normal people, the esophagus or gullet has to pass through a gap in the diaphragm to get through from the chest into the adbomen, where it connects to the stomach proper. The diaphragm is a great spread of muscle that separates those two parts of the body, chest and abdomen. Looked at from the chest, the diaphragm is like a trampoline; looked at from below it resembles a domed cathedral—a wide sweeping cupola. There are gaps in this muscle to allow the body's plumbing through, and sometimes the one that lets the esophagus through is too weak or wide, and part of the stomach slides through alongside the gullet or, more likely, the junction of esophagus and stomach is displaced upwards through the weak ring.

Part of the stomach is then lying in the chest, and more important, it is empty of food, in contrast to the stomach below where food neutralizes acid. The lining in this stomach hernia is usually raw and sore and gives considerable discomfort to patients.

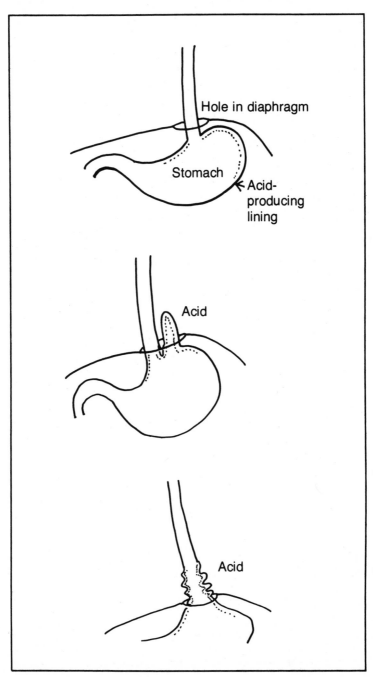

Hiatus hernia.

The symptoms are "heartburn" as if the area behind the breast bone is on fire, "water brash" where sometimes regurgitated acid liquid comes up into the back of the throat, and true indigestion. Symptoms are often intermittent because the hernia is not always consistently in the chest; but the problems are often increased by stooping or bending over or lying down in bed or becoming obese.

Propping up the head of the bed on bricks, on two pound coffee cans full of concrete, or on 10-inch cones, can be very helpful. It takes ten days to get used to the odd sliding-downhill feeling. Extra pillows don't work; they just tilt your neck and head.

Sufferers are often over the age of 50 and men are probably more affected than women. X-rays usually confirm; an *oesphagoscopy-gastroscopy* (telescope-periscope examination) may be necessary and medical treatment is usually adequate.

You need an operation sometimes if the hernia is huge, symptoms crippling, and medical treatment ineffective.

INGUINAL HERNIA

Hernias, or ruptures in the groin, are one of the commonest afflictions of man, and here we do mean *man* as opposed to woman. The problem is five times more common in men. About 5 percent of adult males in America have a rupture or hernia. The problem, however, is worldwide and, over the ages, great surgeons of many nations have tried to clarify the situation. The names read like a Who's Who of Medicine: Russell of Australia; Madyl of Czechoslovakia; Arbos of Spain; Glassow of Canada; Narath of Austria; Hesselbach and Richter of Germany; Poupart, Pare, and Petit of France; Morgagni, Scarpa and Bassini of Italy; Treves, Keith and Cooper of England, and in this country, McArthur in Chicago and Mayo in Rochester.

The principle's somewhat similar to that in hiatal hernia—namely, there is a gap in a muscle, this time the abdominal wall, and through that gap something bulges: sometimes fat, often bowel. Usually the deficit is close to the pubic bone on either side of the groin and represents a weakness at the so-called inguinal ring.

In males, this is the ring through which the testes dropped in the last month or two of intrauterine life. In other words, the normal ring allows the testicles to descend into the scrotum and has to be wide enough for that. Unfortunately, it is often wider and there's not a darned thing you can do about it. That's the way you were born and one day, probably during heavy lifting, you'll feel a tearing sensation in your groin and you've joined the club. If you're lucky, it will

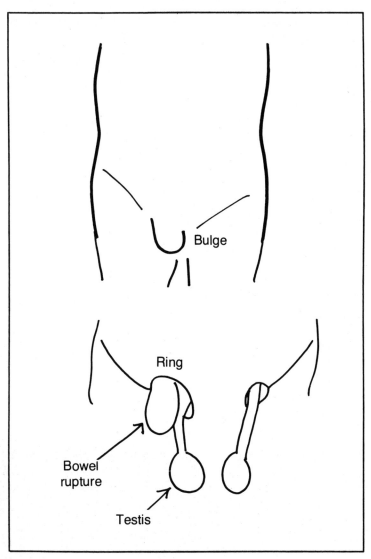

Bulge

Ring

Bowel
rupture

Testis

Inguinal hernia.

happen at work involving workman's compensation, perhaps when you're picking up your Jepp bag. If you're unlucky, it will happen maybe when you're moving a refrigerator for your neighbor's wife and you're on your own financially. Surgery gives you a week in the hospital, six weeks without work, and three months of convalescence without heavy lifting. It can all be expensive.

And if you've got a rupture, you can't avoid surgery. Trusses went out of fashion centuries ago, about the same time as chastity belts. If the surgeon isn't sure whether it's a groin muscle strain or a true rupture, you may wish a second opinion. Why don't you check with your family doctor? But . . .

You got it—you need surgery.

HYSTERECTOMY/D & C

We'll cover this because there are a lot of women pilots, many old enough to be in the age group that needs hysterectomy. We don't have to spend too much time on this because women, probably through Pap smears and because of childbirth, are more familiar with their bodies and have had more chance to ask their private physicians about their health problems. Besides, diseases of the uterus are less likely to threaten the pilot's health than, say, the development of a slipped disc.

The indications for surgery on the uterus are less firm than those for other operations. The D & C (dilation and curettage) is usually done for diagnostic reasons—"Why are my periods crazy and heavy, doctor?"—or for therapeutic purposes to try to straighten out menstruation that is so painful or excessive that the patient's life is miserable.

Hysterectomy is a much more significant procedure. Although the uterus is merely a big empty muscle-bag meant to hold babies, its removal is clearly a big step for any woman. Women can become subdued, even depressed, at the thought that they will never again conceive.

Yet if you somehow performed a hysterectomy on a patient who was, say, unconscious, and you got things all healed before the patient woke up, she would have no post-operative symptoms or complaints other than no periods. All the worries in her head about loss of femininity, loss of interest in sex, premature aging, and so on are exactly that: understandable worries in the patient's head. If the ovaries were conserved, the patient would still go on as before with monthly fluid retention and cyclical changes in her body. Her vagina would be about the same length, its vault would feel normal, and sexual feelings would be unchanged.

Thus, if the ovaries can be spared (and they usually can), a surgical menopause is *not* a hormonal or emotional change.

If you are advised to have a hysterectomy, you may wish a second opinion. But often the second opinion comes from the patient herself and she wants rid of her uterus. However, the Centers for Disease Control reported to the American Public Health Association in 1981 that a review of the 3.5 million elective hysterectomies done on women of childbearing age in this country between 1970 and 1979 suggested that one of every seven had indications for surgery that were "questionable."

While we're talking to women, may we appeal to them to be sensible: Go for regular Pap smears, and please start a program of breast self-examination and do it regularly every month.

SLIPPED DISC SURGERY

Fashions change in medicine just as in women's clothing styles. In 1948 the first operation was carried out for prolapsed disc. The 1960s and 70s were the heyday of disc surgery—I had my two laminectomies in 1965 and 1974—but now from the vantage point of the 1980s, it seems that the operation has been overdone in the past. There were still 200,000 cases done last year.

Many patients who consistently complained of backache have ended up with surgery. This converted them to patients consistently complaining of backache who had a scar on their backs. A study done on a large series of patients, to find out why back surgery had not helped them, discovered that the commonest reason was that the operation was not indicated in the first place. One huge clinic had 400 postoperative patients who still complained of severe symptoms despite surgery. The clinic changed its day for postoperative evaluation from Friday to Thursday.

Asked the reason for the "Thursday clinic" the supervisor answered frankly that after "Friday clinics" the staff would go off depressed for their weekends. Holding the visits on Thursday gave medical attendants an extra day to get over the grumblings of their patients and thus their weekends were less likely to be ruined!

Well, if you have a bad back, it will do more than ruin your *weekend*. You may become unemployable. People such as pilots who sit a lot tend to become obese, develop poor stomach muscles, and get backache. Inactive persons therefore should try to get more exercise. Swimming is ideal, even once a week, and walking is always a good exercise. Jogging and snowmobile riding are bad for anyone with disc problems. I find putting in golf and serving in tennis painful enough to wipe out those sports. I think anyone who would water-ski or skydive with a bad back probably needs his head as well as his back examined. Other sports activities you'll have to test by personal experiment. What one person can handle with a bad back may be too much for another.

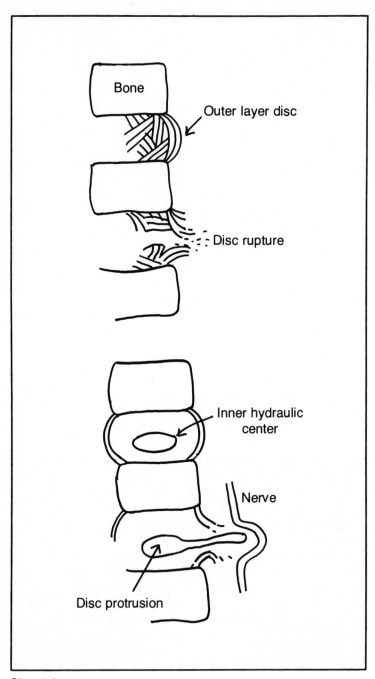

Slipped disc.

What causes degenerative disc disease? Well, we know it's more common in men than women, and in laborers than sedentary workers. About 75 percent of patients with symptoms are aged 35 to 50, an active age group. It seems likely that for some reason the quality of the disc—the cushion or pad between vertebral bodies— deteriorates. Then injury, sometimes acute and sudden and some-times slow and gradual, completes the picture.

Slipped discs tend to occur at the junction of a mobile part of the spine with a more fixed part. By far the most common site is between the two bottom lumbar vertebrae (the fourth and fifth vertebrae), or between the fifth lumbar and the first part of the sacrum—tailbone.

The lumbar spine resembles five children's building blocks placed in a column. Between each bone is a disc or cushion. The outer surface of the disk is a bit like the contents of a golf ball. If you've ever cut the white cover off a golf ball and gazed in fascina-tion at the tightly bunched-up elastic fibers in it, you'll understand the outer skin of the lumbar disc. It forms an exterior layer rather like a pattern of cane or rattan. This outer shell is called the fibrous ring, the *annulus fibrosus*.

Inside is a liquid center like a hydraulic button. This *nucleus pulposus*, or soft center, is about 80 percent water, bound with chemicals. If the disc becomes dehydrated and the rattan outer layer weak, there is less resilience to the disc and suddenly the inner center can push through a fragmented outer layer. The appearance would be as if someone was blowing bubble gum through cracks in an oriental screen.

The pain can vary from constant dull aches in the back or leg to agonizing, disabling spasms. Fortunately, 80 percent of patients with acute disc prolapse will get better with bed rest, usually in ten days. Some medical researchers believe that no matter what is wrong with your back, 90 percent of all complaints are gone in three months in those who will give their back a rest.

Indications for surgery include disc prolapse where recurrent back or leg pain prevents a person from having gainful employment; where severe acute symptoms, cause sudden deterioration in nerve function as shown by, for example, worsening foot drop or nonfunc-tioning bladder or bowel; and where patients genuinely fail proper adequate disciplined bed rest.

Pilots with bad backs should bring the seat a bit further forward towards the instrument panel. This flexes the thighs and relaxes tension on the spine. Check out those exercises that airlines like

SAS publish for passengers to practice while sitting for long journeys. And when you spend overnight stays in hotels, ask the desk clerks to supply bed boards—they are often pleased to offer this service to guests.

At home, get ¾ inch plywood below your mattress top to bottom and all the way across. Waterbeds take the opposite approach, which is also quite effective, but nothing is better than a hard mattress. You'll grow to love it.

Some tips from the Robins drug company are listed here to help you live with your back:

Sitting Advice

At home or work, sit in a straight chair with a firm back.

Sit so that your knees are higher than your hips. To do this you may need a small footstool.

Avoid sitting in swivel chairs and chairs on rollers.

Do not sit in overstuffed chairs or sofas.

Never sit in the same position for prolonged periods. Get up and move around.

Driving Advice

Push the front seat of your car forward so your knees will be higher than your hips. This will reduce the strain on back and shoulder muscles.

Always fasten safety belt and shoulder harness.

A headrest may be helpful.

Standing and Walking Advice

Don't stand in the same position for longer than just a few moments. Shift from one foot to another.

When standing, don't lean back and support your body with your hands. Keep hands in front of body and lean forward slightly.

When turning to walk from a standing position, move the feet first and then the body, as in left and right face in the military.

Open doors wide enough to walk through comfortably.

Carefully judge the height of curbs before stepping up or down.

Women should change to low heels frequently.

Bed Rest Advice

If your doctor prescribes *absolute* bed rest, stay in bed. Raising your body or twisting and turning can put a severe strain on your back.

When lying flat on your back, it may help to put pillows under the knees (unless your physician recommends otherwise).

When sleeping, lie on your side and draw one or both knees up toward your chin.

When lying in bed, don't extend your arms above your head. Relax them at your side.

Do not sleep on your stomach.

Sleep on a flat, firm mattress.

A bed board (½″ to ¾″ thick) placed between the mattress and box springs is an excellent support for the back.

Lifting Advice

When lifting, let the legs do the work, not the back. This applies even if you're picking up a scrap of paper.

Squat directly in front of the object you plan to lift, keeping it close to your body. Then slowly rise to a standing position.

Never lift with your legs straight.

Don't lift from a bending forward position.

Don't lift heavy objects from car trunks.

Don't reach over furniture to open and close windows.

When two or more persons plan to lift something, they should decide in advance what each is going to do, so one of them doesn't get caught with a sudden, unexpected load.

Yard Work Advice

A little exercise every day is far better than a whole lot on the weekend.

Before working in the yard or garden, remember to warm up. To warm up, swing the tool you plan to use (rake, hoe, axe, mattock, etc.) lazily back and forth around your head and shoulders in different positions, gradually working up to the full range of motion and effort needed to do the job. Remember that athletes always warm up before taking vigorous exercise.

Wear protective clothing to keep your perspiring body from getting chilled, except on very warm days. Remember that a baseball pitcher always puts on a warm-up jacket as soon as he leaves the mound.

The weekend golfer, fisherman, or tennis player should take along extra clothing to avoid getting chilled late in the day.

Don't go into an air-conditioned building while you're perspiring.

Miscellaneous Advice

Don't make up beds or run the vacuum cleaner when your back is "acting up."

A prolonged hot bath can be relaxing for a strained back. Be sure the water isn't too hot.

Your doctor may recommend some simple exercises to help strengthen the low-back and stomach muscles. Always follow his directions.

Avoid overweight.

KNEE CARTILAGE INJURY

Another common affliction is knee trauma where the cartilage is injured.

Remember how as kids you used to do an "Indian burn" on the wrist of friends—a rotation of the skin where one part was twisted one way and the other part went the opposite way? It is the same rotating, shearing strain that causes some knee injuries. The cartilage or meniscus is a double pad that separates the *femur* or thigh bone from the *tibia* (shin bone). If you rotate your body on one leg, you are grinding the femur into the tibia. You are prevented from causing damage by the cushion or pad, the cartilage.

Sometimes the cartilage suffers. It is like a flattened plum or tomato and just as a clumsy thumb at the supermarket, checking a fruit for ripeness, will leave the outer skin of the fruit damaged with a surface tear, so the cartilage tested by a twisting stress may rip. It thus becomes thin where before, it was plump and resilient. In a way, it becomes like a homemade quilt not adequately stitched and thinned out at the center.

Partial tears may heal, but now the bones have less protection. It's as if a cushion as thick as a beef steak becomes as thin as a rasher of bacon. Sometimes the tear is like a buttonhole, and occasionally the injured area falls off to the side just as a bucket handle would drop down the edge of a pail. This is more likely to occur at the inside of the knee where the long collateral ligament is attached to the medial or inside cartilage and tends to pull it taut. Strangely, this holds true for Caucasians, where nine times out of ten the inside cartilage is injured. But in Orientals, the outside cartilage is usually damaged.

X-ray of the inside of the knee by injection of radio opaque material or visual examination by arthroscopy may be necessary. If you *ever* injure your knee, get off it, use ice compresses, favor crutches, wear an Ace bandage, and see a doctor.

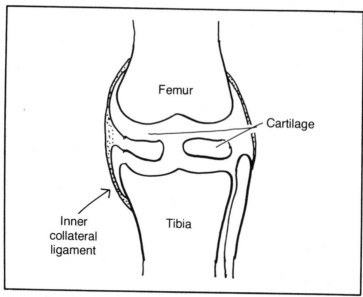

Knee cartilage injury.

You may need an operation if you get recurrent episodes where the knee "locks" and freezes on you. A history of repeated self-manipulation in order to unlock a knee stuck by sitting in a movie or in a chair for a few hours is strongly suggestive that you're coming to surgery.

TENNIS ELBOW

Airline pilots appear always to be fighting the advancing years. I suppose we all are. Pilots try to keep fit, however, more than many other groups. They have to, or the uniforms don't fit. Hence they tend to join raquetball clubs and health spas, and it's no surprise to see them come in with tendonitis, or bursitis problems.

One of the most common is tennis elbow, surely a wretched name to give such a condition. Most people with tennis elbow have never played the game but when the backhand was developed in the 1930s, by Don Budge I believe, doctors started seeing a lot of painful elbows.

The extensor muscles on the back of the forearm are not as strong as the flexor muscles on the front. Furthermore, there is not enough room on the outside of the top part of the elbow for all the chicken-drumstick-like forearm muscles to be attached. Our Maker therefore gave us a long bungee shock cord—the common extensor tendon—and the muscles are inserted onto this. It's rather like the way the parts of a feather join the quill or the persons in a tug-of-war pull on the rope.

This common tendon is then inserted into the bump on the lower humerus just above the outside of the elbow. It represents the pull of many muscles and this is quite a haul. As a result, the insertion at the bone is sometimes irritated even to the point where tiny fragments of the bone are pulled away. Consider an old toothbrush: Some of the fibers will be broken at the junction of the mobile bristles and the immobile plastic, but if you plucked out some of the intact bristles, a few would pull out with tiny bits of plastic attached. With tennis elbow, this is exactly what happens to the bone at the tendon insertion.

The treatment is heat, rest, sling, aspirin, or anti-inflammatory drugs. Sometimes injection is required with local anesthetic and cortisone. It's quite an easy, safe injection but we now know that too many shots—say more than four to six—may denature the protein in the tendon, make it less elastic and render it more prone to snap. This has happened with competitive athletes who have been injected too many times.

In treatment, most doctors try simple things first, then go ahead and inject. The injection may cause a bit of pain for 24 to 36 hours. I usually suggest that the person comes in on a Saturday morning for injection so he can rest the weekend. I remember

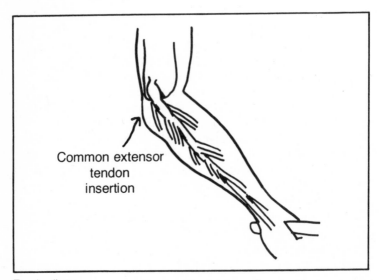

Common extensor
tendon
insertion

Tennis elbow.

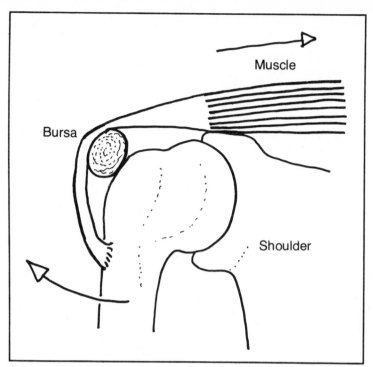

Bursitis.

setting up a PanAm airline pilot for such an appointment, forgetting the odd hours pilots work.

I finished the injection and put on a Band-Aid. The pilot grinned at me with relief and said, "Well doc, I'm off to London. Any messages for your home town?"

I stared at him, puzzled.

"I'm off to London. I'm flying a 747 there tonight . . ."

I had a sudden urgent wish to take my shot back. I mumbled something about not realizing that I'd injected a man about to work an eight-hour shift, and silently prayed to our Maker.

He doesn't always favor the foolish. Next visit, I got the full story of a captain nursing his red-hot elbow all the way across the Atlantic and a copilot flying the entire journey.

BURSITIS

Bursitis is another fairly common problem for people who sit a lot, often in their shirtsleeves in a draft or below an air conditioner. The term is used mostly for shoulder problems although technically a *bursa* is a pad or cushion anywhere in the body. It protects tendons from chafing on bone. In the shoulder, the bursa is a fulcrum or capstan, a pulley that allows the force of a muscle's tendon to go round 90°.

If you had a rope passing over a sharp precipice, it would fray—so would a tendon passing over solid bone. That's why we have bursae. Sometimes the bursa gets inflamed and sore. The reasons can be diverse. The inflammation is painful enough, but sometimes the body tries to cure the problem by depositing calcium in the bursa. This attempted healing effort can produce sudden, agonizing pain in the shoulder and only someone who has had bursitis knows how this ache affects sleep if the shoulder can't get comfortable.

On occasion, the pathology lies in the tired old tendon itself and it too can have deposits of calcium in it. The X-ray appearances can be very similar and the treatment is the same as for tennis elbow.

TIETZE'S SYNDROME

I tend to remember my failures rather than my successes. I hope not too many of my patients read this book. One can't because he now lives in England and won't see it.

He is Belgian, has a sly sense of humor, and sells antique books. Over the course of several years he has been kind enough to send me antique maps of Scotland, old woodcuts of medical scenes, and a magnificent etching of the great Vesalius who was the father of anatomy and who just happened to be a Belgian.

Vesalius has a Mona Lisa grin on his face; I know why he has that superior look. It stems from the strange case of Tietze's syndrome.

Let me go back. Christopher, the patient, came to see me with the complaint of chest pain. The story was vague, the symptoms inconclusive, the examination equivocal. As I helped him back on with his shirt, I noticed, I really did, the crackle made by a piece of paper in his shirt pocket.

I set up an appointment for chest X-ray and EKG, and saw him a few days later. He still had the pain, examination was negative, the lab tests were normal. He returned a few days later. Aha! There *was* a change. Now he felt the pain more if he twisted his body, and he was very definitely tender over the junction of his fifth left rib and the costal cartilage which joins it to the breast bone.

"Oh, Chris, you've got costochondritis: Tietze's syndrome," I said. "This is a simple condition. It'll be gone in six weeks."

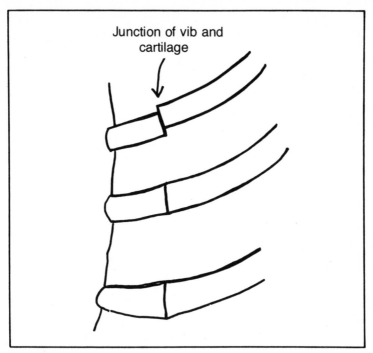

Junction of vib and
cartilage

Tietze's syndrome.

He smiled archly and produced from his breast pocket a piece
of paper, still crackling after two weeks. It was a clipping from a
newspaper—an "ask your doctor" column—yes, and it was a description of Tietze's syndrome.

"I felt this was what I had," my patient said. "I read this in a
newspaper before I came to see you. It took you two weeks to
diagnose what Ann Landers figured out in one day!"

I didn't feel too defensive. His chest wall tenderness had not
been apparent until the last day and you really need that for the
diagnosis. I felt okay about the delay and I felt better when Vesalius
came as a gift to grace my office wall some time later.

Tietze's syndrome occurs in young adults. There, the rib does
not sweep continuously as a piece of bone all the way from the back
to the breast bone. It stops short in the middle of the chest and joins
on to a bar of springy gristle, or cartilage, which gives the chest
greater flexibility. This connects with the sternum or breast bone.

The junction of rib and costal cartilage gives a definite joint that
can be seen in thin young adults. Sometimes the joint gets out of
kilter or becomes so sprung it can wobble. It's as if a superglue

bonding had changed to a joint fixed by mere chewing gum or salt water taffy. This gives a painful chest, local soreness, and a discomfort that will last for a month or two until the joint settles down.

Costochondritis usually responds to simple pain pills or antiinflammatory drugs. Occasionally it needs injections as tennis elbow. It doesn't occur in older persons where the costal cartilages start to ossify as part of the aging process. I'm 51 years old and one of my recent bad experiences was looking at my own chest x-ray and noticing the speckling of calcium which has now developed in my costal cartilages. At least I'll never get Tietze's syndrome.

Another aging sign are the senile kerratoses, the large brown freckles that older persons get on the backs of their hands. My partner, the same age as myself, has a TriPacer, "The Flying Milkstool." He has an instrument rating but his old airplane is pretty bare when it comes to instruments. I asked him once if he'd ever had a bad experience in his TriPacer. "Yes," he said promptly, "I was doing a 180 and I looked down and saw a senile kerratosis on the back of my hand. It gave me quite a bad turn."

ARE SURGEONS KNIFE-HAPPY?

There's no more worse turn perhaps than knowing you need an operation. If you really do, you've got plenty of company. It took the American College of Surgeons about two years to do the counting but in December 1981 they announced that in 1979, Americans had undergone 23.8 million operations.

This contrasted with, for example, 17.3 million in 1972. It now seems that 110 persons in every 1,000 in 1979 received surgery. Presumably the higher figure reflects a population that is forever aging and a technological skill in anesthesia and surgery that is forever improving.

Every year I see in my practice patients who have been operated on in the 1980s who would have been dead when I started medicine in the 1950s. If you have been advised to have an operation and want a second opinion, you can get further information by calling the Department of Health and Human Services at (800) 638-6833.

What about surgeons? Are they knife-happy? We've talked about this a bit in an earlier chapter. Most surgeons I know are busy, dynamic, aggressive people who like to operate, and would, I suspect, operate even if the money crossing palms was going *from* the surgeon *to* the patient. I think those fellows would operate for nothing. Yes, they like to operate. Are they honest? Yes, I feel, scrupulously. If there's any argument about too much surgery in

America, it's not because the surgeons are greedy although it is true that they are the big earners in medicine.

It is, instead, that surgeons tend to look for easy answers. In this land of instant gratification, the surgeons lead the medical establishment. It's their personality—they'd make lousy psychiatrists, where victory is won an inch at a time. Their calling goes back a long way. The world has long required the surgeon to have "a strong and steady hand, as expert with the left hand as with the right, with vision sharp and clear, and spirit undaunted; so far void of pity that while he wishes only to cure his patient, yet is not moved by his cries to go too fast, or cut less than is necessary."

Federal Health requirements, perhaps? Government regulations? Hardly—the words were written about the surgeon by Celsus in AD 30.

Yet surgeons tend to have large egos. They need them when they're up to their elbows in blood, their own hearts at times palpitating as wildly as the patients' on the monitors. If you are a surgeon, it helps to be patronized by kings and beloved by the gods.

At Edinburgh University in Scotland, I was taught surgery by as irascible and flamboyant a figure as that dour green and gentle land ever saw. Sir James Learmonth was my chief—professor of surgery and surgeon to the King. When King George VI came up to Balmoral Castle in Scotland for his autumn vacation (have you seen our heather in the fall?), Sir James would be advised that he was now the local physician for His Majesty.

One day students arrived for lectures in surgery to find that they were cancelled. The notice on the door was brief. It said: "There are no lectures on surgery today because Sir James Learmonth is operating on the King." To the notice one wag, a student, had added "God Save the King."

But surgeons believe not only that they are patronized by kings but they are beloved by the gods. Perhaps they are—sometimes. I remember one surgeon who is still laughed at in Britain by his amused colleagues. This surgeon was a man so calm, so contented, so omnipotent that all illness disappeared before his magic wand.

He was called to a home he knew well, to a family he adored, to a problem he handled easily with his skills. His work done, he then sat on the sofa, sipping a cup of tea, serenely contemplating his weekend off-duty which had now started.

He was distracted from his reverie by the children who sat affectionately at his feet, sharing his love. Would he look at their faithful hamster who was mysteriously ill? They knew he was not a vet, they knew he could not promise a diagnosis, they knew he could not guarantee a cure, but would he, could he, look at their hamster?

Indulgently, he bent over the inert furry shape and gently poked it. Immediately the beast seized his finger in its teeth and bit down hard. The doctor gave an involuntary swing of his arm, the animal let go at the peak of the arc and flew across the room into the open jaws of the German shepherd which caught the tasty morsel as cleanly as any baseball centerfielder ever received a sacrifice fly. One gulp and the hamster was gone, the entire episode taking five seconds.

There was a dreadful wave of disbelief, a frightening scream of horror, then that wonderful warmth which had surrounded the beloved physician for a decade disappeared in a moment.

The doctor picked up his hat and his bag and slunk into the night.

Even if a doctor is without sin, he is still not beloved of the gods.

Chapter 9

Passengers Sick and Healthy

Sam, the first patient I ever carried in an airplane, wasn't very pleased with the arrangements. He crouched on the seat behind me within easy reach of his personal doctor who was sitting in the front right-hand seat. At the beginning of the flight the patient, sedated, slept fitfully and was no problem.

Indeed, I had really forgotten about him and was peering at an approaching squall line when Sam suddenly reminded me of his presence. He licked my ears.

And growled. Sam, a 75-pound German shepherd, was en route from Boston to Ohio for ear surgery. He wasn't happy about the double layer of underpants pulled over two sets of pampers even though the shorts were reversed to allow his tail egress. He wasn't happy about the aftereffects of the sedative he'd previously been given by his veterinarian, Leo Dube, and he sure as hell wasn't happy about the time I was taking to fly a Cessna 182 to Columbus.

He growled again so loudly he even woke Leo. Out came the syringe, on slipped the tourniquet, and off again went Sam into the land of Nod.

With Sam catnapping beside us, if you'll forgive the expression, we finally reached our destination. But I'd seen a vivid example of the rule: You shouldn't fly a patient unless a proper attendant is available.

FLYING PATIENTS

As a pilot, you'll find yourself at times flying patients too. Perhaps one of your passengers will become ill and it will be easier for all concerned to go on. Perhaps you'll get a call from a sick relative who needs a ride. Perhaps you'll be asked to assist a stranger—if so, just hope his brother-in-law is not a lawyer.

There are certain things you should know about the transportation of ill persons, partly for your own interest and partly because those who know of your flying absorptions may be inclined to ask questions.

Ideas are changing now, but for a long time, nobody knew much about the proper handling of sick passengers, and many inadequate situations existed because there were no guidelines and no regulations. One outspoken critic was Wesley W. Bare, MD, an obstetrician and president of North American Air Ambulance, Inc. He pointed out for years that "There is nothing to guard the patient's safety in the air. In terms of regulations, it makes no difference whether you are carrying a critically ill patient or a sack of potatoes."

Another critic was Forrest M. Bird, MD, president of the subsidiary of the 3M Company that makes artificial respirators and appliances which deliver intensive care to patients. Bird felt that too many ill-equipped aircraft were used to carry sick patients and that persons seriously ill deserved more than "a flying bed." He is still particularly concerned about what happens to a patient if the aircraft suddenly undergoes explosive decompression at altitude.

The situation, however, was improving before government agencies started looking into the quality of air ambulances. Allen W. Moberg, MD, president of Airmergency of Minneapolis, sees changes. "There have always been airplanes containing stretchers," says Allen, "but it's not been very long that the process has been dedicated to the care of the patient—with proper personnel and appropriate equipment."

As you can imagine, equipment can be expensive. For example, the Swearingen Aviation Corporation of San Antonio has built Merlin turboprops equipped as flying emergency rooms for the South Africa and the Argentine air forces. The cost (in 1978) was $1,065,000 plus $75,000 for the avionics and $70,000 for the medical equipment.

Moberg didn't buy a Merlin, but when he came out of his residency in medical school in 1973, already with personal debts of $80,000 due to his medical studies, he borrowed more and bought a

1955 seven-seat twin Beechcraft. In his first year as surgeon-pilot he flew about 15 medical missions. Within three years his company was making a thousand trips a year and had acquired eight twin-engine propjets.

There is obviously a need for proper air transportation of the sick. Within the vast reaches of America lie many communities isolated from specialized medical care where emergency transportation becomes of critical importance. There are also many patients stricken miles from home while on vacation. Not only is air transportation faster than road, but beyond a hundred miles it is even cheaper. The patient may pay more per hour for the airplane than for an ambulance, but the savings in salaries per hour for the attendants becomes a big factor. Air travel can be a smoother journey for a sick person, and sometimes more comfortable.

If you are ever a pilot flying medical attendants, remember that doctors, so it is said, like to be in charge. They are uneasy as passengers in light aircraft where they've lost command to a pilot. Lt. Col. Earl D. Provancha, USAF (Ret.), who runs Medical Air Operations of North Carolina, describes his flying doctors: "These people are not in medicine because they're daredevils. They like the closeted atmosphere of the classroom, so we do a lot of hand-holding."

Minor incidents in an airplane can however be very important to sick patients. For example, a very debilitated person without an attendant could vomit if airsick and literally drown in his own vomitus.

We like to consider America more advanced than any other country but a few years ago the Greater Philadelphia Chamber of Commerce surveyed all air ambulances in its area: 47 percent didn't have a stretcher, 43 percent didn't have medical oxygen, and 39 percent didn't even have an emergency drug kit. The same year, Australia's Royal Flying Doctor Service celebrated a birthday by flying in 12 months 2,484,299 miles, providing 88,231 consultations, and evacuating 6569 patients. It was the Australian service's *50th* anniversary.

Yet a study by the American Medical Association of medical equipment and drugs aboard all major airlines showed that most aircraft carried first aid kits containing only bandages and no drugs except aspirin. "Complete emergency kits including drugs are not provided," said the AMA, "because of medicolegal reasons, including the possibility of misuse by non-trained individuals, theft, and outdating."

The US airlines fly 300 million passengers annually. American Airlines has done research suggesting that one life-threatening medical emergency develops for every million passengers. Air France, SAS, and El Al carry kits with essential equipment but United States airlines do not. What's in those bags carried by our national airlines was described once by Stanley R. Mohler, MD, director of aerospace medicine at Wright State University in Dayton, Ohio: "The basic kit carried today was developed in 1915."

A New Orleans surgeon and pilot, Hewitte A. Thian, MD, has formed a medical service for the 36,000 men who work the 200 offshore oil rigs in the Gulf of Mexico: Helicopter Medical Evacuation. The service gives immediate on-site care to injured persons, stabilizes them, keeps them alive, and gets them fast to medical centers. This creates results: Life is preserved and time lost due to injury is reduced; disability is minimized; accidental claims and benefits are decreased; insurance premiums for workers are reduced; morale is increased. Everyone wins.

EVALUATING EMERGENCY AIR SERVICE

If you ever engage an emergency air service to fly a friend or relative, you will find it can be difficult, even for another pilot, to evaluate the service. The Flying Physicians Association suggests you ask these questions:

Who is the medical director of the company?

Where can he be reached?

What training have the attendants had?

What aircraft are available?

What are the qualifications of the pilots?

What experience have they had with ill patients?

What are the charges for the flight?

What help does the company give clients to collect from third party insurance?

What insurance does the company have and does it include aggravation-of-injury coverage for patients known to be "medically at risk"?

MEETING PATIENT NEEDS

Having heard all this—that there are professionals out there better qualified than you to fly ill persons—what can you do if you somehow find yourself in the air flying a passenger who has become an emergency? And what are the concerns?

First, for any flying in the high terrain you have to consider oxygen needs. The usual oxygen supply in a light aircraft is adequate only for healthy persons who are breathing properly, needing merely supplementary oxygen. It is not nearly enough for a sick person with heart or lung disease. If you've got time, you will obviously put in extra oxygen equipment.

Think too of the problems of altitude. Not only may it be too cold up there for your passenger, but the decreased pressure may cause problems for those who have head injuries, blood clots, blocked sinuses, or collapsed lungs. If the patient has a bowel obstruction, altitude creates difficulties. Flying high will allow gas expansion in the intestines and make him more ill. Michael N. Cowan, MD, medical director of Air Ambulance, Inc. of San Carlos, California, reminds pilots also of how unbearable the interior heat can be in an unpressurized aircraft, and how dry the air can become. Thus patients with heatstroke or asthma may markedly worsen.

Get your patient to empty his bladder and bowel before the flight, urges Cowan. If he does so, he'll be much more comfortable at altitude. And finally, concludes Cowan, remember how therapeutic it is to give a patient lots of reassurance.

Even if the persons flying in your plane are not patients, they may become so if you can't keep your passengers healthy. Many of their problems have been covered in the discussions of you, the pilot, but there *are* difficulties peculiar to the health of passengers.

Their frame of mind is important. Any pilot who gives off bad vibrations that he's tense, worried or, even worse, incompetent will not have passengers who lie back in their seats. Show a person a bad first impression of general aviation and you won't see him return for an encore.

A lot of what the pilot takes for granted is new to the passenger. Even on commercial flights, first-time passengers can be startled at the steep angle of climb on takeoff and quite frightened when the jet engines roar in reverse after landing. Likewise, the angles of climb and bank and noises of magneto testing and propeller pitch changing may bother passengers who have not been pre-warned. Reducing power on downwind and changing tanks in mid-flight both produce a strange aircraft sound—silence—and need explanation before or as you do it.

You'll find many aspects of a general aviation flight that can worry a passenger if you'll only put yourself in the passenger's place. If there's a heat shimmer on the runway that makes a 10,000 foot strip of asphalt look only 500 feet long, discuss this with your passengers as you do the runup. Advise that you'll be turning crosswind on departure; that first run turn puts your right-side passenger higher than you and often gives a sensation of centrifugal movement as if the right seat occupant is about to break out through the window. Explain.

Warn about noise. Most non-fliers are frankly astonished at the din in a lightplane. Make sure they know about radio squelch, and how loud the radio can be. Have them wearing sunglasses and maybe a hat with a visor. If you're flying west into the sun you'll be glad, for their sake and your own, that you cleaned your windshield. If you're flying north up the east coast of the United States, remember that *you* may have the interesting coastline off to the left of your seat but all your passenger may have is a hundred miles of horizon out to sea.

Even twitchy pilots have to rise above themselves, relax, and pretend to be Joe Cool if they're flying with passengers.

Motion sickness can be a problem with passengers. Watch out for anyone busy with a camera, especially one with a telephoto lens,

On vacation trips try to plan stopovers where things are happening. If weather closes in, then at least your passengers have something to do. (Mike Hawkins Photo at Gray Rocks Resort)

or for anyone peering through binoculars: This is almost guaranteed to produce nausea. Be careful with heat. Often old planes smell, and the combination of stale cigarette odors with those of dust, oil, burned paint, and other fumes may be too much if the heat is on full blast. Be ready to direct a stream of cool, fresh air at any limp passenger.

Just as any lecture or talk (or book?) tends to run too long, so does the average flight. Passengers would probably appreciate more time on the ground than in the air. To you the flight itself may be the vacation, but not for the others cramped up in your flying cigar. You can therefore redeem yourself with your passengers and help them enjoy flying if you use the airplane as a means to get to a vacation spot quickly, as a convenience for everyone rather than an adult toy for you.

A good discipline, therefore, is planning to get a very early start to your flying day, and to stop early. Not only does this enable everyone, including the pilot, to relax and enjoy the rest of the day if weather is fine, but it gives you the second part of the day still available for flying if the early start is cancelled due to bad weather.

Starting early is like driving with a spare tire—everyone just feels better. A golden rule for general aviation private pilots is that the pilot is always enjoying the flight more than the passengers. As Klemens von Metternich once said, "Only fools want to travel all the time; sensible men want to arrive."

Chapter 10

Survival

Survival after a crash is a subject that seldom enters the minds of pilots. That a crash should happen is, well, unlikely. It would be hard to sit in an airplane, shout "clear propeller," and turn the ignition on if the possibility of crashing rather than flying were foremost in the pilot's head.

Yet it does happen. We may not have "survive a crash" written on our landing checklists but sometimes we do become what Richard Collins once called "aluminum litterbugs." Sometimes we crash.

A lot has been written on the subject of airplane crashes and survival (including my own *Plane Safety and Survival* from Aero Publishers), but in a book dealing with the pilot's health, we are more concerned with the pilot's reactions and attitudes than the airplane's strength and crashability.

In the impact of any airplane crash, probably the most important pilot factor, after luck, is his physical strength. Does he have strong, wiry, spunky physique? He's going to need it if he's badly injured, even if medical attendants get there quickly. Lots of things break when a body comes smashing down from the heavens, but the human frame is capable of great healing powers. Patients mend.

ATTITUDE

If the crash occurred in a distant remote area, and none of the searchers know where, different factors come into effect. Now, clearly what keeps a pilot alive is not his physical shape but his mental attitude. The right emotional outlook saves lives. You can be trained up to a point to respond appropriately to stress—to a very high point, as astronaut programs demonstrate—and you can under some circumstances rise above yourself and do better than might be expected by those who know you, but you are basically the image of how you perceive yourself. You are the reflection in your mirror, except there is an unknown, untapped reservoir of mental strength in most persons which has enabled man to endure and survive for centuries.

Thus the defeated athlete rises and trains for yet another day, the bankrupt financier retreats and rebounds to new successes, the anguished mother survives holocausts and still finds her baby, the disoriented traveler staggers across the desert and falls into civilization. And so the injured pilot, lost in desolate wastes as lonesome as space, copes, plans, acts, and survives because of the right mental attitude.

Experiments have shown that if mice were thrown into a tank of water they would swim around for two to three days. But mice held until they stopped squirming and then dropped into the tank sank immediately. It's as if they had given up and fallen apart. Another feature of rodents is equally interesting. In 1957 Richter reported that if you shave the wiskers off rats, they drown faster in laboratory experiments. He concluded not that the hairs aided in swimming, but that they acted as tactile receptors and prevented the rat from panicking.

Panic in scuba divers has been extensively studied by Michael B. Strauss, MD, a submarine medical officer. He found many incidents that could lead to panic. Breathing difficulties, for many reasons, caused hypoxia and anoxia. Prolonged swimming in strong currents caused fatigue and exhaustion. Sustained exposure to cold water caused hypothermia. Losing contact with a diving partner or catching sight of a shark created fear. All this set the stage for panic if trauma from boats or rocks caused injury, if loss of a mask or aspiration of water gave a fright, if kelp entangled or an eardrum ruptured. The diver could completely lose control and even overlook 'such simple corrective procedures as ditching the weight belt or inflating the life belt."

The parallel between the drowning overwhelmed diver and the injured crashed pilot is close but the pilot is in better shape. He has time to think.

The most important survival tool is always there right between the pilot's ears. Your brain enables you to assess the situation and establish priorities. What are the injuries of the passengers or yourself? Is anyone having difficulty with breathing? If so, straightening the patient's neck may be all that's necessary. Is there bleeding? If so, firm pressure with a clean handkerchief directly on the wound may be appropriate. Are bones broken or lying out of alignment? If so, they should be splinted. Is the patient cold and clammy and weak? If so, get him to shelter and warmth.

Shelter is very important. In extremes of climate, shelter is the most important survival factor after mental attitude. The warmth of a fire comforts in every way. It produces heat, it gives light at night, it shows man's supremacy over his environment, and it psychologically soothes. It's crazy therefore not to fly with some matches in the aircraft or, better, on your person. This is the one time when a smoker may be in better shape than a nonsmoker—at least he's got matches.

And if you're thinking about matches, you may want to think about how poorly most civilian light aircraft are equipped with surivival gear. It's as if nobody wants to believe a crash will ever happen. It's as if placing a small survival kit in an airplane will somehow tempt fate and allow an accident. That's the same sort of reasoning that used to startle me when I was a rural doctor in East Texas. Patients would avoid paying off the last part of their bill to

Bush flying makes demands unknown to the commuter pilot. Flying in remote terrain requires that a survival kit be carried.

A survival kit should include a lightweight tarpaulin. In isolated areas it will have many uses.

their doctor because of the superstition that once the bill was paid in full, the fates would make the patient sick again.

SURVIVAL KITS

It surely makes sense to carry a minimum survival kit every time you fly. Even if you are close to civilization when you crash,

Each terrain you overfly has its own problems. In flying over desert terrain carry flares, ground marking panels and mirror for signaling; and chapstix, sunglasses and headgear for comfort—and water. (courtesy *Plane Safety and Survival*; Aero Publishers)

Flying does have its "moments of terror." Are you healthy enough and tough enough to handle those far from magic moments? (courtesy U.S. Coast Guard)

the plane can disappear into a forest as fast as a beer can vanishes if flung into a clump of bushes. The problem of inappropriate clothing is easily handled by throwing an old ski jacket, a thick pair of socks, a woolen hat, and an old sleeping bag into a plastic bag and leaving them permanently in the back of the plane. The human body cannot function out of a range of about 12°Fahrenheit body temperature — we are almost as vulnerable as snakes to temperature changes.

If you are in fact now stimulated into putting together a small survival kit, then include a steel mirror, a small lens to start a fire, a candle, a razor blade, a knife, some fishing line and hooks, and a whistle. Wrap this in aluminum foil (which you can use for cooking or signaling), and place it in the same plastic bag as your parka. Make sure there are waterproof matches in one of the pockets. A survival pamphlet or book may be worth the extra weight also.

The time you spend right now just thinking about all this may well be time that saves your life. Survival kits need to be personalized for the terrain or climate you tend to fly over. The ski jacket may be more useful in Maine, and several gallon-size containers of water may be more important in Nevada.

You may want to ask yourself about your own health when you preflight the plane for various forms of terrain flying. Take Nevada again, for example. Some skin problems are aggravated by dry air and solar radiation. Allergies can worsen. Eye conditions can deteriorate. In contrast, mountain flying can be bad for patients with heart disease, lung problems, or anemia. Cold weather creates difficulties for patients with angina, asthma, peripheral circulation conditions like Raynaud's Disease, and winter chest infections.

All those considerations can be part of your preflight of the pilot. If you don't know your own health problems, who does? Thinking things through at this time takes a lot of the later confusion out of an emergency landing should it ever happen.

Another very wet pilot, this time in the Gulf of Mexico, owes a debt to a man named Sikorsky. (Tim Stroop Photo courtesy U.S. Coast Guard)

It easily can. As Skip Stoffel of the Washington State Department of Emergency Services has told many of those attending search and rescue conferences:

"Light aircraft users and pilots need to understand priorities and emergency response procedures more than the average mobile traveler because of their total dependence upon a complex mechanical system that defies gravity. Light aircraft can fly only so far, so fast, at the mercy of performance, weather, and human skill. This airborne bucket of bolts is subject to malfunction, misuse, human error, or poor judgement.

"Once this happens, most survivors wish they had learned a little more about how to take the misery out of the challenge to stay alive. Acquired knowledge is man's greatest asset in recognizing, analyzing, and prioritizing his defenses against this unpredictable threat."

Chapter 11

Fatigue and Sleep

The fifth of August 1976 was a bright and sunny day in the Midwest. A gentle wind stroked the cornfields around the town of Abie, Nebraska. A hot sun burned down from the deep blue sky. A whisp of cirrus wandered by at 25,000 feet.

It was a day for swimming at the nearby mill pond, for casting a lazy line at the old fishing hole, for drinking a cool soda at the corner drugstore. It was a day for lying on your back in a meadow with a piece of grass between your teeth, and your bare toes wiggling in warm sand. It was a day for enjoying life.

It was a day for flying.

A Piper PA-18 was flying, twisting and turning in the sky above. The sun reflected off its wings as it wheeled in the heavens, then suddenly darted to the ground like a sparrowhawk after a mouse. In a way the Piper *was* hunting after wildlife in the cornfields—it was crop dusting.

Now *there's* a branch of flying that requires the greatest of skills—crop dusting, a career that truly separates the real pilots from the boys. No fancy footwork, no glossy glamour, no showing off—just grit, tenacity, and skill.

And such skill: Crop dusters are the only modern pilots to recapture the dexterity and talent of World War I pilots. Like them, they soar with the wind in their squinting eyes and the smell of new-mown grass in their nostrils. Like them, their planes are their lives.

In a world full of deceitful bluff and advertising hype, the crop duster is the honest artisan, his ability unquestioned among his peers. And his career permits him the great pleasure of flying. It allows him to move in the company of the gods.

The Piper turned again, caught in the sun. It reared briefly and then crashed to the ground, life extinguished in the flames that follow as surely as in a moth against a candle.

The airplane, examined once the fire was controlled, revealed no secrets to account for the fatal accident. The pilot's logbook did. He had flown 20 hours in the previous 24. The National Transportation Safety Board had no hesitation in citing pilot fatigue as the factor in an accident where a commercial pilot, with 1358 hours including 140 in type, stalled his aircraft.

FATIGUE KILLS

Surely a remote incident? Who would fly so many hours? Who would dare to tempt the skies? What pilots would possibly believe that they were so invincible that rest was not essential?

A *lot* of pilots would. Take, for example, the commercial pilot, with 1900 hours, who fatally attempted a nonstop distance record flight of 3080 miles in a Cessna 170. He took off from Port Angeles, Washington, and impacted at Billings, Montana, *22 hours* after takeoff.

His plane was completely destroyed. Less heavily damaged was a Molino glider that crashed at Hobbs, New Mexico. The private pilot, with 1150 hours, had been competing in a soaring event and had been aloft grabbing the wind for 8½ hours.

It's usually not pleasure but grim duty that fells the pilot with fatigue. And if it's not duty, it's the pilot's perception of it that traps him and causes disaster. And sometimes it's not a pilot but an airport manager, a dispatcher, or company official who goes home eyes downward with an ache caused by putting schedules and duty before common sense and human life.

The commercial pilot, with 1446 hours, who crashed his air-cargo Cessna 310 at Antwerp, Ohio, had been on duty for almost 19 hours. The crop duster, with 1022 hours, whose Grumman collided with a ditch at Fisk, Missouri, had flown 18 hours in the last 24. The Grumman American AA1 destroyed attempting to land at Unity, Maryland, was piloted by a 294-hour private pilot who had been on duty for at least 17 hours. Youth does not protect against fatigue; this last pilot was only 23 years old.

And so the random list goes on: A tired commercial pilot, 6784 total hours, killed with his passengers when his Piper PA-23 collided with trees at Pellston, Michigan, on final approach. He'd been working for 16 hours. An enthusiastic student pilot, 100 hours, with fuel exhaustion making an off-airport landing at Madera, California. It was half-past midnight and he'd been flying for 15 hours in the previous 24.

Brook Park, Ohio: Beech 3NM; ATR, 3891 hours, age 30; killed—stalled on landing IFR; on duty 13 hours.

Lostine, Oregon: Bell 47G-4A; crop duster pilot, 5550 hours, age 46; injured, high density altitude, VFR; on duty 13 hours.

Albrightsville, Pennsylvania: Beech B55; commercial pilot, 1389 hours, age 34; damaged aircraft substantially, overshooting landing at wrong airport; on duty 13 hours.

Thirteen hours doesn't seem to be the real unlucky number. That place is claimed, like Bo Derek, with a "10." Ten hours' labor seems enough for anyone. It is an especially tiring amount of work for pilots, where an hour at the controls of a plane is clearly more fatiguing than, say an hour spent by an assistant librarian at the desk of a museum.

The weariness of ten hours' flying has downed a lot of commercial pilots. Look at some—Montrose, Colorado: Cessna 177 landing roll with fuel exhaustion. Etna, Wyoming: Hughes helicopter, go-around with high density altitude. Greensboro, North Carolina: Cessna 182 landing roll with overshoot. Pasco, Washington: Piper PA-25 crop dusting over obstructions. Adrian, Oregon: Callair A9B spraying grain on a dark night. Othello, Washington: Piper PA-25 starting swath run stalled on a calm day. Ellaville, Georgia: Cessna 188 aborted takeoff and hit trees. Geraldine, Montana: Piper PA-18 landing, nosed over in snow.

Some people don't understand their own bodies; they're not aware of their deficiencies. Perhaps it would take an MD degree to help pilots understand when they should call it quits. Really? An instrument-rated private pilot with 3000 hours destroyed his Piper PA-31T in a fatal accident when he lost control climbing to cruise at Lamar, Colorado. It was 9:40 p.m. He was probably tired from the previous six hours' flying and the two operations he had performed that day. The pilot was an MD.

It's not only the recent hours flown that create fatigue. The symptoms can be insidious, creeping up due to accumulated periods of concentrated activity. For example, the animal-herding work season is short in Alaska. Pilots grab the jobs when they can. A student pilot aged 58 killed himself in a hard landing at Nome, Alaska, when his Bradley helicopter developed rotor failure. The NTSB found that fatigue prevented his making the correct in-flight decisions. He had flown *190 hours* in the past month!

Sometimes it's not so much the amount of previous work, it's the lack of opportunity to rest from it that invites a tragedy. Thus it is no surprise to find inadequate sleep as a factor prior to flying mishaps. Planning a long cross-country is tiring and exciting. Like athletes before a great race, pilots sometimes sleep fitfully, not getting the rest they so desperately need to endure the work that lies ahead.

Often, overnighting in strange beds and noisy hotels with routines out of sequence and diurnal behavior out of whack, pilots sometimes start the next day in less than their best shape.

The commercial pilot who destroyed his Beech in blowing snow at Amidon, North Dakota, had not slept for 18 hours. The private pilot stalling in with his Cessna 337 at Bunkie, Louisiana, had been up late the night before. The private pilot impacting his Piper PA-28 at Greenfield, Oklahoma, in a thunderstorm had received only a few minutes' sleep the previous night. The commercial pilot who aborted his takeoff at Dekalb, Illinois, causing his Aero Commander to collide with a ditch, had managed no rest or sleep in the prior 24 hours. Nor had his colleague at Orocovis, Puerto Rica, who died at the controls of his Norman Britt at the age of 22 with 4180 flying hours behind him, but no sleep in the last 27 hours.

Drivers who have caught themselves nodding at the wheel of their cars will not be surprised to hear the NTSB has found pilots asleep at the yoke of aircraft. A 23-year-old pilot, observed sleeping at the controls on previous flights, allowed his Piper PA-23 to make a gentle constant-rate descending turn into the Kentucky earth at Marion. Investigators of this fatal accident surmised the pilot fell asleep during the flight.

There was no such suspicion at Blythe, California; Bismarck, North Dakota; or at Lamar, Colorado, where each pilot admitted falling asleep. Indeed, in the last two cases, the autopilot was found engaged at the impact site.

Not for them was sleep that gentle thing described by Coleridge as beloved from pole to pole. Not for them was it the gentle sleep from Heaven that slid into their soul. For them it was the earth-shattering, neck-snapping explosion, the reality that the

It's the good life, but you still need your sleep if it's an early start the next day. (courtesy Cessna Aircraft Co.)

skies have a price. Yet the way seems clear to avoid paying this price: Understand your body, be aware of its messages, accept its limitations. Rest. Sleep.

SLEEP STATISTICS

But it's not quite as easy as that. Indeed, some notable opinions emerged in a Gallup Poll of 1550 adults in America. Although 8 to 8½ hours of sleep was regarded as ideal by 48 percent of respondents, only 26 percent reported obtaining this amount.

Strangely, white-collar workers got less sleep than blue-collar workers, Easterners got less than those from any other region, and men got less than women (interestingly enough, women working full-time sleep less than women working part-time).

Another survey, this time of 4451 physicians, found the incidence of insomnia at about 17 percent in their practices. However, when Frank Sinatra sings, "I didn't sleep a wink last night," he was probably exaggerating. Researchers into sleep and its problems feel that about one-third of insomniacs in fact sleep well and just *feel* that they don't. The problem of sleep disorders is real nevertheless, and many of the patients whom doctors see in the office with multiple complaints are in fact simply exhausted because they sleep poorly.

One physician tells all his "tired housewife syndrome" patients that they may have a sleep deficit and should not come to see him until they have made the effort to get to bed early for ten consecutive nights. He claims, probably accurately, that we are all jazzed up, overstimulated and underslept.

The other side of the spectrum is the patient who makes a good night's sleep a lifelong quest as if for the Golden Fleece. And golden fleece is exactly what he gets as he indulges himself with over-the-counter items all designed to make him feel that the answer to any problem, even if nonexistent, is the open wallet and the closed mind. Americans in fact spend $200 million a year for over-the-counter aids to sleep.

Sometimes the patient is not much better off going to a doctor. Often the problem of poor sleeping pattern is treated superficially with a prescription for sleeping pills, which only compounds the problem. Those medications generally are effective against insomnia for only a few nights and lose their power within two weeks.

Then, the patient falls into the trap of increasing the dose in order to get the benefit so eagerly sought as the exhausted person tries to fall asleep. Multiple studies have shown that chronic users of hypnotics sleep no better than insomniacs who take no drugs. Yet doctors write 30 million prescriptions a year for sleeping pills.

Says Ian Oswald, MD, a psychiatrist at the University of Edinburgh: "Too often, sleeping pills are prescribed to allay feelings of uneasiness within the doctor, rather than for the patient's own good." Oswald, a dour Scot from my land of porridge and oatmeal, actually believes that a cereal food drink with warm milk at bedtime is the best nightcap, and that it tends to keep the person asleep in the latter half of the night.

150

While deeply interested in the problems of insomniacs, Oswald nevertheless believes that just as "our forefathers overvalued regular bowel actions [so] today many patients overvalue the idea of eight hours of sleep."

Who says we need eight hours? There are wide variations in nature. The shark never sleeps, the tree shrew hardly ever; however, the rabbit drops off for a minute every five, and the bat sleeps away a good five-sixths of its life. Salvador Dali was said to manage with very little sleep; Thomas Edison got by with four hours; Albert Einstein needed ten.

SLEEP FACTS

There are probably more misconceptions about sleep than any other body function. The book should have been called *All You Ever Wanted to Know about Sleep But Were Afraid to Ask*.

Let's look at some of the misguided ideas.

Adults require at least seven hours sleep. If they don't get it, they won't have normal psychological and physiological functioning. False: Studies suggest that requirements vary from 5.5 hours to 8.5 hours. Short sleepers seem to be more efficient but too busy, whereas long sleepers tend to be more tense and withdrawn, yet more original and creative.

Most people get enough sleep. False—probably: If you are functioning well and feel fine, then you're okay. But many people are sleep-deprived like brainwashed political prisoners. Dr. William Dement, of the Stanford University Medical School, says, "Most adults are substantially sleepy all the time." He feels that Americans should pay as much attention to sleep as they give to exercise and nutrition.

It is interesting to note that more than half the people of the world practice the habit of the afternoon nap—the *siesta*—but America is too sophisticated to take time off for forty winks.

Sleep is quiescent. The brain turns off. False: Although blood pressure drops, the pulse slows, muscles relax, metabolism slides, and temperature sags, during sleep the brain continues working and remains active and busy even as we tumble into oblivion. The brain indeed may turn our bodies on 30 or 40 occasions during the night and waken us as often as five to 15 times with no subsequent memory of waking. And it controls a most complicated program of alternating depths of drowsiness which have only recently been understood.

All stages of sleep have been investigated in depth only since

1953 when a professor at the University of Chicago, Dr. Nathaniel Kleitman, noticed rapid eye movements during sleep in —of all things—infants. William Dement, then one of Kleitman's students, was later to call this phenomenon REM or rapid eye movement sleep. Researchers found during REM sleep that the sleeper dreamed and that the event occurred in 90 minute cycles as sleep lightened. The amount of REM sleep in adults tends to total about 100 minutes a night. Subjects experimentally deprived of REM sleep become anxious, tense, and irritable.

The body thus *needs* REM sleep. In a way, you sleep to dream, not dream to sleep. Your brain is not just idling, although it doesn't seem to respond to cues, noises, or outside factors during sleep. Nor do you incorporate your current environment in dreams. The brain isn't programmed to work that way.

Sleep remains a mystery. False: Sleep clinics have sprung up all over America. To them have come chronic insomniacs with problems of every kind. Doctors find in the 50 million Americans afflicted with inability to sleep that there are two females distressed for every one male. Insomniacs come from all walks of life; there are as many blue-collar as white-collar workers.

Some scientific facts soon become apparent. Most hypnotics—sleeping pills—suppress REM sleep and gradually reduce the deepest stages of sleep. Alcohol does the same in amounts larger than six ounces although smaller amounts may cause brief drowsiness. Chronic pain and acid indigestion can spoil sleep. The elderly sleep less but need less. Unfortunately, they are prone to self-medicate with over-the-counter items.

SLEEP DISORDERS

Misuse of medication is a common cause of insomnia. Other factors include underlying anxiety or depression, illnesses that are more than simple moodiness. In general, anxious people have more trouble *getting* to sleep while depressed patients have problems *staying* asleep. The poor sleep pattern of an anxious person can vary from the busy brain syndrome of the sleeping pilot, flying so far ahead of the aircraft that he or she is actually preflying the flight in bed the night before, to the exhausted exasperation of the individual beset with constant stress who really does hear every hour strike all through the night.

Depressed patients differ. Their problem is staying asleep. Typically tired and worn out, they fall asleep relatively easily, then waken at about 3:00 a.m. to find themselves unable to sleep thereafter. This altered sleep pattern is so typically that of depression that anyone with it should ask himself whether there are other features of depression—despondency, apathy, loss of appetite, loss of libido.

Sexual problems themselves can create sleep difficulties. During REM sleep, penile tumescence and erection occurs normally, as does clitoral distention and vaginal lubrication. With this come increases in respiration and heart rate and a rise in blood pressure. Those features, somewhat typical of sexual arousal, occur in all groups, even the elderly.

Sleeping pill abuse, anxiety, and depression are common factors in insomnia and usually need the help of a physician. Another sleep mystery revealed by research is the problem of *nocturnal myoclonus*. This is *not* the common harmless twitching in the legs that occurs as we fall asleep, but a persistent, repetitive jerking of the leg muscles which can occur as often as every 30 seconds to waken the sleeper constantly through the night.

Patients with this problem are unaware of it but their bed partners know—they often get wakened too. Somewhat different is the restless leg syndrome, equally ill-understood by physicians, which wakens the patient and is relieved only by getting up and walking about briefly.

Mild tranquilizers seem to help both these conditions, which are relatively unimportant in contrast to *sleep apnea*. Patients with this serious condition notice their difficulty in the day rather than their problems of the night. They often complain of severe headache, poor memory and fatigue, and of being excessively sleepy during the day. They can drop off at dinner or watching a movie; they can even fall asleep waiting at a red traffic light, or sitting in a public rest room.

Sleep apnea strikes one million Americans, mostly males over the age of 40. Usually they are found to be overweight. Sometimes they have elevated blood pressure that may actually be the result of the sleep disorder. They tend to snore very heavily. I had a patient with this problem once whose family loved camping. They awoke one day at Acadia National Park to find a rude note pinned to their tent and an empty campsite next door. Their fellow campers had struck their tent and relocated their campsite in the middle of the night in order to have a quieter time of it.

Men with sleep apnea sometimes snore so loudly that no one hears the baby cry or even the telephone ring. But the problem with sleep apnea is not so much the snoring, tiring though that is for the bed partner. It lies in the periods of not breathing that follow: Sometimes the snorer will hold his breath for 30 or 40 seconds dozens of times during the night. Patients at sleep clinics have been discovered who stop breathing hundreds of times a night.

Doctor Michael Biber, the director of the Sleep Unit of Boston's Sleep Unit of Boston's Beth Israel Hospital, had one patient with sleep apnea who was found on testing to stop breathing 350 times a night. So tired was the patient, a soldier, that he fell asleep on a machine-gun range at Army practice sessions.

Says Biber of those patients' respiratory problems: "The oxygen saturation in the blood goes way down to the basement. It's as though they're jumping from sea level to the top of Mount Everest every few minutes."

The sequence of events in sleep apnea characteristically starts during sleep with the muscles at the back of the throat and base of the tongue closing off tight. The sleeping person struggles to get air in, and opens his airway a little. Then the excessively heavy snoring starts. The patient half-wakens, moves around, turns over (or gets kicked over by his wife), and goes back to sleep. The cycle then begins again.

The periods where the patient doesn't breathe are the clue to diagnosing this problem, which differs clearly from just snoring itself. The wife may be able to tape-record the sounds for the doctor to make the diagnosis, or the patient may have to be observed during a nap at a sleep clinic.

This condition is important if there are more than five attacks in an hour. It is one cause of high blood pressure and heart irregularities. It may predispose to heart attacks.

Weight reduction in the obese may help. Drugs may be necessary. Even tracheostomy can be required. In this procedure, a hole is made in the windpipe above the breast bone and left open during sleep. It can be life-saving.

More common and less frightening than sleep apnea is *circadian rhythm disruption*, a phenomenon well-known to the shift workers of the nation and the travelers and flight crews of the world.

For centuries, man has lain down with the night, his behavior based on stimuli provided by his surroundings. Deprived of those cadances of the clock, man can be confused, even bereft of purpose.

The rhythm of the day guides and cues our movements. It is our internal clock, our inner metronome, our synchronizing signal. Some insomniacs sleep late because they sleep so badly. If they lack economic or social pressures to rise from bed, they can fall into random schedules that are independent of the 24-hour circadian rhythms. Thus deprived of their *zeitgeber*, those insomniacs develop "free-running desynchronized cycles" where the body and the clock can be at variance.

Research done on isolated subjects such as Michel Siffre, 375 feet underground for 63 days, shows an interesting phenomenon: The human body seems to prefer a 25-hour rhythm. On weekends, many people in fact follow such 25-hour tempos. They go to bed an hour later on Friday night and even later on Saturday night. The return to the conventional cycle at the start of the regular week may well be part of the problem of "blue Monday."

Studies at the Max Planck Institute in Germany, at Montefiore Hospital and Medical Center, New York, at Harvard, and at many other centers have shown that not only do volunteers extend their rhythm to 25 hours, but they will develop even longer days if the experiments continue for several months. At times, bed is not sought for 36 or even 50 hours, although occasionally at intervals a shortened day can result.

It is known that temperature drops during sleep. Our lowest ebb is about 4:00 a.m., a time when we are at our most vulnerable because our ability to function matches our body temperature. In a normal cycle, body temperature peaks about mid-day although, for most of us, our best performance comes in the early evening—say about 8:00 to 9:00 p.m.

The scientists who explored the oddity of those longer days found that the volunteers slept for a length of time according to whether they were at a high or low body temperature when they fell asleep. Those who fell asleep at a low body temperature slept for only half the time of those who dropped off when their body temperatures were high.

Thus the time when people fall asleep may be more important than how much sleep deficit they have. The amount of sleep required by a person clearly is not proportional to how much has been lost. All this may seem academic to any jet-lagged air crew. Yet industry is carrying out considerable research to help executives and other travelers diminish the problems caused by crossing time zones.

Exhausted airline pilots may be startled to find that in 1977, an English woman, Maureen Weston, went without sleep for almost 19 days in a "rocking chair marathon." Although she endured brief hallucinations, she suffered no apparent long-term consequences.

Sleep-deprived persons show other phenomena: A volunteer

at the department of psychology, University of Illinois, after a prolonged period of sleep deprivation, set a record for the greatest amount of REM or dreaming sleep at one time—2 hours, 23 minutes.

JET LAG

Does any of this research help people avoid jet lag? Travel dysrhythmia can alter as many as 200 different body functions. The sleep pattern can take two days to reregulate; the temperature rhythm may need five to stabilize. Many of the earliest record flights brought fatigue problems. Wiley Post found in his historic circumnavigation of the globe in 1931 that eating lightly helped him avoid drowsiness in a flight where he slept only 15 hours in 8½ days. Nevertheless, over Germany, the time zone displacement caught up with Post.

He and Harold Gatty in the *Winnie Mae* had considerable difficulty following a magnetic course to Hanover, and on taking off for Berlin were so tired they forgot to check their fuel. Post returned (you might say post-haste) to Hanover to rectify this striking error, surely one of the first documented stories of time zone exhaustion.

Post needed eight days in 1931 to fly around the world. The astronauts in 1965 took 88 minutes to orbit the Earth. Much of the science applied to help our men in space was actually developed from many earlier flights. Joe Engle and Richard Truly, the astronauts who brought the Columbia space shuttle down to Earth in November, 1981, trained for their countdown and the pending circadian dysrhythmia by going to bed in the afternoon and rising long before dawn. On the morning of their launch, they rose at 2:40 a.m. for a steak-and-eggs breakfast and a brief physical examination. Engle was described as being "in a terrific mood, hugging everybody," and Truly as saying, "Columbia is ready and so are we."

Discipline and training can thus master jet lag but the two astronauts had group support—they had others working and living those odd hours. Research on submarine crews has shown that people cope with disturbance of their body clocks better if they have company, persons with whom they work and suffer. Indeed, it appears that group-travel programs, which have large numbers of tourists flying together across time zones, enable passengers to adjust more easily than situations where solitary air travelers have to cope by themselves. It has been said that those on business or diplomatic negotiations should always travel with colleagues or even family members in order to adjust faster to the new biological rhythms.

Ross A. McFarland, Guggenheim Professor of Aerospace Health and Safety, Emeritus, at Harvard School of Public Health, compared the strain on flight crews flying from San Francisco to Manila at the present time with the duress on Pan Am aircrews in 1937-39, when the Pacific routes were first opened. As a younger physician, he had checked those Pan American aircrews for pulse rate and blood pressure, for arterial blood gases and venous blood counts, for biochemical and hormonal levels, and for general degree of fitness. He found everything normal in those flying boat operations over the Pacific, but the crew had overnight stops at every island station, with a two-day layover in Manila and seven days in Honolulu.

Despite a total review of 1222 hours in the air, there was no circadian disturbance. Because the flights were slow in those pre-jet aircraft days, there was no difficulty in adjustment.

McFarland feels that some jet lag is due to the combined effects of high altitude, low humidity, cigarette smoke pollution, carbon monoxide increase, excessive food and alcohol intake, and even the age of the traveler.

Confirmation of those problems today was obtained by testing 315 senior executives in 29 British and 20 American companies. Eighty-seven percent of the travelers had sleep disturbances following a flight, although 50 percent had to conduct business negotiations before getting to bed. For many, their trip to Europe was truly the longest day.

Yet Dr. Elliot D. Weitzman, the director of the Sleep Disorders Unit at Montefiore Hospital, feels that there is no biological requirement that we follow the duration of the day. He points out that we are simply entrained to it by social time demands and the alarm clock. "Sleep," he says, "is the most powerful organizer of our lives."

One of the greatest examples of a person organized by sleep—or rather its abnormalities—was United Airlines flight attendant Irene Anker, who came in despair hoping Montefiore could reset her body's sleep clock. The procedure, labelled *chronotherapy,* is used in people who are in perpetually out of synch with their physiological rhythms as are the twin engines in a student pilot's multiengine flight test.

Anker, who suffered from insomnia of the delayed sleep-onset type, was studied in a room without windows, without clock, without radio, TV, or newspapers. She lived there for three weeks with attendants who brought her meals but never referred to the time of day. She might have been an astronaut in space, as lonely as a lunar command-module pilot 2200 miles above the moon.

Unknown to the flight attendant, her days were increased to 27 hours and her bedtime advanced three hours a day. Finally she was converted from a person who could sleep only at dawn to a person whose biological bedtime coincided with midnight. She was then, apparently successfully, stabilized on that schedule.

What can the pilot or his passengers do to avoid jet lag? We can't all behave like Aeroflot crews, who allegedly keep to Soviet time no matter where they are in the world. Nor can we always fly Concordes, so fast that we hardly have to alter our watches. Captain Michel Butel, a Concorde pilot, feels that jet lag requires four hours in the air and, since his transatlantic flight takes less than that, he does not see flight fatigue in his crew or passengers.

Exercise probably diminishes jet lag—both exercise done for a few days before the flight and during. Many airlines have developed programs for inflight activities. Continental, SAS, and Lufthansa are examples. Of course, staggering off a plane carrying a flight bag laden with Jepp plates is hardly what is meant by exercise.

Sleep during the flight appears in some people to diminish the exhaustion from airline travel, but grabbing some shuteye as soon as you land may not be biologically sensible. Weitzman, at Montefiore, advises that you force yourself to stay awake and synchronize your bedtime with the new environment's time.

The easiest suggestions come with reference to diet. Nobody knows anything about the subject of jet lag and diet, but there are plenty of theories. Peter Wood, who has been flying with British Airways for more than 25 years, has the most sensible advice: "Eat and drink alcohol sparingly. It's so easy to overindulge, especially if you're traveling first class." Because of the low two percent humidity of cabin air and the risk of dehydration, you should, however, force plenty of fluids: at least eight ounces of liquid per hour of flight. Remember, this is water or tonic water, *not* alcohol, and remember, too, that drinks at altitude appear to have more potency than at ground level.

The interesting ideas about preventing jet lag, however, involve the dietetic manipulations of chronobiologists like Dr. Charles Ehret. He has complicated programs depending on whether you are tracking east or west. If you head west, you are going into a longer day; thus extra caffeine in the morning will keep you active. That seems logical.

On the other hand, his techniques for flying toward the rising sun are as complicated as those programs for field sports athletes and professional boxers. They consist of days of high-protein breakfasts and lunches with a high-carbohydrate dinner, alternating with days of three light meals, all starting four days before departure.

It's a long story. Somehow it reminds us of the old saw: "When there's too much, something is missing."

Doctors seem on stronger ground with more basic advice on how to improve your sleeping pattern. Most of the suggestions are sensible and time-proven. Although Dement, at Stanford University, is prone to tell his students that text books of medicine are the results of three centuries of study of the human body in the waking state, "What we need," he says, "is three hundred years' study of the human body during sleep."

In fact, we sleep 220,000 hours in our lifetime—a time in bed formerly a mystery to physicians.

Dr. Allan Hobson of the Massachusetts Mental Health Center has studied sleep for so long that he challenges Freud's interpretation of dreams and sleep. Freud felt that dreams are bizarre in order to disguise forbidden wishes that might disturb.

"The nervous system doesn't work that way," says Hobson, "it never did, and as far as we know it never will. Dreaming is not the guardian of sleep."

Ralph B. Little, MD, a psychiatrist at the Philadelphia Psychoanalytic Institute partly agrees. "Dreams are not disturbers of sleep," he says, "they are *preservers* of sleep." Little feels that many of his patients are not so much troubled by insomnia as reacting to the worry of the significance of poor sleep. He tells his patients to keep a sleep diary. He wants to know their rituals before going to bed.

SLEEP TIPS

All those rituals have a place. Most sleep authorities agree that certain instructions improve sleep patterns. For example: Don't cat-nap during the day. Try to get some daily exercise. Avoid caffeine drinks in the evening. Be aware that studies at Pennsylvania State University showed that cigarette smoking impaired sleeping ability.

Don't exercise or eat a heavy meal within two hours of bedtime. Try a warm bath or shower at bedtime. Sleep in a cool room in summer, and in winter be prepared to use a humidifier, especially if the house is dry and you're using a wood stove.

Go to bed at the regular time and precede this event with the same habits or idiosyncracies: Comb your hair, drink a glass of milk (yes, there *is* actually some evidence that warm milk encourages sleep), read one chapter of a not-too-exciting book. But whatever you do, do it each night. Try to get rid of tension before you go to bed, but don't overuse alcohol.

Don't go to bed if you feel wide awake. Blank out your mind from the moment your head hits the pillow. If you *start* calculating and thinking, you will never finish.

If you can't sleep, get up. Don't just lie there worrying. If you do get out of bed, do something useful: write a letter, read a book, watch a movie—preferably a dull one.

Don't extend your time of rising in the morning; still get up at the same time. Continue the program. You'll be sleeping in a few nights. Don't worry if you can't sleep. It is almost always a temporary situation.

Chapter 12

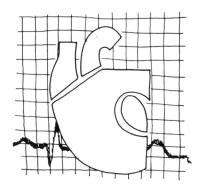

The Heart of the Matter

Your heart will beat around 100,000 times a day—about 36 million beats a year, every year. Without the heart, there can be no life. No wonder the ancients ascribed such powers to it: The Babylonians felt the heart was the seat of reason; the Greeks and Romans likewise described the heart as the source of human intelligence; the Aztecs ended some of their ceremonies of worship to the setting sun by offering a beating heart in the belief that this would ensure the sun's return in the morning.

The Dark Ages were penetrated finally by the anatomical studies of Leonardo da Vinci, by the meticulous dissections of Vesalius, and especially by the almost blasphemous experiments of the great Harvey.

William Harvey died in 1657 one of the grand men of medicine. He gave his first lecture to medical students in London in 1616, a week before the death of Shakespeare. The notes of that lecture are preserved in the British Museum and show that even then, twelve years before he published *De Moto Cordis*, the most famous book in medical history, he believed the movement of blood was in a circle and followed the beat of the heart.

Such was Harvey's contribution to medical knowledge. He demonstrated a simple fact understood today by every Cub Scout, yet to prove his contention, Harvey had to step into the unknown and even defy the church.

A modern Harvey and student of the pilot's health is Robert S. Eliot, MD, professor of medicine and director of the cardiovascular center at the University of Nebraska Medical Center in Omaha. Dr. Eliot was called to the Kennedy Space Center in Florida in the mid-1960s as a consultant because of the high rate of heart attacks among the aerospace engineers and technicians.

As an authority on heart disease, Eliot was crouched over a telemetry monitor when Ed White "walked" in space, the first astronaut to leave a space capsule. The monitor crackled with a flurry of *extra* heart beats transmitted from the ether above. The cardiologist frowned. No one had walked in space before. What were the problems, the strains, the challenges to man? Was it normal for the human heart to beat thus in space? With only one patient as an example, the doctor's series of cases had started with a 100 percent incidence of palpitations once the patient was outside the space capsule. Would this happen every time, and with every astronaut? The physician had no way of knowing.

Again Eliot studied the monitor. His patient, White, on Earth could outperform a pentathlon athlete, but no man had ever before been given a test of space walking, a combination of physical exertion and terror.

The palpitations increased. Part of the EKG called the T wave went upside down and a segment called the QRS complex, which is normally about 0.1 seconds long, widened to 0.6 seconds. Was White in trouble?

He rubbed his chin thoughtfully and stared again as the irregular contractions flipped across the screen. Two Air Force generals noted his concern and crossed over. They studied the oscilloscope, then spoke.

"Say, doctor. What does this mean?"

Eliot answered promptly. "I don't know," he said.

The two officers looked at each other and walked away. Eliot told me later what he overheard one say: "Jeez," declared one general looking back over his shoulder, "We spend billions for space and nickels for cardiologists!"

This military opinion of doctors is shared by a lot of airline pilots who feel that medical machines are taking over the assessments and the opinions of their health. And nowhere are those pilots more concerned than with this machine—the electrocardiogram. In the arena of medicine, if technology has now created a stage where science is supreme, then the EKG is god.

Careers flourish or falter depending on the tiny squiggles charred on sensitive paper by a hot needle. And yet the machine is not perfect.

Results *can* be consistent: You can walk into an intensive care

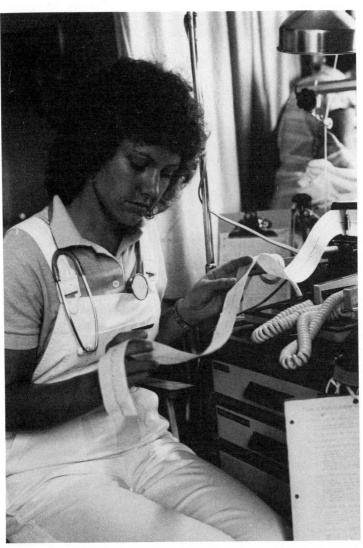

Today's coronary care nurse will soon know more about your body than your wife. Nevertheless, why not try to stay out of intensive care units and stay healthy?

unit of, say, three patients, and study the electrocardiograms of that day and, without even looking at the names, allocate one EKG to each patient just because you know what each one's EKG looked like the day before.

You can look at an EKG and suspect that the patient is young, skinny, and tall with a thin chest wall. Here's another EKG: This patient is probably black. And this one shows the patient has a pacemaker. And here we're getting a strange result—ah, it's an artifact from the electric bed. And what's going on here? The patient has just drunk a Coke which has both elevated his blood sugar and chilled the stomach against which the lower wall of the heart rests.

There are changes on EKGs sometimes from too much caffeine and too much nicotine—and sometimes from too little rest. The resulting premature ventricular contractions can be felt on occasion by the patient as a flutter or thump, or a feeling that the heart has stopped or turned over. A concerned patient might worry, but worry itself can cause those extra beats.

Thus, if you are a commercial pilot heading for your physical and worried about it, the resultant anxiety can make abnormalities appear. And so the circle continues. If the pilot slept badly the night before, this also may predispose to irregularity on the EKG.

At the time of the Vietnam conflict, as students were called for military physicals, the word went round the colleges through the underground grapevine: Students learned that if they smoked 60 cigarettes, drank 20 cups of black coffee and exercised before their physicals, they would have so many palpitations when the doctors listened to their hearts that they would fail their physicals.

This was an interesting twist to military medicine, because during the War Between the States, many recruits were considered to have heart disease, yet the problem was really that of cardiac neurosis—the patient believing or even pretending that his vague symptoms in the chest were due to heart disease.

A Civil War physician, Jacob DaCosta of Philadelphia, did much to clarify this situation, the term *DaCosta syndrome* or Soldier's Heart often being used for the picture of this cardiac anxiety.

It was understandable that patients with chest symptoms would be anxious, although it took a long time for physicians to share their concern. Fifty years ago, no American medical student knew about heart attack even although Jeremiah had said in the Hebrew Bible: "And the heart of strong men will feel pains like the pain of a woman in labor," and Hippocrates, the father of Medicine, had reported that "angina is serious . . . and may suffocate the patient even on the first day."

ANGINA PECTORIS

The first contemporary description of *angina pectoris* (temporary pain due to poor circulation in the heart) came in 1772 from William Heberden, the eminent physician, who on his deathbed at the age of 91 was described by Dr. Samuel Johnson, his patient, as "the last of the Romans."

In this century things slowly became more clear. In Chicago, Herrick described the picture of heart attacks in 1912. Levine followed in 1929 in Boston with a careful study of 145 patients, and in the same city in 1944 Wilson developed the technique of EKG leads placed over the chest itself to clarify what happened when a heart attack occurred.

The coronary consciousness of American doctors, for so long undeveloped, has now swung so far in the opposite direction that there is a real tendency to overdiagnose the presence of ischemic heart disease, common though the problem is.

The risk that a private pilot might have a heart attack while flying is a particular concern to all lightplane passengers, although there is a tendency for the pilots themselves not to think about it. They should: The results can be shattering—literally.

Consider the Beech 35 that was turning from downwind to base at St. Charles, Missouri. The pilot, age 49, sustained a heart attack and spiraled in.

Or the Cessna 170 that took off from Beaver Falls, Pennsylvania. The pilot, age 61, suffered a heart attack and collided in midair with a Stinson.

Maybe it would be easier on the ground? Don't count on it. A Cessna 337 was rolling at Grass Valley, California. The pilot, age 61, was felled by a heart attack on takeoff and ran into a ditch.

Would landing be easier? A Cessna 150 came into a cow pasture at Kissimee, Florida, and wiped out. The pilot, age 46, experiencing a heart attack had attempted in vain an off-airport precautionary landing.

Perhaps younger men are safer? A Cessna 411 left St. Louis, Illinois, and in level flight over Delevan, Wisconsin, fell out of the skies. The pilot, who'd had a heart attack, was age 23.

Possibly the Lord smiles on experience? An ATR, flight instructor, crashed a Lockheed at Burns Flat, Oklahoma, after a heart attack. Not only did he have 15,955 hours flying time, but he had taken off from the hallowed ground itself: Oklahoma City.

If those favored by the gods are still vulnerable, what can we less-fancied mortals do to protect our flying future? What problems can pilots and their passengers expect since heart disease is so common? It's not so simple as it is on cruise ships, that's for sure.

Nigel Roberts, MD, the principal medical officer of the *Queen Elizabeth II*, hears very early, on his ship, about passengers who may be having heart attacks. "I get my cardiacs early," he told me, "because a moment of 'indigestion' and the spouse is calling me on the telephone. Passengers don't spend a lot of money on a cruise and not act promptly if symptoms threaten to spoil things."

His passengers are luckier than those flying with lightplane pilots. Just as pilots can deceive themselves about weather by taking off and wishing for better things, so they can deny the significance of chest symptoms and ignore warning signals in their bodies that they might have noticed had they not been so preoccupied.

Small airports don't have doctors, don't have convenient ground transportation to the inner city, and don't have easy access to community hospitals. Pilots can't wait endlessly like other transients in city emergency rooms while the weather changes. NOTAMS alter, and airports close down. Pilots can't receive medication with side effects, accept a few precautionery days in an intensive care unit, or acknowledge and permit damning diagnostic labels on their health records.

How would their passengers get home? Who would collect the plane? What if the aircraft is rented?

No wonder it's simpler to call it a *stomach* pain.

There's no easy answer to this. There's probably *no* answers. Passengers should have some rudimentary pinch-hitting flying skills. They should have attended the basic cardiopulmonary resuscitation courses (CPR) put on by the American Heart Association or the Red Cross, although attempting CPR on a pilot sitting behind the yoke would be unlikely to have a successful outcome. Passengers should never give off vibrations that their wish to get home takes precedence over the weather or the pilot's health.

Pilots need to know more about heart disease. They should carry—even those who need only a Class III medical certificate—a small copy of their EKG, and they should be informed about family and past personal health. They need to be as intimate with those marvelous machines that are their bodies as they are with those crazy inventions of Wilbur and Orville Wright.

While the present epidemic proportions of heart disease cross all frontiers and while many considerations are important—family history, diabetes, obesity, inactivity, loneliness, and stress—it seems clear from the ongoing study at Framingham, Massachusetts, that the three important factors are cholesterol levels, high blood pressure, and cigarette smoking.

CHOLESTROL

You can reduce cholestrol and other fats in your blood only to a degree. Weight reduction, diet adjustment, and exercise all help a bit, and there are drugs (not without side effects) that are sometimes indicated. However, despite the interest scientists have shown in chloresterol for more than a quarter of a century, they still have no advice for consumers that does not conflict with the opinion of other researchers.

Nevertheless, Americans would be wise to reduce the fat in their diet. The only people who eat more fat are the Finns and they live on blubber. Coronary heart disease is relatively rare among the Chinese, a nation that gets most of its calories from rice. This is one of the reasons suggesting that carbohydrates are less important than fat in contributing to cardiovascular diseases.

Stamler and his group in Chicago have shown that patients on a low-fat diet, and followed for 20 years, had a 20 to 30 percent reduction in coronary disease. This is no surprise today because a National Diet Heart Study as far back as 1968 had estimated that a ten percent reduction in cholesterol blood levels would give a 24 percent decrease in the incidence of coronary artery disease in America. However, to achieve proof of this point, the statisticians found that 50,000 middle-aged men would have to be studied for more than three years, an impractical consideration then.

The Air Force, nevertheless, started a heart disease screening program in January 1982. Not only are such tests practical for the military, they are even necessary. Heart disease, the Air Force's leading non-accidental cause of death, is believed to cost that branch of the service $50 million a year in terms of health, disability, and death benefits.

HYPERTENSION

High blood pressure is a problem more amenable to treatment.

Unfortunately, half the 45 million Americans who have it are unaware of the problem. At a time when so many hospitals, drug stores, and community clinics offer free blood pressure readings, it defies belief that people can walk the streets unaware they carry this ticking time bomb.

In contrast to some well-publicized diseases which, though important, are rare, high blood pressure is common—and life-threatening. But it's treatable. It's a terribly important disease. It's

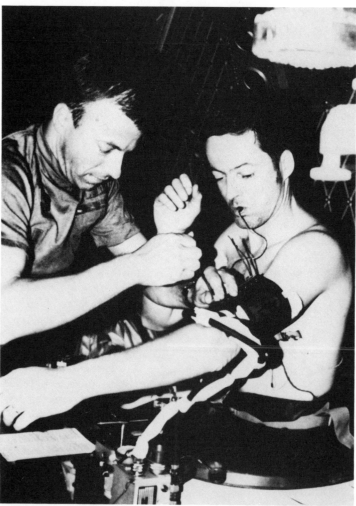

The blood pressure of astronaut Joseph P. Kerwin, MD, (right) is monitored by fellow astronaut Paul J. Weitz on board Skylab II (courtesy NASA)

the commonest form of death amongst blacks, but it strikes *every* family in America. One million deaths a year in the United States are either caused by it or associated with it. One American in five has the problem, and in an odd way, the treatment becomes the doctor's problem.

For example, I saw a patient the other day in my office. He had twisted his ankle. His blood pressure was 170/110 (conventionally we take 140/90 as the upper limit of normal). Six months ago, on blood pressure medication, it was 140/85. What was happening?

I could guess, but I asked him. "Shoot, doc," he said, "Your medicine made me feel lousy. I flushed it down the toilet, called you a few names, and now I feel great!"

Anderson strikes out again. Why? There's a reason for what in present medical jargon is called this "patient non-compliance," and it's a pretty basic one. If you take medicine today because you have high blood pressure, you won't necessarily feel any better today. You may in fact, feel so different that you interpret the sensation as being unwell, and *that* does not help you take your medication.

Yet it's so important to take it. Jeffrey B. Neilson, MD, a private pilot, a member of the New Hampshire Academy of Family Physicians and a past president of the New Hampshire Heart Association, points out that "Hypertension is a lifetime problem, and the cause of strokes, heart disease, and kidney failure. There is no cure for most forms, but it can be controlled by daily treatment. Early hypertension does not cause symptoms. Therefore, you must take your medicine regularly *even* if you feel well."

You don't take blood pressure medication in 1984 to make you feel better in 1984. You take it so you're here in 1994 and maybe 2024. You take it to stop the relentless pounding of your blood pressure in the vessels of heart, kidneys, and brain—especially the brain. Hit a trampoline with a mallet, day after day after day, and finally something gives. It's the same inside the human body.

Doctors *are* seeing improvements. More people who have it are now aware of the problem of high blood pressure. We've gone from 50 percent patient awareness ten years ago to 70 percent awareness. As a result of treatment, stroke deaths are down by 20 percent since 1970 and heart disease death by 15 percent.

Nevertheless, a study in Washington, D.C., showed a frightening lack of awareness by professionals—doctors, nurses, and hospitals—as to the importance of the diagnosis of hypertension. In a city hospital, trained paramedics checked the blood pressure of all patients who were not on the obstetrics or general medical wards. Out of 1300 patients, they found 400 with pressure greater than 150/100; of those, 285 did not know they had a problem and only eight were on treatment. And those were persons already caught up by the medical machine in a well-run hospital.

Why, until recently, was the picture so unsatisfactory? I guess everyone's to blame, especially doctors. Physicians had to be taught by insurance companies from statistics that even mild hypertension should be treated and that the disease is a killer. Doctors can be as lazy as the next person. If a patient comes in with a sore throat, it is quicker to treat him for that than to harass him, perhaps for life, about his blood pressure.

Yet high blood pressure does its damage for life. It enlarges the heart muscle, which has to push against its resistance. It thus increases the oxygen demands of this working muscle pump.

If the patient with high blood pressure is a recreational pilot whose pleasure is to fly around the Rockies VFR at 10,000 feet, he's at a double disadvantage. His heart is requiring his lungs to provide more oxygen at a time when the air actually contains less. If he is a smoker, he's *triple* compromised.

Cigarette smoking was not invented for pilots. The contribution to disease by tobacco is pretty well accepted by everyone including smokers themselves. The cigarette makers have allowed themselves to be struck off television advertising without any legal posturing. For such big business to accept so unprecedented an action without rushing to the lawyers for a stay of execution strongly suggests that the tobacco companies know the facts and the satistics better than the average consumer.

But not better than the doctors, Physicians, notoriously lax at following their own advice, have not run true to form on the subject of cigarettes. More than 100,000 doctors have somehow quit smoking in the last decade.

I attended a county medical society meeting in Huntsville, Texas, in 1964. The speaker, a chest specialist, scolded the audience of doctors: 18 were smoking out of a total of 21. Ten years later, in New Hampshire, another lung specialist said, at a hospital staff dinner, that he had just returned from a convention of chest physicians in Atlantic City. In an audience of nearly three thousand doctors specializing in lung diseases, only three were found smoking at dinner.

Cigarettes are dangerous for older women on birth control pills. They are unsafe for patients with poor circulation in the legs.

They are risky for people prone to palpitation. And they are bad news for pilots who like to fly at night or at altitude.

Nevertheless, smokers don't always quit cigarettes, even if they have advanced lung disease. Sometimes it's because they don't believe that the odds apply to them. Says Dr. Peter N. Herbert, professor of medicine at Brown University, "Tobacco provides immediate gratification for the man grabbing all the gusto today has to offer. And not every roulette player loses."

The country loses—thirteen billion dollars for direct care of smoking-related diseases; twenty-five billion dollars in earnings lost from sickness or death. This is the true tobacco blight.

SALT

One thing a patient can do to keep him winning in this hypertensive game of life is to reduce salt. We all eat too much salt. A *cordon bleu* chef wandering into McDonald's would be horrified— not at the food, which isn't actually too bad, but at the way our little Americans throw the salt around.

If every housewife in her kitchen put the salt shaker on a top shelf rather than on the table, the nation's health would be the better for it.

But we get salt in snack foods like potato chips, nuts, crackers, and pretzels. We get it in canned foods like soups and vegetables. We get it in bacon, ham and pork; cheese, sausage, and pickles; and frozen foods. We even get it in saccharin and some antacids (read the label for sodium content; it can vary from 0.3 mg/5 ml in Riopan to 13.0 in Gaviscon).

Try to use less salt in cooking, stop all salt at the table, avoid heavily salted processed foods, and try herbs and spices instead of seasoned salts like garlic, onion, catsup or soysauce.

The National Institutes of Health feel that we should reduce our sodium intake daily to about two grams—which is equal to the amount found in one teaspoonful of salt. Most Americans eat at least four times that.

Indeed, it is felt that some of the migration studies that demonstrate increasing blood pressure as primitive societies to adopt more modern ways of life show results that are due essentially to the fact that increased salt intake often follows, too.

Certainly, hypertension is almost absent in some remote native cultures that do not use much salt as, for example, the Kalahari bushmen of Africa or the Melanesian tribes of New Guinea.

CAFFEINE

We've mentioned caffeine already. Most consumers are aware that caffeine is found not only in coffee but in tea, cocoa, chocolate, and cola drinks. But did you know that a single dose of Excedrin for a headache will give you as much caffeine as two cups of regular instant coffee? Or that a 12-ounce can of Mountain Dew has one-and-a-half times as much caffeine as the same size can of Coca-Cola? Indeed, the can of Mountain Dew contains 52 mg caffeine, about the same as a 5-ounce cup of regular instant coffee. However, the most common sources of caffeine are drip coffee, which as 146 mg in a 5-ounce cup, and percolated coffee which contains 110 mg.

You can reduce your caffeine intake a bit by avoiding coffee brewed for a long time, and by changing to percolated coffee. Switching to instant or even decaffeinated makes a much more significant improvement.

Quite apart from the inconclusive evidence linking caffeine with stomach ulcer, breast fibrocystic disease, and pancreatic cancer in adult humans, with possible overstimulation in children drinking too many sodas, and with birth defects in rats force-fed high doses when pregnant, is the whole spectrum of whether our national drink, coffee, is not somehow poisoning our population, producing a Jazz Age America—lifted up, restless, busy, alert, palpitating for the chase and not quite knowing why. Coffee makes us speed up our lives. We need coffee *brakes*, not coffee *breaks*.

If FDR drank water at his desk, why do you have to knock back coffee at yours? (author photo courtesy FDR Library)

Most of the problems seen by practicing physicians are either excessive palpitations of the heart or increased irritability of the nerves. A valid experiment for any patient who gets periods of cardiac irregularity or episodes of nervous tension is to examine his caffeine intake and see what happens when it is reduced.

You don't need to become evangelistic and totally opposed to coffee. *Just cut down.*

So you've cut down your salt and coffee. What else can you do to reduce the chance that you might get a heart attack? We'll talk about some of this in the next chapter, but in the meantime listen to George V. Mann, ScD, MD, professor of medicine and biochemistry at Vanderbilt University school of medicine, Nashville, Tennesse who seems a bit overprecise and overconfident to some front-line doctors. Nevertheless, he has a "Decalogue of Lifestyle" that he presents to his patients:

1. Avoid excessive fats. This means grill rather than fry; use lean meats rather than the traditional ones.

2. Avoid sodium and seek potassium because a high ratio of sodium to potassium in our usual diet is the *sine qua non* for high blood pressure.

3. Try to get a small portion of red meat each day for its iron supply. This is essentially important for young women who are thin and lean and often anemic.

4. Avoid phosphorus and seek calcium because a high ratio of phosphorus to calcium in the diet seems to predispose to osteoporosis. In practical terms, this means seeking dairy products and avoiding soft drinks. (This is considered an oversimplification by other practicing physicians.)

5. Get some form of vigorous exercise three times each week. There is persuasive evidence that vigorous exercise during leisure time protects people from coronary disease. Avoid carbon monoxide. This means no smoking and try to exercise in fresh air rather than in city streets.

6. Seek fiber. This is best done by eating five servings of fruit a day. This practice will also supply potassium.

7. Seek out seafood. Marine animals contain an unusual five double-bond, 20 carbon fatty acid, which is the precursor for prostacyclins (substances that improve blood flow).

8. Avoid drinking too many alcoholic beverages, especially the colored liquors, because of their contamination with congeners (chemicals which have pharmacological results on brain and nervous tissue). If you must drink, choose the white liquors.

9. Eat small portions, and include only one major meal in your diet each day if you are a sedentary urbanite.

10. Select a varied diet each day. This means consuming dairy products, meat and legumes, fruit, vegetables, and cereal grains.

"Despite our high coronary rate, it is this kind of lifestyle in this abundant and vigorous nation that has made us the best nourished people in the world."

Mann's message to man is a bit altruistic, but if we were to follow even some of those commandments, we would probably be the better for them.

Chapter 13

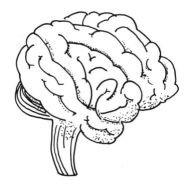

Stress

My patient was concerned, and no wonder. A commercial pilot needs a stout heart and *he* was convinced that his was diseased. His symptoms worried him: chest tightness, shortness of breath, arm pains, and general malaise.

Examination was negative.

Just out of medical school, I hadn't any equipment yet in my office, newly established in Groveton, a small town in Texas. I looked around at the empty room, then faced my patient.

"I can see how worried you are," I said. "I understand how important this all is to you. You're thinking of your career and your family. I'd like to run an EKG but it will be a week before my stuff arrives."

I laid my hand on the telephone.

"Let me call an internist in Lufkin. He'll check you over and answer your questions. Okay?"

The pilot licked his lips anxiously then nodded.

"Go ahead, doc."

I made the arrangements, and sent him on his way.

An hour and a half later I met him downtown on the street.

"Geez, have you not gone yet?" I said. "It will take you 30 to 40 minutes to get up to Lufkin. The doctor is waiting for you."

The patient grinned from ear to ear. "I've been."

"Been?"

"Yep. Been. He didn't even take an EKG. Listened to my story. Got me to breathe fast. It brought back all my symptoms. He told me all about it. Sent me back home."

He grinned again and disappeared.

HYPERVENTILATION SYNDROME

I'd missed my first case of hyperventilation syndrome. Somehow, I don't think I've missed one since.

Hyperventilation symptoms haunt us all. It's a very easy condition to understand. The blood contains CO_2 (carbon dioxide) in solution.

It combines with water to form carbonic acid:

$$H_2O + CO_2 \rightarrow H_2O_3$$

This makes the blood and the body briefly acid. That's the way the body functions. Reduce the acidity of the body and a lot of weird symptoms result. Some of those features could appear in the old days before antacids, when baking soda, an alkali, was widely used for indigestion. The sodium bicarbonate effectively stopped stomach problems but created others by making the blood less acid, indeed alkaline.

In hyperventilation states, the fast breathing, caused usually by anxiety, blows out all the CO_2 available in the lungs—all the stale air. Because the person keeps breathing, the lungs have no choice. They have to continue yielding CO_2 and end up stealing it from the blood circulating past each air sac. Some of the blood deprived of the gas cannot continue to make carbonic acid and becomes less acid—in fact, water.

$$H_2O_3 \rightleftharpoons CO_2 \uparrow + H_2O \text{ (water)}$$

As a result, a syndrome unfolds due to a less acid blood. The fingers may tingle, even the toes. They may go into spasm as if the hand is making an imitation of an ostrich head. This carpal spasm can be quite frightening to patients.

A feeling of lightheadedness or dizziness may develop, difficult to distinguish from true vertigo. There may be chest pain or tightness. A sense of apprehension may smother the person.

Patients almost always think they are getting a heart attack. The tipoff is the respiration rate, which is best measured by another person who does not reveal to the patient that the breaths are being

176

counted. You can take your own *pulse*, but it's hard to count your own breaths.

The respiration rate at rest is quite low—say 14 to 16; it is certainly never up in the 20s as you commonly find in hyperventilation patients. You see the syndrome in women in labor (and sometimes in their husbands), in kids breathing hard before they dive into a cold pool, in tense people who just breathe too fast. You see it in student pilots, with white knuckles clamped on the yoke.

The doctor sometimes gets a clue from the amount of sighing his patient does, or from the hands which start to grip the side of the examination table as the stethoscope, moving over the chest, makes the patient—already at the edge of the hyperventilation syndrome—breathe faster and become dizzy and symptomatic.

Everyone has heard about hyperventilation. People have all seen Goldie Hawn in *Shampoo* and Burt Reynolds in *Starting Over*. The kids at the nearby high school know about it. They've formed kinky hyperventilation clubs to freak out without drugs: breathe fast, pop your ears by doing a Valsalva, and you faint.

Everyone has heard about it, except my patients. It's usually a woman and she's convinced that she's having a heart attack. You see, doctor, chest pain and funny feeling in my left arm: That *has* to be a heart attack.

Wrong.

The treatment is twofold. The doctor has to prove to the patient that overbreathing causes the symptoms. Usually breathing fast every second for about a minute or so will reproduce all or most of the symptoms. This test can be done at home with the spouse present to supervise and remind the patient to breathe again after the test. Or it can be carried out with the doctor moving things along. It probably is necessary to show that the symptoms are caused by fast breathing because otherwise the patient won't believe it.

They often say that they don't breathe as fast as 60 a minute and therefore the experiment is not valid, but all the test is doing is accelerating the pace to produce faster results. Overbreathing is accumulative; even a few extra breaths per minute add up soon to create symptoms.

The second part of treatment is to show that the symptoms are easily treated. For example, try to stop breathing; hold your breath for as long as possible. Then take one breath. Stop and hold. Slow down your breathing for the next 30 minutes.

If you have a small paper bag handy, place it over your nose and mouth, bunch it up, and breathe into it. Rebreathe the stale expired air; it is rich in CO_2. If you don't have a paper bag and are in a conspicuous place such as on a bus, in a movie theater, or walking down a street, you can hold your cupped hands in front of you and rebreathe into them. The paper bag approach is best, however.

Once the syndrome is revealed and explained, it will often go away as if worry itself about it was perpetuating the problem.

A physician who has investigated more than 700 patients with this syndrome is Dr. L. C. Lum of Cambridge, England. Lum thinks that the anxiety exhibited by the patient, so apparent to onlookers, is the result rather than the cause of the problem. I find that hard to believe. Lum, however, feels that some patients simply have bad breathing habits and, like asthmatics; need to be taught slow-breathing diaphragmatic exercises.

Herbert E. Walker, MD, of New York University school of medicine, has studied more than two hundred patients and teaches them a simple method of breathing slowly through the nose with the mouth tightly closed.

"This is a paradoxical illness," he says, "even though you feel as if you don't have enough oxygen, you have too much."

It takes time for patients to come to grips with the diagnosis. They need to be shown that overbreathing causes the symptoms and that slow breathing or using a paper bag makes them well again. But although the ailment is a very simple affair, it is however a very common presentation in the doctor's office. It's as if the stress of living was suffocating the patients of today.

WHAT IS STRESS?

What is stress? What is this intrusion into our daily lives? What is this modern challenge that so swamps the people of our times?

Stress is *not* a modern affront, although the term has become a buzzword in this decade. Stress has been around as long as *homo sapiens*. A caveman about to be trampled on by some giant mastodon no doubt felt pretty well stressed, as did some village oaf in the pillory at the market square.

Stress has always been with us. But, as thousands of phys-chologists have pointed out recently, in the old days problems were speedily resolved. Stress was acute. Life was basic. It was all sink or swim, fight or die, fight or flee. You didn't smolder with resentment at work under a superior you disliked; you went up to him with your caveman club and biffed him—*hard*. Or got zonked yourself.

In such primitive times, the alarm signals from your body were noted and a response was made. Once the incident was over, the animal-man could return to a less-aggressive state. But try zapping your chief pilot or your flight instructor now and see what happens.

Actually, what happens is that you don't try. Social and cultural barriers surround people today. It is inappropriate for one person to assess the situation from his vantage point alone, then take physical action to resolve an imagined problem.

And therein lies the difficult for some: They exist in a state of such irritation, tension, and anger that this very mood defeats their ability to live. They virtually can't cope because they are dominated by survival instincts, just as a computer sometimes can't perform because its circuits are overloaded.

The reference is valid. Russian psychologists believe that for every year we are alive today, we live the sensory-input equivalent of a thousand years of our great-grandparents.

The pace of life has surely speeded up, and with these faster tempos have indeed come problems. It is, however, wrong to speculate that the stress itself is the issue. It is not. What is important, even crucial, is the *reaction* of the person to the stress. Because people vary.

In Montreal, the original world-authority on stress, the late Dr. Hans Selye, made this clear. Having studied stress for more than 40 years, he reached this conclusion: "Some people are stress seekers. They need it to live and be happy. This is good, and they should seek it. They are like race horses."

Other people, he suggested, were stress avoiders: "They want to be placid and easy-going," he said. "This is what they need to live, and they should avoid stress. We call them turtles."

Two doctors, Friedman and Rosenman, tried to be a bit more scientific and published their theories in the 1970s. They attempted to differentiate the behavior of people into two types. Type A was the person who came across as dynamic, aggressive, and with a sense of time-urgency. This would be Dr. Selye's race horse. The Type B personality they considered more mellow and relaxed. Such B behavior persons did not seek achievement like the Type As but avoided stress, indeed like Selye's turtles.

While there is still a lot of interest in this classification, we now realize in the 1980s that this division was an oversimplification. First, it appears that 65 percent of the population is Type A, thus it is no surprise to find that two-thirds of patients having heart attacks are Type A. Probably all airline pilots and all doctors are Type A. If they weren't, they couldn't have survived the selection process. Secondly, some Type A's thrive on stress.

Type A behavior can be modified to a degree if the individual is willing and the doctor is patient. The person has to be taught to change his interpretation that the environment is a challenge, because in the 1980s it is not likely that the environment itself can be altered. A type A cannot be tempered into a pure Type B, but he or she can be converted a bit.

Some change may be enough. The very personality of a Type A could make him accept the change itself as a challenge for him to conquer, and thus make him propose vast, impossible turnabouts that would be quite unrealistic but so typical of Type A behavior.

Rosenman, with the help of Margaret A. Chesney, PhD, director of the Behavorial Medical Program, Menlo Park, California, has encouraged Type A personalities to identify, select, and change some characteristics of their behavior.

The two doctors give written lists to their patients thus:

Plan one event that encourages humor or friendship each week.

Avoid becoming angry at local association meetings by keeping in perspective the issues discussed.

Replace the regular "business" meal with a quiet lunch alone.

Allow more time for commuting to work, thereby avoiding the rush.

Practice setting priorities and purposely postpone one activity each day to another time.

Spend 15 minutes once a day relaxing quietly.

Select the longest lines in stores and practice smiling at passersby or chat with others in line rather than becoming impatient and angry.

It is too soon to say whether this program will be productive. Perhaps only a Type A personality could endure the agony and frustration of trying to tamper with a Type A personality!

Yet even a Type A can be made to admit that life should have some quiet moments, some passive relaxation. Herbert Benson, MD, an associate professor of medicine at Harvard and director of the hypertension section at Beth Israel Hospital, Boston, using biofeedback mechanisms once taught monkeys how to lower their blood pressure.

He was then approached by a group of people practicing transcendental meditation who demonstrated their techniques, which were simpler than the monkey methods. Indeed, Benson found that TM diminished oxygen consumption by 17 to 18 percent, reduced other biochemical activities, and dropped blood pressure.

Benson simplified the relaxation process and found that a secret TM *mantra* or restful word was not required to induce this state but that any word, even a number like "one," would suffice.

The technique he taught hypertensives he called the *relaxation response*. It was a simple program, especially compared to the rather extravagant trappings of TM. His advice was precise:

1. Sit quietly and in a comfortable position.

2. Close your eyes.

3. Deeply relax all your muscles, beginning at your feet and progressing up to your face. Keep them deeply relaxed.

4. Breathe through your nose. Become aware of your breathing. As you breathe out, say the word "one" silently to yourself. For example, breathe in . . . out, *one*; in . . . out, *one*; etc.

5. Continue for 20 minutes. You may open your eyes to check the time, but do not use an alarm. When you finish, sit quietly for several minutes, at first with your eyes closed, then with them open.

6. Do not worry about whether you are successful in achieving a deep level of relaxation. Maintain a passive attitude and permit relaxation to occur at its own pace. Expect distracting thoughts. When these distracting thoughts occur, ignore them and continue repeating "one." Practice the technique once or twice daily and not within two hours after any meal, since the digestive processes seem to interfere with the elicitation of anticipated changes.

It works. There is clear evidence that persons who try this relaxation response do benefit—without drugs, without dependence on others, by doing it themselves for themselves.

Remember, high blood pressure is a killer. But besides that, there has been quite a bit of research to suggest that patients with hypertension because they are Type A persons don't really enjoy life as much as others.

Harris and Forsythe, two psychiatrists at the cardiovascular research institute at the University of California, San Francisco, in studies of college women found hypertensives to be tense, restless, anxious, and irritable persons who perceived "many kinds of personal interactions as stressful and as the occasion for emotional arousal." They considered those patients to have mental outbursts that were more common, more intense, and longer-lasting than the emotional upsets of other persons.

Although most physicians in private practice don't feel that there truly is a "hypertensive personality," it is instructive to find that scientists in a study of employees of one insurance company considered the hypertensives they found to be "emotionally more responsive, guarded, apprehensive, and unwilling to talk about themselves." This fits in with a review of United States Air Force officers where personnel with the highest blood pressure were labelled as "dominant, assertive, and decisive, with narrow ranges of interest, over-controlling, rigid, and obtuse in their social relationships." But I bet they were excellent pilots. Indeed, some of the worst traits for personality may well be the best for flying skills.

Rigid rules may prevent fatigue, not cause it. Dr. Kevin Wand, the flight surgeon to the Navy's precision aerobatic team, the Blue Angels, believes his greatest responsibility is safety.

"I try to keep the pilots aware that stress and fatigue can slow reaction time," he says. "Usually the pilots receive eight to ten hours sleep each night." Training at Pensacola, Florida, starts at 6:00 a.m. and ends in the early afternoon. Then pilots are free to fill the rest of the day with personal fitness programs and periods of complete relaxation.

Lest there be any student pilots out there who somehow imagine that only sissies would plan relaxation procedures for themselves, let them hear the opinions of Champe C. Pool, MD, who was medical consultant and team physician to the United States aerobatic team in 1972. He found those pilots to be critical, cool, and reserved. They showed characteristics of emotional detachment, tough-mindedness, self-reliance, psychological endurance, and old-fashioned tenacity. Other common traits were unconventional independence yet a need for professionalism, for achievement, and for recognition.

Along with a colleague, Bruce C. Ogilvie, PhD, professor of psychology at California State University, San Jose, Pool discovered other unusual psychological attributes of successful aerobatic pilots: "They rate high in deference, which is the inclination to take or accept suggestions, to follow instructions, praise others, and to conform to customs. They also score high in the need for order and organization, indicating that this is a highly developed aspect of their personalities. Within this trait is a concern for detail, a tendency to plan ahead, to live by some system. But there is a definite trend toward exhibitionism."

It is no surprise to find, in those who display themselves so openly in the skies, the need for exhibitionism or for organization, but it must be hard for flying teams to plan ahead when, like the Blue Angels, they spend only three months annually on their home base and nine months of the year on the performance circuit.

Will Rogers wasn't being fair when he said, "When you get into trouble five thousand miles from home, you've got to be looking for it." Travel itself can be a stressor. Several authorities have recognized this for decades long before circadian rhythm disturbance became a buzzword among aircrews. Adolph Meyer, MD, professor of psychiatry at Johns Hopkins at the turn of the century, noted how illness tended to strike his patients if they had moved away from their usual routines. Since World War II, Harold G. Wolff, MD, professor of neurology and psychiatry at Cornell University Medical College, then Thomas H. Holmes, MD, professor of psychiatry and behavorial sciences at the University of Washington School of Medicine, and Richard H. Rahe, adjunct professor of psychiatry at UCLA School of Medicine and commanding officer of the Naval Health Research Center in San Diego, have all studied the effect of change in their fellow man.

Rahe, for example, looked at patients in locations as diverse as Sweden and Oklahoma, taking inventory of what recent life-style changes had occurred in cardiac patients prior to their heart attack. The results were fascinating. They suggested that variations from patients' normal life-patterns constituted a duress for those persons, a strain sometimes provocative enough to bring on a heart attack.

Rahe also considered the illness patterns of about 2,500 officers and enlisted men aboard three Navy warships. He found consistently that the 30 percent of men with the highest life-change scores developed almost 90 percent more first illnesses in the initial month of the cruise than the 30 percent of the men with the lowest scores.

With Holmes, he published in 1968 a rating scale for major life events where the figure of 50 points was given for marriage, 100 for death, and 25 for any change in living conditions. Divorce was rated 73, jail 63, personal injury 53; retirement earned 45 points, pregnancy 40, foreclosure of a loan or mortgage 30, and so on.

Interestingly enough, a vacation brought in a stress factor of 13 points, Christmas 12 points, and a child leaving home 29 points.

The list has been published in just about every woman's magazine but still remains as a fresh and viable attempt to put a rating on duress. Those doctors felt that if you scored below 150 in any year you had one chance in three of a serious health change in the next two years. If you collected between 150 and 300 points, your chances rose to 50-50 and if you hit more than 300 you were almost 90 percent certain to become ill.

The list makes rather grim reading for a peripatetic traveler like a commercial pilot, to whom change is common rather than the exception. However, a change is not always a stress if if can be anticipated or controlled, and even then, as we've seen before, it's the perception of the individual to the change that is important.

Says Herman K. Hellerstein, MD, professor of medicine at Case Western Reserve University School of Medicine, "Stress is an input . . . Strain is a deformation produced by a stress . . . Actually, everything in life could be considered a stressor—working, loving, thinking, eating. So not all stressors are necessarily harmful. It's very subjective. What is stressful to one person may be pleasurable to another."

Another cardiologist, Robert S. Eliot, MD, of Nebraska (who you met in the last chapter), has attempted to distinguish between the groups who respond to stress so differently. He works surrounded by the most complicated of technical machines at the University of Nebraska Medical Center. He once joked that he wanted to build a cardiovascular center in Nebraska that the football squad could be proud of.

Among all his expensive equipment is an ATARI electronic video game, Breakout. He has it rigged by computer so that the competitor can never win, although he or she can come close. Challenging himself against the game, the player tends to exhibit most of his characteristics and may show several of the factors apparently associated with coronary-prone behavior: competitiveness, impatience, and hostility.

During the game, Eliot measures (by noninvasive means from outside the body) the blood pressure, the volume of blood pushed out by each heartbeat, and the amount of resistance the peripheral blood vessels give to the heartbeat.

Based on those determinations, he divides his subjects into two categories that he calls *cold reactors* and *hot reactors*. The cold reactors he's not concerned about—they are the lucky Joe Cools of this world. He is worried about one subgroup of the hot reactors where both the blood pressure and the peripheral resistance goes up. He sees those competitive people preparing as if for war but with an autonomic nervous system that paradoxically increases the resistance to the heartbeat "as if a clamp were to be forced down on a garden hose." It's as if the person "was driving a car with the brakes on. The motor begins to burn out."

The motor in those hot reactors is the heart, the organ, with the gut, most susceptible to stress.

Eliot believes that one person in three, despite a negative physical examination by a doctor, will show this worrying over-reactivity if exposed to psychological stress. What would he make of the regular check flights undergone by airline pilots?

Yet Eliot understands the realities of life. "We know the only way to totally avoid stress is to be dead," he says. "Properly used, stress is essential to a life of élan and rigor." However he does ask his patients why they want to pay the price of rage when a little anger will do the job nicely.

Eliot himself had his own heart attack at the age of 44 while he was lecturing to a group on how to avoid a heart attack! The increased insight from his own illness has added to the value of the views of this articulate professor who still crosses the world—"the high priest of stress management"—to educate others.

One of Eliot's challenges at the Kennedy Space Center in the 1960s was to find out why aerospace engineers and technicians were dropping dead of heart attacks at the inordinately low age of 31 years. It took Eliot and his medical team about eight years to be sure. Indeed, they found there *was* a 44 percent increased risk of dying among those young aerospace personnel.

All the physical risk factors checked out satisfactorily. The emotional factors were then considered. The mental attitudes of the technicians did indeed reveal that they were under great stress.

The strain, however, was not the cause of their responsibility to get men in space and bring them back safely. No, the pressure lay at a more primitive level. The technicians were in fear for their own futures.

Those specially trained young persons had "unique jobs in a unique profession." They knew nothing else and the prospects, indeed the certainty, that they would in a few years lose their jobs created a chronic alarm system of tension, worry, and fear. The results, in some, were alcoholism, divorce, mental breakdown—and death.

Of course there were many survivors. This resilience to survive, this ability to cope has always fascinated psychiatrists. Dr. Thomas P. Hackett, the chief of psychiatry at Massachusetts General Hospital, was intrigued by the factors that enabled World War I pilots to survive an era where no young aviator could expect to live more than ten weeks in the hostile skies of war.

He paid particular study to the American pilots in the Lafayette Escadrille. He found that those who lived had "confidence, optimism, and a strong reason for wanting to survive." They were marked by great self-assurance in their flying and engineering skills. There was an absence of depression and a lack of self-pity. There was great toughness of mind. And there was often, "someone to love, or a family to live for."

This is an opinion starting to emerge from the work of Selye in Montreal, the scientist, previously mentioned, who really started it all. Selye said that the best way to alleviate stress is to make ourselves loved, to become necessary: "Man, with his highly developed central nervous system, is especially vulnerable to phychic insults."

We are especially vulnerable to stress whether the insults are random and unexpected or whether they are repetitive and anticipated. Any reader of Tom Wolfe's *The Right Stuff* has an idea of what astronaut selection was like but it is even more interesting to hear from an astronaut who was also an MD. The thoughts of Astronaut Joe Kerwin, a doctor who walked in space, as revealed in an interview with newspaper reporter David Nyhan in 1977, are still absorbing. Said Kerwin:

"Physiological stress that your environment causes is measureable: lack of oxygen, weightlessness, and so on. They are mechanical stresses. When you begin to talk about emotional stress, I don't know how to define it, or how to state those characteristics of personality that would enable you to overcome it.

"We haven't gone that route in the space program. We get people with experience, and let their own supervisors evaluate them. We screen out only identifiable personal or neurotic traits, but only negative things," he said.

"We select people who have demonstrated they can handle it, whether in their education, combat experience, aviational training, and so forth. Then they have to withstand the stresses of training. At the end, by some magic, you've got yourself someone who can do the job. There's no simple mechanical way to do it. You can't give a guy a 10-page test to be an astronaut."

"Maybe there are too many different kinds of stress for that. For example, the personality you might want in a wartime versus a peacetime pilot. Maybe for your wartime pilot you want a guy who seeks risks, whereas in the peacetime military, and to a good extent in NASA, you want a stable, cautious, conservative individual to protect your expensive hardware and machinery.

"The selection process drove us to selecting relatively mature individuals, in age as well as experience. They had demonstrated in combat, space, their own work or school that they were pretty capable people. They had accumulated good records."

Kerwin pointed out that the astronaut training program, while rigorous and demanding, was very supportive to those who had survived the recruitment hurdles.

"When guys came in, people looked at them as capable. An assumption of capability exists when such a person walks in the door. The people around him assume that he is going to do it. It is a relaxed attitude in which a guy can do his best."

The need to have peer approval, the necessity for man to be acknowledged—even loved—by his colleagues is one cause of stress and if, in turn, the esteem of one's associates pours forth, it does indeed appear to assuage the tension of one's times.

This is actually what the Institute of Stress in Canada has been saying for years. Man should not hoard wordly goods but instead "should collect a huge capital of goodwill that protects him against personal attack by his fellow men." Selye always felt that each of us had, as if in a bank account, a great wealth of what he regarded as "adaption energy" on which we could draw in crisis. We can spend this capital but not replenish it. "Complete restoration is probably impossible, since every bilogical activity leaves some irreversible chemical scars."

The chemistry involved in stress is starting to become apparent. We are woefully ignorant about the human brain and our tests are so crude they will be scorned by the scientists of the 21st century. At times, it seems as if we hardly have progressed in understanding psychiatric disease since Freud once said in 1889 that there were "powerful mental processes which nevertheless remained hidden from the consciousness of men."

We know now as little about nerve activity as we did in prior days about tuberculosis. With TB there were so many theories about treatment—offer fresh air, open the windows, improve the nutrition, set a fine table, get longer sleep, go to bed early. Yet when streptomycin was discovered, and the "magic bullet" to treat the disease became available, the effete theories were discarded and the practical solutions were applied.

In some ways, the variables of stress have a similarity to the degrees of tuberculous infection that occurred in the past. Dr.

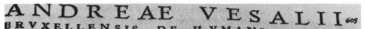

ANDREAE VESALII
BRVXELLENSIS, DE HVMANI CORPO-
RIS FABRICA LIBER SEPTIMVS, CEREBRO ANL-
malis facultatis fedi & fenfuum organis dedicatus,& mox in initio omnes
propemodum ipfius figuras, uti & duo proxime praeceden
tes libri, commonftrans.

PRIMA SEPTIMI LIBRI FIGVRA·

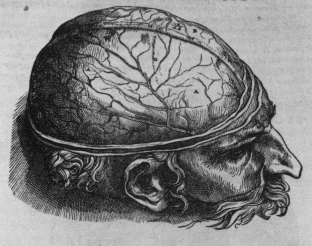

PRIMAE FIGVRAE, EIVSDEMQVE CHARACTERVM
INDEX.

R I M A feptimi libri figura humanū caput ita adaptatū exprimit, quemadmo
o oftendēdo opportune à collo ey inferiori maxilla diffecātibus liberatur. Praete
luariae partē orbiculatim ferra abstulimus, quanta quoq; omniū quae in caluariae
plitudine uidendorū gratia, auferri folet. quanta uerò illa fit, liquidò dijudicabi
gurā fexti capitis libri primi examinaueris, quae hinc ablatā caluariae partem i
e exprimit. Quēadmodū itaq; praefens figura fectionis ferie caeteras omnes inui
ntes praecedit, ita quoq; illā feptimi libri figurarū primā non inopportune inf
ā cerebri cōmonftrat membranam adhuc illaefam, neq; aliqua ex parte pertu
e. quamuis interim ipfius membranae uincula diuulfimus, quae per capitis futur

We knew little enough about the brain in 1543 when Vesalius produced his classic anatomy text. We still know very little at a time when never has there been so much stress placed on it.

Arnold Rich pointed out in 1945 that tuberculosis infection reflected the virulence of the organism, the magnitude of the infecting dose, and the resistance and degree of reactivity of the patient.

This concept compares with our awareness of how different people react dissimilarly to the varied forms with which stress impacts. Hall and Malone published in 1976 a study with a two year followup into the consequences of continued stress. They looked at the stress of captivity on American military personnel. They found, among some, intellectual slowing and indecisiveness, emotional withdrawal and regression, and difficulty in communication with depression.

Somewhat similar findings had been described in 1974 by Popkin, Stillner, and Osborn among individuals who had lived for a year in Antarctica. This apparently is the response to protracted stress, but it doesn't apply to all persons.

Why not? Again, we're back to the theory that it's not stress itself but the individual's *perception* of it that counts. Does the person see the stress as a tiring danger or an exciting challenge?

A nationwide survey at the University of Michigan's Institute for Social Research showed where the subjects of the study found their stress. The affected employees were middle-managers. Thirty-five percent complained about a lack of clarity in their responsibilities; 45 percent mentioned having too much to do, and 48 percent felt caught in the middle between persons with different desires and different expectations of them.

That not all were affected by work-stress tells us again how individual variations occur. Although physical well-being may indeed trace back to the genes, it has been shown in military situations that people can be trained to survive under stress. In fact, in industry now, one of the big concerns is that white-collar workers have been educated to cope with the demands of their work while blue-collar workers may well have been promoted from the ranks without training and are suffering duress because they are underqualified for their present situations.

"Human beings are magnificent," says Dr. Mark D. Van Slyke, chairman of the Human Factors Department at the University of Southern California. "They can handle a lot of pressure and a lot of overload but typically not for long periods of time. The whole thing just breaks down."

Industry has probably exaggerated the prevalence of this professional "burnout" but it's in the present jargon along with "midlife crisis" and a few other cocktail party conversation pieces of pop psychology. Yet there is an entity, a phenomenon, that can hit us all when we get bored and restless and lose our zest for our present work.

True burnout, however, produces a patient with a similar lack of enthusiasm for even his recreational activities. Van Slyke lists the warning pointers:

"If you find day in and day out you are exhausted, feel your work is a drudgery and complain that no one appreciates what you're doing, it may be time to check under the hood and see if everything's ticking like it used to."

It sometimes takes professional help to overcome the impact of job burnout. An objective counselor can help you identify the causes and map out a strategy to overcome the problem, which is often the result of unrealistic goals that create unnecessary pressures.

Van Slyke notes that unyielding inflexibility is a common denominator in many executives who are facing a need for change but who are too rigid to respond. Again, as in survival, it's that old matter of mental attitude. Successful career persons picture themselves as winning and they keep trying. They know sometimes they will fall down, but that doesn't stop a further new attack. Van Slyke feels that executives should be resilient enough to continue with constant forays into work and life. "Winners lose more often than losers lose," he says. "The trick is they don't stop and they don't let it all cave in on top of them."

Some of those claiming burnout may in fact merely be opportunists, sometimes subconscious ones. It has been said that the Chinese word for crisis is represented by writing the symbol for opportunity combined with that for danger. It seems unnecessarily provocative to comment on the air traffic controllers' strike at this point but from my vantage point as a commercial pilot and family physician, I've never seen any more stress in the working day of the air traffic controllers I've observed and treated than I've discovered in the hectic days of many in the service industries.

Agreed that the rush hours in the sky are congested, that the radar screen with 15 targets is busy, that a six-second wait for two blips to separate again can be purgatory—but so can the moment when a policeman looks *up* the barrel of a sawed-off shotgun, a fireman sees his only exit a flaming hell, or a coronary care nurse suddenly sees the soul leave the patient she's been guarding for three intensive days and nights.

Donald Watkin, MD, the chief of the FAA's Occupational Health Division, has been quoted as saying: "Any group of 16,000 to 18,000 people are (*sic*) going to have a number of cases of hypertension and high blood pressure".

"We find," he continued, "that the controller is not disabled, that the person wanted to get out with a pension. We devote so much time to investigating 'wolf' that (I'm afraid) we'll miss the legitimate ones which you'll have in any population."

When I look at the action of those air traffic controllers who went on strike and read their complaints, I'm reminded of a marvelous RN administrator with whom I worked in Trinity Memorial Hospital, Texas. If I chose to grumble about my lot, she would face me squarely and mouth the phrase that so often in the next four years I would learn to lip-read on her face: "Nobody forced you to become a doctor."

Clearly there was no resemblance between the worries of the air traffic controllers in 1981 and the experiences of aircrews in combat. Of those men, André Malraux said, "Aviation united them as maternity makes all women one." In their unity they supported each other throughout their personal war of personal challenge and personal danger. Yet they could fall wounded and helpless from psychological scars, just as their trusted airplanes could fall spinning and shuddering from the exploding skies.

An American psychiatrist, Douglas D. Bond, MD, studied the emotional problems of military pilots and noted in World War II that three different groups of aviators found it difficult, even impossible, to continue to fly into combat. One group became mentally decompensated as a result of traumatic combat conditions; a second because its psychological defenses had been overcome by the severe anxiety of flight fatigue; and a third in all ill-understood manner: The trauma of strain has been minimal and the person was medically able to fly but somehow chose not so.

It was hard for any World War II airman to believe that war existed for him only when he was in his plane and that it ended each time he landed safely when at the same time he saw, so often, his friends and fellow pilots die in action. It was easier in Korea. In that conflict, there were few combat losses because of air superiority, and pilots were rotated after a certain number of missions before they suffered combat fatigue.

Yet many requested to be allowed to stay on in action. The pilots were so highly qualified in Korea and of such superior caliber that their great morale—conceit, if you like—did not have them as stressed as, for example, the young flying officers in France in 1917. So inexperienced were the subalterns of World War I that their men would sing, as each new replacement arrived, the hymn: "A little child shall lead us."

Training is everything. It beats the hell out of experience which, you will recall, has been described as the worst teacher,

There is less stress to life if people are prepared for it. Professional flight personnel can be brought by training to a fine edge of awareness. Readiness reduces stress. (courtesy Civil Aeromedical Institute)

giving the test before presenting the lesson. Training prepares a person. It hardens him.

COPING

Training can be why one person remains cool in a situation, his vital signs normal, his reaction insignificant, his response modest. Yet another recoils, turns on an alarm system, and pumps out those mysterious high-energy chemicals to meet a low-energy situation.

Stress makes blood cholesterol leap into the sky. It doesn't make sense to try to diet your cholesterol down in your body if strain is putting it up in your blood.

The answer is to handle the stress, not to engage in fad diets. Says Eliot at Nebraska, "Who is going to carry a brown paper bag full of concentration-camp food throughout life?" He has followed medical students through examinations, accountants through tax seasons, and Air Force pilots through training. His opinion: "Stress turns on the body's cholesterol faucets; dieting alone doesn't turn them off."

192

Stress can kill because some people can't handle it. Of the million Americans dying each year of heart attacks, half die within 24 hours. And of those sudden deaths, almost half—43 percent—occur on a Monday. Dragging back to work with the Monday blues may indeed be fatal for some.

Thus, learning ways to avoid stress, or to face it and conquer it, becomes an urgent consideration. We should be acquiring methods to reduce stress, yet many professions with their own self-imposed pressures seem to encourage it. Earl R. Gardner, PhD, has made a study of how professional people can become burned out under protracted stress.

This psychologist at the Medical College of Wisconsin, Milwaukee, finds, not surprisingly, that professionals have their pride, their conceit, their ego. They are dynamic (there's that Type A behavior word again) with great professional and career expectations and they have relatively high social and economic strains bearing down on them.

A professional who continues despite this stress may burn out to become a person who denies his own responsibilities for his problems, and who projects the blame to others, and thus tends not to be receptive to offers of help or advice. He thereby becomes withdrawn, bored, and resentful. He flares up with anger readily, says Gardner.

A professional pilot with this problem may see himself as merely tired and, indeed, chronic fatigue is invariably the complaint those patients bring to their personal physicians. A doctor, noting signs of anxiety and irritability in his patient and finding the blood pressure elevated, may put it all down to transient nervousness. However, life insurance companies are beginning to realize that if the doctor's simple examination is nerve-wracking enough to raise pulse and blood pressure, then probably during the patient's day there are equal stresses to duplicate those responses.

Experiments have been carried out with taxi drivers who had blood pressure cuffs fastened on them all day. At intervals the cuff was automatically inflated from a source of compressed air, the blood pressure taken, and the results recorded. The data showed surprising effects—huge jumps in blood pressure when the taxi gets a red light or the driver a fussy passenger.

Eliot once reported to the American Heart Association the consequences of trying to modify the behavior of anxious people in order to reduce their stress. Those persons he sees symbolically as a clenched fist holding a stopwatch: people hounded by a sense of urgency. He makes practical suggestions: If a person is so driven by his wristwatch, then perhaps he can put a small red sticker on it as a reminder of its stress-provoking capabilities. If a patient's enemy is the telephone, he could use a red label on that.

This Nebraska cardiologist believes that some people are so rigid and inflexible in their working day, and have every moment so organized and spoken for, that they cannot handle any extra demands unless it can be resolved very quickly. This "adds extra circuit-breaking dimensions to an already full load with no time for adjustment, consideration, reflection, or setting priorities." To cope, the patient accelerates the other parts of his day—sometimes beyond the speed of reason. "When he reaches that point," says Eliot, "he is headed for disaster."

An effective way to help a busy executive is to reduce the number of cues intruding into his working day. And the easiest way to reduce cues is to reduce the total number of hours the patient works. Business tycoons perhaps can be brought down from 90 hours a week to 50 with significant reduction in stress if they will only accept this "shorter" work week.

Fortunately, many heads of corporations are Type B personalities with a sense of the value of family and recreation; they are actually sympathetic to the doctor who wishes to modify their executives. It is fortunate that airline pilots are already limited in their number of flying hours. Research into fatigue of pilots has surely led experimentation into other fields of employment.

Eliot has a simpler way of dealing with his time-urgent patients. He sometimes asks them to suppose they have only six months to live and to divide their activities into three groups ranging from what they have to do and like, to what is unnecessary and unliked. He finds that people who go along with this thought are often able to reduce their activities and their stress by 50 percent.

He is like an evangelist when he says: "Last year alone, piecing together the 140,000 victims of ischemic heart disease by coronary artery vein bypass surgery cost $2 billion. There has to be a better way."

The better way is not through chemistry, through pills and potions. It is by learning to conquer stress. Want the remedy?

Here's my *Seven-Day Prescription to Fight Stress.*

We sure need remedies because we have become the Valium generation. Life is a struggle, a daily battle. The bad days are wars and even the good days are skirmishes. And if we're in a fight, who is our adversary? Ourselves—we are our own enemies.

If we are both the cause and the result of ourselves, it's time we changed because our environment can't—that environment of accelerated pace which compresses the excitements, the joys and pains of years into months, and sometimes into the mere time from sun up to sundown.

But not even dusk relieves the pressure as we switch to the insidious, relentless pounding of television.

I had a patient who was constantly anxious and as a result exhausted. To him English was a second language but his complaints were eloquent. "Doctor," he said, "I would like to draw to a sudden shut." We all know what he meant. We get too many times at bat—we need a time in the dugout.

Being buffeted by the blows of life is a common coast-to-coast experience. Eliot says: "The alarm reaction without resolution is the typical lifestyle of today." The caveman solved his problems in an immediate, direct fashion—brutally and with no residual tension, but "modern man with his nerves twanging is a physiological Edsel."

A Beth Israel Hospital, Boston, psychiatrist talking about persons of our time said: "People no longer feel good about themselves. They live in a depersonalized society and never establish the community contacts which would help them with problems. For many, life is despair."

How do we get off this treadmill?

There was once a hamster who spent his day spinning a drum in a cage. When the family went on vacation the child stuck a picture postcard in front of the animal to give him a change of scenery too.

It should be easier for us to step off our shrill, shrieking, senseless, spinning world. We are smarter than hamsters. *Get off.* There's a way, you know, with seven simple suggestions, one for each day of the next week of your life.

Day 1: Find Time for Yourself

Look around and take—yes *demand*—time for yourself. This is the success of transcendental meditation, yoga, the Relaxation Response and self-hypnotism. The time need not be spent obsessionally in deep thought, but it should be private and sacred. All must know that you cannot be disturbed; neither friend, Fuller Brush man, nor family cat should cut into this moment. Take the telephone off the hook and ignore the door. *This is your life.*

Day 2: Find Out Who You Are

Use this time productively. Indulge yourself. You inquire kindly after an acquaintance or neighbor; are you not equally important?

Once an exhausted patient said, "I've come to the end of myself; there's no more of me left." Not so! We have tremendous reserves, as Roger Bannister demonstrated when he broke the four-minute mile that first time in 1954.

"My body," he said, "had long since exhausted its energy but it went on running just the same. The physical overdraft came only from greater willpower."

What are your weaknesses, what do you abhor, what are your pleasures, what are your needs, what requires little effort yet gives you much enjoyment? Find out. Ask yourself.

Day 3: Are You Winning?

How is life going? Are you doing well—not with reference to a good job, a comfortable home, and material possessions, but in terms of the intangibles of life? What is the quality of your existence? Are you pleased with yourself? Eliot in Nebraska is disappointed with the number of patients he sees in his coronary care units who have the "Peggy Lee/Is That All There Is Syndrome."

If he finds a patient with an aggressive temperament and associated heart disease, he asks his patient: "Is your lifestyle worth fighting for, or dying for—Because, by God, you may do just that?"

John Hunter, the so-called Father of Human Anatomy, a victim of angina, used to say "My life is in the hands of any rascal who chooses to annoy me." Is it worth dying for? Dr. Hans Selye, at the Institute of Stress, Montreal, puts it succinctly: "Don't waste time on lost causes."

Don't fight City Hall. Don't be the one always jumping up in anger at the PTA or the Town Meeting. Don't always be the constant, tiresome writer of tirades to your local newspaper. *Is it worth dying for?*

Day 4: Experiment and Change?

Learn a new word—it's called *"NO."* Decline offers that would engage you in frantic efforts to stay on time and which would ruin your routines. Decentralize, yes, pass the buck—you're not Harry Truman. Use other family members, especially young ones, for definite duties. Establish rules and priorities for your life, then be consistent.

If you are a full-time homemaker, get out into a part-time job. It need not pay magnificently, but it should be interesting and enjoyable. It should offer a change from your usual routine. Indeed, doctors are lucky who hear their patients say: "I feel great; I threw away your medicine and got a part-time job."

Day 5: Plan for the Future

Have goals and discuss them with your spouse. Plan your retirement. Learn skills or hobbies that will sustain you and entertain you as you cut back.

While doing that, keep living for today. Remember, the good old days of tomorrow are here right now. *Enjoy them.*

Day 6: Spread Out Your Stress

There is great psychological impact in the epochs that change our lives. Marriage, birth, death, change of job or location, selling a home, injury, illness, even going on vacation—all create stress.

If a family has already suffered much stress recently, go slow with new busy ideas.

Day 7: Learn to Live and Endure

Assess your evaluations: Try to improve your non-likable qualities. Be less envious of others. Be content with simplicity. Be less hostile and angry. Be fair to yourself and stress your good points.

Be less critical of imperfection.

A doctor building a professional office haunted, almost persecuted his builder about trivial details in the construction. (Yes, it was me.) The builder rolled his cigarette slowly, tapped it thoughtfully, and spoke up: "Doc, I accept 90 percent perfection. That's good enough for me. If I demand 100 percent, my men would quit. I'm quite content with myself."

He sounded exactly like our Boson psychiatrist: "Psychotherapy is a process by which people learn to feel good about themselves."

Chapter 14

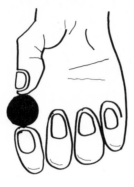

Drug and Alcohol Abuse

The darkness of night slowly fades. The sky lightens. The east glows orange; then that golden orb, without which there can be no life on Earth, leaps into the heavens.

It is midsummer. Like a laser beam, the bright light strikes Cadillac Mountain on Mt. Desert Island in Maine. Below, there is a cheer from those hardy souls at Acadia National Park who have climbed the mountain in darkness to be the first in the nation this morning to see the sunrise.

Another day has dawned in America.

But today's sunrises differ from the billions before. Just as America now lies uneasily in a nuclear age, so it squirms under other problems. One is that we have taken too seriously DuPont's slogan: *Better Living Through Chemistry*. We now live in the Chemical Age. But whereas Edison in the electrical age brought us light, the chemists threaten to bring darkness.

Drug abuse is not a modern problem, but never before have its ramifications been so widespread. In Britain, a special commission on internal pollution summarized the issue thus:

"Each year, perfectly healthy men, women, and children in the developed nations swallow hundreds of tons of pharmaceutical products, presumably for relief from the almost incurable disease of being alive."

DRUGS

Yet man has lived on Earth for, shall we say, two million years.

Why *now* this problem? If man could survive in the Omo basin of the Great Rift Valley, if he could endure in the primordial land of Taung, if his ancestors *adapis, aegyptopithecus,* and *ramapithecus* could cope with primeval life, why now this problem?

Drugs have always been with us. Except for alcohol, opium is probably the oldest known pharmaceutical. In 5000 BC the Sumerians in Southern Mesopotamia (Iraq) were using opiates. There is reference, about the year 1000 BC, in Homer's *Odyssey* to "a drug to lull all pain and anger, and bring forgetfulness of every sorrow."

Yet Homer knew the other side too: "Suppose a brawl starts up when you've been drinking—you might in madness let each other's blood . . ."

Opium, the drug from the poppy from which comes modern morphine, was widely taken in the 18th century in Europe. As Blue Cross/Blue Shield points out, it was "the first wonder drug because it was used to treat venereal disease, cancer, diarrhea, tetanus, gallstones, typhus, childbirth, toothache, and probably at one time or another every other kind of illness and injury."

Of course, opium and its derivatives only relieved the *pain* of suffering, but so effectively that not even the technology of the 1980s has produced anything better. In the 19th century the drug was brought to China by European sea captains. "Opium was to the China traders what beads and mirrors were to American frontiersmen." And as China fell, so opium addiction ended one of the world's oldest and most enduring civilizations.

In America, problems with morphine started after the Civil War. The drug was widely prescribed not only for the carnage on the battlefield but for the dysentery that followed. Strangely, although the addiction that resulted was called the "army disease" it was more prevalent amongst middle-and upper-class women. Narcotics were used in every quack remedy, every snake oil promise, every patent cure.

The Harrison Act of 1914 attempted to correct the situation. It made illegal the use of narcotics at about the same time as the medical schools of our nation were cleaning out their own houses. Yet heroin, discovered in 1898, had about 60,000 addicts by 1930 in America. That number increased after World War II, Korea, and the VietNam conflict to reach an estimate of 600,000 today. Imagine that number—600,000!

The Blue Shield Association believes that this is only a fraction of those who have used the drug once or occasionally. There is no real medical indication for heroin. Thus heroin usage contrasts with the drug abuse of all those legitimate medications that have some genuine value.

People get caught up in heroin for a multitude of reasons. David Smith, MD, of the Haight-Ashbury Free Medical Clinic in San Francisco treats nearly 100 addicts a day who show "poor self-image, low self-esteem, and impaired social skills."

We tend to think of drugs as a West Coast phenomenon and certainly the 29-year-old man interviewed by columnist Jack Anderson was from California. He explained why he was into heroin: "Life is just boring without it. I've got the Porsche, the swimming pool, the Jacuzzi spouting champagne. But there's no comparison with the *good* I get from smack."

But California is just a more obvious part—and perhaps even a more *honest* part—of America. There are 110,000 heroin addicts in New York City alone. The annual death rate from heroin in New York has doubled in three years, and quintupled in Washington DC. Admissions to treatment centers in Newark, New Jersey, have increased by 54 percent in the same time. At New Haven, Connecticut, in the Yale program, there is a waiting list of four to six months for methadone treatment of heroin addiction.

As bad as these statistics are, they fail to emphasize the social aspects of this $57 billion dollar drug-trafficking industry. Dr. John Ball of Temple University, Philadelphia, once interviewed 243 known addicts from Baltimore. They admitted to an unbelievable 473,000 crimes in the previous 11 years—248 crimes per junkie per year to meet a $100-a-day drug addiction.

In addition, it is said that eight million Americans use cocaine. Narcotics agents believe about $20 billion worth of cocaine was smuggled into the United States in 1979 to sell for $30 a snort for a twenty minute high. A drug once so fashionable that "bartenders would, on request, add a dash of cocaine to one's shot of whiskey," cocaine was sold door-to-door 100 years ago, enjoyed by Sigmund Freud himself, and sniffed even by Dr. Arthur Conan Doyle's famous creation Sherlock Holmes. It has now come back. *MD* magazine calls it "The Lethal Status Symbol"; *TV Guide* says "It's Snowing in Hollywood Every Day"; and *Time* itself describes cocaine as "Middle-Class High."

Said one addict to *Time*: "After one hit of cocaine I feel like a new man. The only problem is, the first thing the new man wants is another hit."

Then there's PCP—phencyclidine, or Angel Dust. Supposedly taken by one million every week and tried by ten million Americans, it's a drug that can take seven days to six *months* to leave your body.

Pilots are probably less prone to experiment with drugs than any other group. They have so much to lose. They are conditioned to be cautious about flying under medications. They are also the very antithesis of the type of personality that uses drugs. Pilots like to be in command of situations whether it's the jet stream or their blood stream.

They should, however, be aware of the results of a government study of college drug users. The students offered these varying reasons as to why *they* use drugs:

- ☐ To relieve boredom, tension, nervousness, anger.
- ☐ To reduce appetite; to improve sex.
- ☐ To increase physical performance; to come closer to God.
- ☐ To prepare for stress; to feel less afraid; to keep from going crazy.
- ☐ To make a good mood last longer.
- ☐ To augment learning.
- ☐ To improve self-analysis.
- ☐ To satisfy a strong compulsion.

A stronger compulsion for pilots is to pass their FAA physicals. They are better motivated to stay healthy and avoid drugs. The peer pressure is to stay away from chemicals, not to go seek.

ALCOHOL

Each year Americans drink almost five billion gallons of the oldest drug of all: alcohol.

And among them are pilots, like the man with the Taylorcraft at Liberty, North Carolina, one summer day in June, seen drinking several beers before takeoff with empty tanks. Results? Pilot seriously injured, aircraft substantially damaged. Consider a Cessna 182 at Holbrook, Arizona: the plane destroyed and the pilot killed though those who observed his drinking in that not-so-merry month of May advised him not to fly. Or how about the Grumman American AA5 in Puerto Rico? The pilot, seen drinking from a bottle of whiskey, took off, buzzed the harbor, and somehow "came to rest in the water."

Of course it's no mystery that reason goes out the door or off into the sky when alcohol dulls the brain. Most State Police officials consider that blood alcohol levels above 50 mg are relevant and that figures above 100 mg (0.1G) are *prima facie* evidence of intoxication.

See what levels above 50 do to pilots:

Investigators found a level of 58 in the dead body of a student pilot who stalled his Beechcraft near Newton Falls, Ohio. The corpse of the private pilot, who was the true pilot in command, was found in the *rear* seat. Both had been drinking.

Maybe if the private pilot had been a flight instructor he would have had more wisdom. Really? The Cessna 337 that crashed in the hands of a private pilot one September near Atlanta, Georgia, was on a multi-engine check ride. The pilot had only 161 hours, 18 in type. The pilot-examiner's blood alcohol was 160!

Drunk pilots do not perform rational acts. Consider:

- ☐ Private pilot, aged 59, Luscombe, buzzing friends at Fairfield, North Carolina, struck a tree—blood alcohol 60.
- ☐ ATR, aged 42, Bellanca, aerobatics near Lake Dallas, Texas, hit water—blood level 130.
- ☐ Private pilot, aged 29, Cessna 182, in Dierks, Arkansas, crashed landing on top of a parked log train—blood alcohol 130.
- ☐ Private pilot, aged 33, Piper PA-28, not instrument rated, climbing out IFR at Rockwall, Texas, impacted in fog with ¼ mile visibility—blood 157.
- ☐ Commercial pilot, aged 46, Cessna 120, 4500 total hours, buzzing duck blind at Covington, Tennessee, and stalled in—blood 160.
- ☐ Private pilot, aged 23, PA-22, collided with automobile at Cataract, Wisconsin, in low pass over car park—alcohol level 164.

When the blood alcohol levels get way up, the situation suggests that perhaps these persons are beyond caring—killing themselves one way or another with alcohol, people who just happen to be in the plane at the time instead of a car or even a bus. For example, persons coming in with a blood alcohol level of 234 to Charlotte, North Carolina, on final approach in fog with 500 foot ceiling. Persons with a blood alcohol of 260 impacting at Wasco, California, in a stolen aircraft. (Ironically, since the flight was non-commercial it had to be classified by the NTSB as "flight purpose: pleasure.")

A pleasure trip was also the purpose of the flight of the Beech 35-C33 which in normal cruise near Morengo, California, flew into a box canyon. Pilot's blood: 269.

Not pleasure but duty brought disaster to a Piper PA-11 near Turner, Montana. The Search and Rescue mission stalled in. Pilot's blood: 316.

The list goes on: Student crashing at Cheswold, Delaware, after "erratic flying"—blood 330. Bush pilot impacting on flat tundra near Fairbanks, Alaska. Jeez—*flat* tundra? And in an Aeronca—how in the hell can you crash an Aeronca? Easy—just get your blood up to 366. And if your blood is boiling with 373 mg alcohol you can surely expect to collide with the Texas prairie at Cameron if you're doing aerobatics.

The ledger is indeed endless. The only question is how did those people get safely to the airport? Did anyone try to stop them? Yet anyone who has fought a drunken spouse for control of the car keys knows the frustration. The only redeeming factor here is that usually the pilot's passengers had been drinking too and in their oblivion never knew what killed them or the agony of that last spiral.

I recall an incident in the 1970s when a drunken group staggered out of a bar and headed for an airport. Then, while the intoxicated pilot started up the plane, the happy gang lay down on the wings. A few minutes later, after the plane took off, they were all *wearing* wings. John MacGee, the pilot who "touched the face of God," would have shuddered.

It's crazy to drink and fly. Alcohol by itself can be a dangerous poison even if you're just sitting on a bar stool. A Canadian widow sued both a restaurant in Calgary and its bartender because her husband died after being served eight doubles of tequila within two hours.

But there is another hazard for those who drink: the terrible potency that drugs develop if added to the effect of alcohol. In Chicago, 60 percent of all drug overdose deaths are found to be associated with alcohol. Drink makes a person careless with any medication, and not only are multidrug abusers lax but they have often been dealt drugs other than what they believed they bought. As one drug abuse counsellor put it: "It is much harder to stay alive when you don't know what drug you're taking."

No sedative drugs are safe with alcohol, yet people combine the two—often. I worked once at a "drying-out farm" for alcoholics. Emptying the patients' pockets would often reveal a cornucopia of pharmaceutical confusion: every color, every size, every kind of tranquilizer or sleeping pill. We never found empty pockets—ever. It was someone called "the supermarket approach to feeling mellow."

Neither psychiatrists nor organizations like Alcoholics Anonymous agree with the concept that an alcoholic be prescribed drugs for anxiety or tension. It leads to abuse. Every physician—

indeed every coroner—has seen the proof.

However, there are situations where a patient who is taking, for example, a benzodiazepine like Valium will ask if or when he can have a drink. Daniel X. Freedman, MD, chairman of the department of psychiatry at the University of Chicago School of Medicine, once was moderator of a clinical roundtable which applied itself to that question. Remember, the group was *not* talking about persons who wanted to drive or fly. This was how the panel responded to the patient's question: "Can I have a drink now and then?"

If you are a light drinker and on benzodiazepine therapy, here is some practical advice on alcohol use:

1. Are you over age 60? If so, do not drink at all.

2. Does your medication disturb your physical coordination or mental concentration: If it does, do not drink at all.

3. If your age and effects of the medication allow for occasional alcohol use, you may have one or two ounces of alcohol (never more) on occasion, if you observe the following precautions:

—Skip your medication on the day you plan to have an alcoholic drink.

—Always allow at least three hours between the time you take your medication and the time you have a drink—or vice versa.

I believe the panel's instructions are a bit generous. There is some evidence that even if alcohol is consumed up to 11 hours after the Valium, there is still an enhancement of the drug's effect.

Dr. Herbert Moskowitz, director of the Southern California Research Institute, as a result of studies on volunteers using driving simulators, estimates that one dose of 4.5 mgs of Valium was equivalent to a blood alcohol concentration of 70. Indeed, one physician, Vernelle Fox, MD, calls Valium "dehydrated gin."

I'm used to the smell of alcohol in emergency rooms when I'm called in to treat victims of automobile accidents. As a medical student, until I caught on, I thought this smell was the odor of blood. Even so, I'm staggered to find the true incidence of alcohol abuse in road accidents. In 1980, Canada published an epidemiological survey of all traffic deaths of drivers and pedestrians in Ontario. In the post mortem examinations, Dr. Herbert Simpson of Ottawa's Traffic Injury Research Foundation detected alcohol alone in 41 percent of cases, alcohol and drugs in 14 percent, and drugs alone in 12 percent.

No wonder Norway requires pharmacists to label certain prescription drugs with a red triangle on a white background to indicate that they might represent a possible danger to motorists.

What about the benefits claimed for caffeine in restoring function to a person who has been drinking alcohol? Many physicians are cynical, stating that all black coffee does to a sleepy drunk is create a wide-awake drunk. Dr. William Haddon, Jr., president of the Insurance Institute for Highway Safety, believes however that 1981 research showed "caffeine may help when the alcohol ingestion is small to moderate."

Nevertheless, Ernest P. Noble, MD, who was chosen for the first endowed chair in alcoholism in the country (at UCLA) points out that persons who drink even just a little and then take caffeine still do poorly in "information processing," the very skill needed in heavy traffic on the highways and presumably while flying.

There is *no* drug suitable or safe to take with alcohol. A pilot who doesn't believe this is, like the kid riding his bike without using his hands, an accident on its way to happen.

As was the student pilot in November 1971 when he stalled in at Big Bear, California. The post mortem showed both alcohol and barbiturates. The pilot was age 63—a reminder that drugs are even more potent in the brains of older persons.

Doriden, a sleeping pill, was the drug found with alcohol in a student who collided with trees on a low pass at Andrews, South Carolina, in 1973. It may be okay to have a sleeping pill in your blood at 8:40 p.m., but not if you're flying a Cessna 150.

Phenobarbital, a less-commonly prescribed medication now, was discovered associated with a blood alcohol in Williams, California; in Hilo, Hawaii; and in Glen Ellen, California, in three accidents all happening within three months.

In every case the alcohol potentiated the problem. But alcohol is not safe around aircraft, even if you're not flying. A bystander, swaying in front of a Beech B90 at Olympia, Washington, had a blood alcohol level of 235. He walked into the prop.

People of course, vary in their ability to handle alcohol. The record for alcoholism is the story of one Vanhorn of London, England, who is believed to have drunk 35,688 bottles of ruby port over a period of 23 years before he died in 1811 at the age of 61. England was also the source of the highest blood alcohol level found—1200 mg percent—in the blood of Samuel Riley, who died in 1979.

Of nations, the Germans are considered to drink the most beer and the French the most wine. The Poles consume the most spirits despite the saying "God invented whiskey so the Irish don't rule the world."

There seems to be no dispute that alcohol is involved in accidents. When Michigan increased the legal drinking age from 18 to 21 years, the police reported in 1979 that the incidence of alcohol-associated automobile accidents in this age group dropped 30.7 percent.

In this same year in Massachusetts, when the legal drinking age was increased from 18 to 20, the number of traffic fatalities involving teenagers dropped by 39 percent.

The difficulty is getting the *pilot* who may be drinking to stop flying.

As a drunk pilot said in a famous medical experiment: "I'm flying all right—I *think*. But I don't really care." This was just one of the shattering moments in a medical study as to how alcohol affects pilot performance, a trial actually carried out in flight.

The investigator's interest began in 1968 and the testing ran for 2½ years. Two hundred flying hours were recorded in a Cessna 172 equipped to keep a log of all control movements including throttle, all aircraft variables including airspeed, and exact conditions at all times with respect to glideslope, localizer, and marker beacons. The equipment, which cost ten times the price of the plane, could also monitor the physiological changes in the pilots.

Robert L. Wick, Jr., MD, a pilot later to become the president of the Flying Physician Association, started the study interested in the effect of low blood alcohol levels on flying skills. He used sixteen pilot volunteers and explained to them: "The subject pilot occupies the normal left front seat, and I fly in the right seat to ensure that we don't make any headlines." All subjects had current instrument ratings, and flew four ILS approaches at night to Port Columbus airport. Each pilot was compared to himself sober and with different levels of blood alcohol.

The FAA issued a special exemption from the regulations to allow those supervised pilots to drink and fly.

The results were frightening. Especially badly handled by the drinking pilots were the ancillary tasks which are part of safe flying. The pilots at low blood alcohol levels coped to a degree with the challenge of glideslope and localizer, but had no capability left for the secondary tasks like answering radar controllers, turning on navigation lights, or using carburetor heat. On occasion they taxied too fast, took off with full flaps, and misread altimeters; once, a drinking pilot passed over the middle marker exactly on glideslope and localizer but headed *90 degrees to the runway.*

There was one episode of total loss of orientation to the air, and says Wick, "we began what might have been Cessna's version of an outside loop before I took control."

Reported in the *AOPA Pilot* in January 1974, Wick's historic experiment on the effect of alcohol has not been duplicated with other drugs because they are more difficult to measure. It is easy to find the strength of any alcohol-containing liquid and to check for the presence of alcohol in the blood. Testing is indeed simple—just note what it says on the bottle label and read the LED display on the laboratory machine.

Other drugs are more complicated to test, and the results somewhat anecdotal and subjective.

MARIJUANA

Nevertheless, the study attempted by Mike Knepper when he was editor of *Car and Driver* remains of considerable interest. Published in June 1980, the articles described how four magazine writers handled driving a car after smoking marijuana.

Knepper's own conclusion was: Don't dope and drive. But the test showed more than that.

The results could be summarized thus: The subjects became more sensitive to their surroundings while driving but they couldn't handle and use all this increased information. They didn't lose their coordination for the short time of the test, but decision-making became difficult. The drivers also became drowsy.

The test drivers had many comments. One had a "feeling of good will toward men, punctuated by throat irritation." He enjoyed himself but was subject to distraction.

Another stated that behind the wheel he felt more like an observer than a participant.

Said a third: "Smoking marijuana heightens all your perceptions. Trouble is, you can't process the information efficiently." He felt he would be okay to go bowling but not to play chess.

The fourth driver, a technical editor, felt he could still control a car under the influence of this drug but to stay awake to do so was, for him, impossible. "Dope may not hamper your driving ability," he said, "but it will kill your long-term concentration. And probably you too, if you're foolish enough to dope and drive."

Another subject summarized the role of pot in driving: "Dope just puts you in a better frame of mind to accept the inevitable accident."

Indeed, an increased number of road traffic violations occurred frequently in 97 chronic marijuana users studied by Dr. Ronald A. Weller and Dr. James A. Halikas. Those two psychiatrists, while at the Washington University School of Medicine, St. Louis, also found that although marijuana enhanced appreciation of some aspects of sex, it didn't alter the performance itself. The drug certainly didn't prolong the duration of sexual intercourse, it didn't affect the frequency or quality of orgasm, nor improve the ability to have repeat coitus. It did not increase sexual desire but it did seem to enhance the feeling of "emotional closeness."

Cannabis sativa has had aphrodisiac properties ascribed to it for centuries. In India and Islamic countries, men have long claimed increased amorous prowess, but studies have not supported this.

Research workers seem to have tested the action of pot on sexual prowess more than flying skills. It is surprising that data are so scanty. With 30 million marijuana smokers in the United States caught up in a $25 billion a year industry, you would expect science to offer more solid facts to lay before the public. About the only certain consideration is that the drug hasn't been used long enough in America for the long-term effects to be known. We are about where we were with tobacco in 1920—it took a half century to prove the problems that existed.

We don't even know *who's* smoking pot. The conflicting tales leap out of the medical journals. George Farnham, the political director for the National Organization of the Reform of Marijuana Laws, says, "There are now more parents in this country who smoke marijuana than adolescents. The number of marijuana smokers increases yearly but the increase is not among adolescents, but among those over 30."

Yet the Harvard Medical School Health Letter declared in June 1980 that the problem was increasing more in young teenagers, with four million youngsters between the ages of 12 and 17 admitting that they used the drug. That number is 15 percent of the total population of that age. Ten percent of high school seniors claim to be daily users.

However, a study by the University of Michigan showed that only 50 percent of those who smoked the drug as high school seniors in 1975 were still smoking it in 1980. The same survey revealed that 42 percent of the daily smokers said that pot reduced their energy and 28 percent suspected that the drug caused them to "think less clearly."

After the 1981 crash on the aircraft carrier *Nimitz*, investigators found that the body of the pilot had 11 times the recommended dosage of a cold remedy (*brompheniramine*) in his system and that six of the 14 crewmen killed had used marijuana. A subsequent spot-check of enlisted Navy personnel at Norfolk, Virginia, and San Diego, California, indicated that 48 percent had smoked pot during the previous ten days. As a result, Admiral Thomas Hayward, Chief of Naval Operations, ordered every ship in the U.S. Navy to carry the equipment necessary to allow its captain to run random urine tests on personnel.

The situation is serious. General William Louisell feels that two-thirds of Americans aged 18 to 25 have used pot at least once. He has a problem, as does our nation: "We simply cannot ignore two out of every three potential recruits," he says, "and still defend the United States."

Harvard research suggests marijuana clearly interferes with driving or piloting skills (although it does not appear to stimulate aggressiveness behind the wheel as does alcohol). Moreover, the effect on driving skills lasts several hours beyond the period when a person feels high—even someone who feels normal drives worse than usual.

Dr. Alan C. Donelson, of the Highway Safety Research Institute at Ann Arbor, says that psychomoter coordination is not impaired by dope but judgment apparently is. Like the *Car and Driver* writers, he feels that the subject's information-processing is delayed: "It's part of the altered sense of time most smokers experience."

This is about what the previously mentioned studies also suggested and, indeed, research by a Boston University accident team showed that marijuana users had more fatal car accidents than non-users.

So what does it all mean? What do we know about marijuana?

It is metabolized slowly. The active components of marijuana are still found in the plasma after three days and are excreted in the stool after eight days. The drug will persist in certain fat stores of the body for about two weeks. The action is, however, fast. Its effects peak in ten minutes and are gone within three hours.

Delta-9-tetrahydrocannabinol (THC), the active ingredient in marijuana, has been studied the most. A present worry to drug abuse officials is the discovery that, while in 1975 the concentration of THC in street marijuana seldom topped 1 percent, now concentrations of more than 5 percent are quite common.

The symptoms from the drug therefore vary according to the dose taken. The age and perhaps the previous personality of the user are also relevant factors. For instance, an "amotivational syndrome" has been described in heavy users if they suffer a loss of motivation with apathy and narrowing of interest. Young people thus touched may drop out of school. However, depressed persons are more likely to use marijuana than others, and the inertia of such people may be due to the basic character rather than the drug.

Acknowledged adverse effects include drowsiness severe enough to be disabling. Dry mouth, dizziness, disorientation, and depression are common. Anxiety and agitation, panic and paranoia, hallucinations and palpitations can all happen.

Some investigators claim flashback phenomena occur; others say this develops only where the subject is using other hallucinogens. Delayed or prolonged reactions have been described but the observers were uncertain as to whether the persons were not already psychotic.

Tolerance to marijuana develops in some persons—they have to increase the dose and hence the risk of adverse effects. Yet the drug does not seem to addict like heroin or opiates. At the time of the induced high, users may become clumsy and more slow to react. They have a shorter attention span, and can develop defects in memory and calculation.

Most of those statements are accepted as valid by users of the drug.

More controversial and more hotly debated are questions about chromosome damage. The original work at the University of Utah Medical Center was not confirmed at the University of California Medical Center. The Utah findings suggested that white blood cells (which fight infection) suffered 3.4 chromosome breaks per 100 in pot users compared to the normal breakage figure of 1.2. However, a variety of stimula from aspirin to color TV can cause breakage to some degree.

Since white blood cells fight germs, are pot smokers more at risk of disease? Columbia University felt so when a study revealed a 40 percent drop in some cells that fight infection, the T-lymphocytes. Again, West Coast studies, this time at University of California at Los Angeles, disputed those findings.

The study of marijuana in pregnancy again produced contradictory findings as did the effect of the drug on causing or treating cancer. More accepted are the findings from the Biology Research Foundation that the level of male hormone testosterone dropped 44 percent in heavy users. Occasional impotence in heavy users was also discovered by Dr. Robert Kolodny in that study. Males may show some decrease in their sperm count. This has been long known: Galen in the second century AD said: "Cannabis dries up the semen."

What research has been done into long-term use? In 1975, the National Institute of Mental Health studied two groups of 30 people in Jamaica, where the use of marijuana is commonplace. One group was the control; it had never used the drug. The other group had averaged seven cigarettes a day for 17 years. There was no difference in health provided the drug users did not also smoke tobacco.

UCLA scientists published research on long-term use in *Science* magazine in 1981 and concluded that there was no chronic brain damage in ten members of a religious sect who took marijuana, often on a daily basis, but otherwise did not touch drugs, alcohol, or psychoactive herbs.

Dr. Jeffrey Shaeffer, a UCLA neuropsychologist, felt that habituation had reduced side effects and prevented long-term complications. This suggests that you can't translate side effects of an acute nature into long-term expectations.

Long-term problems may require a generation or two before finite answers are given. This consideration is becoming important since there may be medical uses for THC or its derivatives. Dr. Ralphael Mechoulam, president of the academic faculty at Hebrew University, Jerusalem, and the scientist who first isolated and identified THC, believes that the drug may be helpful in about 25 therapeutic roles.

Present areas of his interest encompass high blood pressure, insomnia, infection, immunosuppression, seizure disorders, multiple sclerosis, glaucoma, cancer-chemotherapy nausea, migraine, narcotic-withdrawal symptoms, and asthma. Its possible use in asthma is particularly confusing. The drug seems to open the bronchial tubes in the lungs briefly in acute use but the effect is not sustained. Heavy smoking of pot appears to have the opposite effect: It narrows the air passages and irritates the lining of the lungs. Marijuana smoke contains more than 400 chemicals beside THC and some of them look very much like the tars that contribute to lung cancer. Use of marijuana seems to decrease the ability of the lungs to dispose of germs, debris, and foreign matter. In fact,

Robert L. DuPont, MD, former director of the National Institute on Drug Abuse, has called pot smoking "the single greatest new threat to healthy lungs in U.S. history."

A HEW report in 1980 cited one study which suggested that one marijuana cigarette was worse than 16 regular tobacco cigarettes in decreasing vital capacity, the ability of the lungs to breathe in and out.

And so, we have no new ideas about marijuana, no news for the zealots who would add it to mother's milk, no ammunition for those who would oppose even its clinical trial. Is it safe in conservative use? How should one respond to children who want to join in with parents? Is it safe for one family and a disaster for another? Does experience with other, older drugs offer any suggestions?

Dr. Norm Zinberg, clinical professor of psychiatry at Harvard Medical School, believes that, when alcohol became socially acceptable, moderation bred moderation. "Both abstinent and alcoholic families breed alcoholics," he says, "more than families which use alcohol in moderation, apparently because kids learn how to use it."

However, if the drug is legalized, the jump in users will not be in teenagers but in those of the age group 21 to 40 who, should they be arrested now, have everything to lose: status, reputation, job. And this is probably the group already heavily into nicotine, yet the percentage of Americans who smoke tobacco is now the lowest in about 37 years. A recent Gallup Poll found that 35 percent of Americans had smoked in the previous week. In 1972, 43 percent of adults were classified as smokers. In the last five years, two-pack smokers have decreased from 13 percent in 1977 to 2 percent now. There were, however, 600 billion cigarettes consumed last year in America. This justifies talking about smoking yet again, even though we've discussed it before.

The difficulties caused by cigarette smoking are too well-known to need listing here but you might be interested in knowing that other Gallup Polls have shown that one-third of the 65 percent of adult Americans who don't smoke used to do so. Eight in ten current smokers have tried to quit, but one-third of those were back smoking again within a week, and only one-fourth lasted six months.

Smokers are surprisingly poorly informed about the symptoms of nicotine withdrawal. Commonly, patients experience irritability, anxiety, restlessness, drowsiness, stomach upsets, difficulty in concentration, and headache.

Headache is an odd symptom from quitting cigarettes. I once

had a patient who stopped smoking to find an increasing ability to smell flowers, taste food, and enjoy sex—except for the headache. He told me he got tired of saying to his wife: "Not tonight dear, I've got a headache."

Pilots who think they're charismatic and intriguing when they glance up over their Porsche Carrera sunglasses and urbanely light a cigarette might be disappointed in the charting of a smoker's psyche done by Nicola Cherry and Kathy Kierman, of the London School of Economics Medical Research Council. Over a nine-year period they followed a group of 2753 smokers from the age of 16 through 25 years. Their conclusions: Smokers are more extroverted but more neurotic than nonsmokers.

The reasons for smoking must be diverse. But why this drug culture? Why this sick perversion of the American dream? Everyone must share the blame: doctors who overprescribe and leave prescription blanks around; careless or permissive parents who allow cabinets to bulge with unused pills; TV advertisers who make our narcissistic youth think there is an instant fix for every real or imagined problem. We may always have some kind of drug culture, mostly in our youth.

And if the young person's experience with alcohol is any guide, then we can expect problems. It has been found that permanent liver damage as a consequence of alcohol abuse occurs more rapidly in teenagers than any other age group. It may take 10 to 15 years of heavy alcohol intake to produce cirrhosis in an adult, but tragically only 10 to 15 *months* in a teenager.

It's hard to help adolescents. Psychologists point out the futility of trying to get rational responses from teenagers when we can't even get adults to have rational attitudes with concepts like wearing seat belts. In fact, one of the difficulties psychologists have is in educating their social workers to have rational expectations in treating drug addicts. Now, a "cure" may be defined as getting an addict back to work rather than having him lying around enjoying his high.

Richard H. Blum, PhD, who has carried out considerable research in drug addiction, feels that those who are treating patients are becoming much less moral and more specific in their outlooks. He feels professionals with realistic goals can be successful in handling addicts, provided success is not defined as a cure. As in alcoholism, "Success must be measured," he says, "in reduction of bouts, reduction in social consequences, reduction in associated illness."

Yet the earlier you catch a problem and the younger the patient, the more useful any medical intervention may be.

What should make you suspicious that a child or friend is into drugs?

First, don't expect honesty if you initiate discussions. Says one drug counselor: "If their lips are moving, they're lying."

Clues to behavior may come from the patient's history, says Charles Buissison, a drug abuse counselor at New Hampshire's Center for Life Management. Be suspicious of the patients who have frequent accidents or fires in the house. Fifty percent of domestic problems are alcohol-related and you will find a *family* history of similar problems in the past because the behavior pattern is often learned.

Depression is often a tipoff. Certainly, numerous researchers have noted that alcoholics and drug addicts often have a poor opinion of themselves. Depression is one of the strange common undiagnosed problems of our time. It brings patients to the doctor often with no symptoms other than tiredness. Questioning will often elicit symptoms of poor appetite and constipation, feeling of unworthiness and despondency, and complaints of a poor sleep pattern with early morning awakening. There is often loss of libido and a general apathy.

It is always important to judge whether a depressed person is suicidal. It's especially important if the patient has ease of possession of a lethal dose or assortment of drugs. It's even more serious if the depressed person has access to an aircraft.

NTSB investigators realized this when they checked the wreckage of a North American SNJ-3 that collided with trees during aerobatics at Wilmington, Massachusetts, in August, 1975. They found a 45-year-old private pilot whose logbook showed 450 total hours, whose blood alcohol revealed a level of 180, and whose wallet contained a note with the words: "I therefore want to die."

Maybe there was once a time in pioneer America when grizzled mountain men ate bear, chewed corn, drank from glacier-cold streams, went to bed bright-eyed at sundown and woke at dawn to sniff the air from a virgin land. But it's gone, that time. We've "advanced." Says Louis Lasagna, MD, professor of pharmacology at the University of Rochester "The mind of man has removed the stopper from the medicine jar. The chemical genie, formerly imprisoned within, now stands before us. He is a spirit known to work miracles, but also to create havoc—to improve life or destroy it. It is quite clear that we can never wish him back into the jar."

you've just bought an extra EKG and a few other geegaws that make pathologists rich. The secret is to mention any blessed worry you've got at the beginning, not at the end.

SKIP YOUR ANNUAL PHYSICAL

Let's be clear about this. Probably the only people gung-ho on annual physicals are health nuts and people who make a living doing them. Sure, such examinations catch a few problems but they're not cost-effective, and at a time when the size of the national debt would impress even J.P. Morgan, they are just not appropriate.

We've discussed this a bit in an earlier chapter, but remember we're not talking about regular checks for infants and children, routine visits for pregnant women, school health exams, college physicals, insurance physicals, ICC physicals, FAA physicals, pap smears, or appropriate interval examinations scheduled for individual patients by their regular physicians. We're talking about the "annual physical" that every wife wants her husband to take each year, those visits where anxious obese people who smoke too much, drink too much, and drive too fast come timidly to submit to expensive examinations and listen carefully to the same litany of suggestions on lifestyle—and then just as carefully ignore them for another 12 months.

Save your money.

It's on this basis—money—that we're talking. You should feel good if you've been pronounced well by your physician but the buzzword these days to doctors from Washington is "cost-effectiveness." We've seen in an earlier chapter that it's not cost-effective to X-ray the chest of every hospital admission. Nor is it to X-ray routinely the chest of outpatients without symptoms. The Kaiser-Permanente Group in San Francisco gave this up recently when an eleven-year study showed few benefits. Eastman Kodak employee health records reveal that only two of 3266 applicants for jobs were deferred because of X-ray results, and of those two, one had a history of tuberculosis anyway that would have been detected by the normal screening procedures on every job applicant.

It was therefore no surprise to American doctors to see a draft in late 1981 from the 14-member Chest X-ray Referral Criteria Panel of the Food and Drug Administration recommending that routine chest X-ray screening for unsuspected disease be discontinued.

Two years ago, a Canadian Task Force on the Periodic Health Examination found little value in annual checkups as a method in preventing 78 different diseases. The medical specialists involved advised that "the annual checkup, as practiced almost ritualistically for several decades in North America, be abandoned."

The Canadian group, headed by Walter O. Spitzer, MD, of Montreal, argued that "the routine general annual checkup is nonspecific and casts a searching net far too broadly, particularly in the adult, is inefficient and at times potentially harmful."

Harmful, presumably in the sense that persons may be encouraged if they've "passed" a recent annual physical and later may fail to report a new important symptom.

Richard F. Spark, MD, an associate clinical professor of medicine at Harvard, is against the annual examination "because it falsely reassures patients and it's an easy way for doctors to be gainfully employed. It's automatic."

Well, if the annual checkup is debunked, what is valuable to the patient and useful to the doctor? There *are* some simple tests or procedures that seem worth the money. On occasion, get your blood pressure taken, your hearing checked, your vision measured. If you're over the age of 40, get tonometry pressure in your eyes tested every three years, and annually if there's a family history of glaucoma.

Bring your immunizations up to date. Ask your doctor how he or she feels about pneumonia vaccine and flu shots. Consider a skin test for tuberculosis every five years till age 35, a test for venereal disease every two to three years if you're young and sexually active, a stool test for "hidden blood" every two years, and a pap smear every year—unless you are content with the confusing advice from the American Cancer Society about going every third year.

Mammography for breast cancer you'll want to discuss with your own doctor, but probably getting a complete blood count and urinalysis every three years makes sense. Maybe some blood chemistry like blood sugar and chlorestrol every five years and an electrocardiogram every ten years in appropriate. Sigmoidoscopy, or examination of the last ten inches of the large bowel, has varying medical supporters. Ask your doctor. In fact, get individualized advice about all I've said in the last page or so from your personal physician. He may well say that I've just been pulling numbers out of a hat.

A practical point about the new attitudes that a "complete physical" is not necessary is that it removes a lot of guilt from those who have not been conscientious about regularly visiting their doctors for those annual examinations when they feel well.

style of clinical pharmacy that is emerging in the 1980s. The newly qualified pharmacists are trained to explain drugs' actions and intend to find the time to do just that with their patients. Look for a new approach in drug stores where patients will have explanations read to them by interested pharmacists just as prisoners now have a list of rights read to them by arresting officers.

We've come a long way from the early Middle Ages and the Arabian physicians who read in the Moslem books that the Prophet himself had written: "O servant of God, use medicine, because God hath not created a pain without a remedy for it."

Chapter 18

You Can Take It with You: First Aid Kit

An old doctor retiring from medicine once wrote his swan song—a letter to the British Medical Journal. "I've practiced for 52 years," he said, "and never used a thermometer once. What d'you think of that?"

Patients consumed with the idea that the thermometer is all-important will be startled to find that there was only one reply. A young family physician wrote in, somewhat puzzled. "I don't understand," he complained. "How can you do pediatrics without a thermometer? How can you carry out a full examination on a child without a thermometer? How can you check a child without sticking the thermometer in the *mother's* mouth to get peace for the examination?

Nobody bothered to reply. He'd made his point.

The thermometer can be the most unnecessary item in your first-aid kit. It has, however, its uses for the physician and the parent. When the doctor wonders if his patient's long list of symptoms is a sign of neurosis, when the parent considers that the child's symptoms that prevent his going to school might be imaginary, it always proves something to pop a thermometer in a mouth and get a reading of 103.

The thermometer may thus be useful for pilots stuck in some Holiday Inn in Smalltown, USA. Why does he feel lousy? Why is she so tired? Why are they aching all over? Should they fly?

Of more practical value are items like Band-Aids and Ace

Percussing, 5-7
Peripheral vascular diseases, 23
Peripheral vision, 79-80
Perityphlitis, 108
Pfeiffer, Eric, 26
Phenergan, 58
Phenobarbital, 205
Phlebitis, 11
Photophobia, 92
Photostimulation, 67
Physical, annual, 219-221
Piles, 104-105
Pinel, Philippe, 93
Polarized glass, 80-81
Pool, Champe C., 182
Post, Wiley, 156
Postdural edema, 11
Postural hypotension, 83
Preflight inspection, cold weather, 47
Provancha, Earl D., 133
Pulmonary embolus, 87

R

Rahe, Richard H., 183
Raynaud's disease, 143
Rectal itch, 11
Reflexes, 9, 128
Reich, Theobald, 35
Relaxation response, 181
REM sleep, 152
Respiration rate, 64-65
Reynolds, Burt, 177
Rich, Arnold, 188
Rickover, Hyman, 25
Riley, Samuel, 205
Riopan, 171
Roberts, Nigel, 166
Robitussin, 85
Rods, 80
Rogers, Richard, 25
Rogers, Will, 183
Rolaids, 97
Rose, Darrell E., 70
Rupture, 9

S

Salt, 171
Salt tablets, 51
Salt-water sniffing, 85-86
Schnore, Morris M., 24
Scopolamine, 58
Scuba diving, 87
Selye, Hans, 179
Senile kerratoses, 128
Shaeffer, Jeffrey, 211
Shelter, 140

Sherwin, John M., 69
Shingles, 78
Siffre, Michel, 155
Silson, Ove, 47
Simpson, Herbert, 204
Sinusitis, 85
Sinutab, 84
Sleep, 149-160
Sleep apnea, 153
Sleep disorders, 152-156
Sleep tips, 159-160
Slipped disc, 117-120
Smell, 68-69
Smith, David, 200
Smoking, 19-24, 170, 212-213
Smoking, cigar, 24
Smoking, pipe, 24
Smoking, stopping, 20-21
Snoring, 153-154
Snow, Crocker, 25
Socialized medicine, 224-227
Spark, Richard F., 220
Spastic colon, 96
Sphygmomanometer, 8
Spiral, 61
Spitzer, Walter O., 220
Squier, Carl, 10
Statement of Demonstrated Ability, 38
Stethoscope, 7
Stock, Nancy, 1
Stoffel, Skip, 144
Strauss, Michael B., 87-88, 139
Stress, 175-197
Stress, coping with, 192-197
Subclinical migraine, 91
Sunburn, 53
Sunburn, winter, 48
Sunglasses, 48-49, 79
Surgeons, 128-130
Survival, 138-144
Survival kits, 141-144
Sutton, William, 34
Systolic pressure, 8

T

Tanning, 53
Tar, 22
Taste, 68
Tennis elbow, 123-125
Tests, lab, 217-219
THC, 209
Thermogenesis, 13
Thian, Hewitte A., 134
Thomas, Lowell, 25
Thrush, 98-99

Tibia, 122
Tietze's syndrome, 126-128
Tinnitus, 84
Titralac, 97
Tracheostomy, 154
Transcendental meditation, 181
Transderm-Scop, 59
Treves, Sir Frederick, 108
Trichomoniasis, 99
Trippe, Juan, 41
Truly, Richard, 59, 156
Truman, Harry, 196
Trundle, Stuart A., 73
Tuberculosis, 187
Tums, 97
Turista, 95-97
Type A personality, 179-180
Type B personality, 179-180

U

Ulcers, 23
Uric acid, 15
Urinary tract infection, 97

V

Vaginitis, 98-100
Valium, 204
Valsalva procedure, 8
Van Slyke, Mark D., 189
Van Wittenberger, Robert, 34
Varicose veins, 11
Vasodilation, 92
Vertigo, 60-62, 83
Vestibular balance center, 53-53
Vestibule, 55
Vibramycin, 95
Vibrations, propeller, 71
Viral vaginitis, 99
Vision, 73-82
Vision, peripheral, 79-80

Visual cortex, 89
Visual references, 56
Vitamins, 235-237
Voltaire, 26
Vomiting, 96-97

W

Waiver, 38
Walker, Herbert E., 178
Wand, Kevin, 182
Washington, George, 88
Water, needs in heat, 51
Watkin, Donald, 190-191
Watkins, Gareth, 69
Wax, ear, 73
Weight, 11-19
Weitzman, Elliot D., 157
Weller, Ronald A., 208
Weston, Maureen, 155
White, Ed, 162
Wick, Robert L., 206
Willard, Mary Joan, 35-36
Winchell, Walter, 13
Wolf, C. Richard, 87
Wolfe, Tom, 186
Wolff, Harold G., 183
Wood, Peter, 158
Wright brothers, 167
Wyanoid, 105

Y

Yeast eczema, 11
Yeast infection, 98-99
Young, James Harvey, 230

Z

Zinberg, Norm, 212
Zondlo, Frank, 35

Edited by Steven Mesner